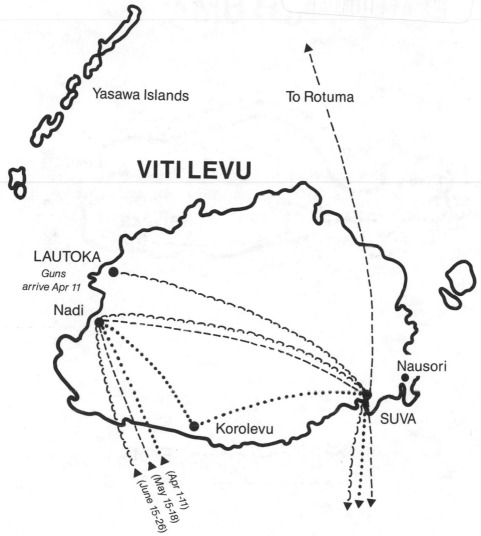

Yasawa Islands

To Rotuma

VITI LEVU

LAUTOKA
*Guns
arrive Apr 11*

Nadi

Nausori

Korolevu

SUVA

(Apr 1-11)
(May 15-18)
(June 15-26)

To Auckland

0   10   20   30   40   50   60   70   80   90   100 km

ROTUMA

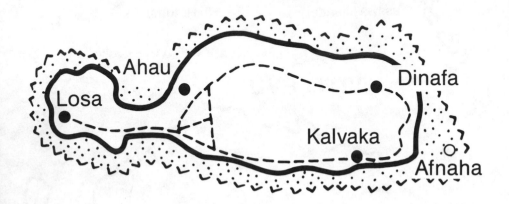

Losa • Ahau • Dinafa • Kalvaka • Afnaha

Key

Reef
Road

0 1 2 3 4 5 6 7 8 9 10 km

THE GUNS OF LAUTOKA
(The Defence of Kahan)

CHRISTOPHER HARDER

This Book is Published by
SUNSHINE PRESS NZ LTD
Remuera, Auckland.

Also written by Christopher Harder

THE CLAYTONS MANUAL
A Look Inside a Policeman's Head.
Interrogation Techniques.

This book is dedicated,

To my good ally and friend Mr Justice Speight for his bold letter in aid of a 'bonny fighter';

To Mr Justice Sinclair for his bouquet to counsel directing my energy to another climate;

To My wife for her patience, understanding and never ending tolerance;

To Countrywide Bank, Visa and Air New Zealand without whose help none of this would have been possible;

And the Commissioner of Inland Revenue for his patience.

Copyright 1988 Christopher Harder
This edition first published 1988

ISBN 0 9597901 0 1

Cover designed by Christopher Harder and Rosemary Sharp.
Cover Artwork by Stag Art Studio, Parnell, Auckland.
Word processor/typesetter conversion by Rennies Illustrations Ltd, Parnell, Auckland.
Printed and Bound in New Zealand by Devon Colour Printers Ltd, Auckland.
Edited by the Ghosts of Aqualine Publishing.

GREAT SPIRITS HAVE ALWAYS ENCOUNTERED
VIOLENT OPPOSITION FROM MEDIOCRE MINDS.

Albert Einstein.

FOREWORD

When Colonel Sitiveni Rabuka lead a squad of armed and balaclava-clad soldiers into the debating chamber of Fiji's Parliament at ten o'clock on the morning of May 14, 1987 it seemed more like an adolescent adventure story than a real life coup d'etat. It was a while before the reality of revolution in the South Pacific hit home to many of us.

Officially Rabuka said he had acted to pre-empt racial strife because there had been an outcry from the Fijian traditionalists when the Coalition Government of Dr Timoci Bavadra won the April election. The Coalition received a majority of its support from Indian voters.

Late last century Indians began arriving in Fiji as indentured workers in the British colonial sugar industry. As labourers they were much more compliant than the fierce and physical Melanesian tribesmen who had lived in the islands for thousands of years.

But Rabuka, and many of his Fijian countrymen believe they have a right to assert a racial dominance. Underlying this scene are many currents in a system that has long offered privilege to a few.

The story behind the Guns of Lautoka started with the reality of the revolution when the Fiji military forces began a systematic campaign to harass the Indian community.

Road blocks were set up to search vehicles. People were watched by neighbours and there were actions reported back to Military Intelligence. The harassment included people in the business world who the military thought might finance opposition to the coup.

Members of the sugar cane council, trade union officials,

teachers and other professional people were harangued day and night by the military.

The Indians felt insecure. They were defenseless. Fijians were attacking them with impunity from the law. Indians calling for police help were given the cold shoulder, matters which should have been investigated were not.

There was even favouritism in the courts. It was the last straw for the Indians. Helplessness was creeping into the Indian mind.

CONTENTS

CHAPTER ONE

THE GUNS OF LAUTOKA
Saturday, April 16, 1988

One shot, then another, thundered across the mangroves. Mynahs in the trees screeched; seagulls, winging their way to an early breakfast down river, called out in blind panic, even the nocturnal fruit bats flashed terror-stricken in the early light. Never before had the upper reaches of this estuary been shattered by the wicked sound of high velocity rifle fire.

Down by the water two Indian men with Soviet pattern AK 47 military rifles in their hands shuddered at the sound which had rent the pre-dawn chatter as nature's daylight shift took over.

One of the men staggered back clasping his shoulder. These were not hardened Fijian troops loosing off a few rounds to test their weapons. The men wore civilian clothes and the one with the sore shoulder did not even know the rudiments of handling a high powered rifle. He had been belted by the butt as the weapon recoiled.

An era of innocence in Fiji had been violated with those first few rounds.

The man who had organised the test firing, Mohammed Kahan, stepped out towards them. He was about five feet, eight inches tall, balding and dressed in a dark blue suit.

"I wanted you to test the guns that we are going to supply to our brothers here because Fiji is making a fool of itself in the world. There are traitors running this country . . ." He spoke with the passion of a man with little to lose.

"I will not forgive them till we take over the government."

His confidence was boosted by the knowledge that prominent

people and persons of high rank were implicated in the arms shipment. Ratu Mosese Tuisawau, the brother-in-law of Prime Minister Ratu Sir Kamisese Mara, was shown as his partner on the shipping documents for the container used to smuggle the weapons into Fiji — at least so said an Indian Customs Official.

Two army officers, one from Ratu Mara's home territory in the Lau Islands supervised the transporting of the container between Carpenter Shipping's bond storage area and Nagan's Steel Pressing Mill, half an hour's drive out of Lautoka.

It was getting dark as the small white Ford van wound its way along the dirt track running to the home of Mohammed Rafiq. He lived well up Tavakubu Road opposite the golf course, several miles outside the port of Lautoka on the West Coast of Viti Levu, Fiji's main island.

Entering his yard the headlights lit up part of a two room concrete block home with a badly rusted corrugated iron roof. An awning spanned a gap of about 15 feet between the house and a small animal shed. An old stove stood beside one wall of the home, alongside a stand with a 20 gallon fuel drum, diesel for Rafiq's old blue Datsun parked in the yard.

A dog barked, darting out in front of the white van to reappear yelping on the other side. Underneath a big mango tree near the middle of the yard stood a heavy duty Mitsubishi rental truck with four large wooden crates on its tray.

The van came to a halt and out stepped Mohammed Kahan and two other Indians. They moved straight over to the big truck. One jumped up onto the tray and started sorting out a block and tackle lying there. The other tossed a rope over a sturdy branch of the mango tree, repeating the process three times in readiness for hoisting the block and tackle into place.

Rafiq and two friends joined in, preparing to lift the heavy wooden crate off the truck. They were working in the flickering light of a gas lantern placed on the cab of the truck and a couple of other lanterns in the yard.

Rafiq's house overlooked a mangrove swamp. The mosquitos were thick, but they did not bother the five men gathered about the back of the rental truck.

2

These were the boxes that had been spirited away from the shipping container at Nagan's Steel Mill.

It was only five days since the container had been aboard the freighter Capitaine Cook III as it nudged up to Lautoka's main cargo wharf after a voyage from Sydney. The cargo manifest listed six boxes of used machinery, shipped from Sydney. Yemen in the Middle East was listed as the originating port of the six plywood boxes.

The branch of the mango tree swayed with the weight of the first crate as it was swung away from the truck and lowered to the ground. There was grunting and cursing as the men heaved the crate aside and then slid the next crate back along the truck ready for unloading.

This one was heavier or perhaps the men belaying the rope lost their concentration. Whatever the reason, the crate plunged the last couple of feet to the ground, whipping the line from the block and tackle through the men's hands, leaving a raw and painful rope burn across the palm of one.

It crashed into the container already unloaded, bursting wide open. Out tumbled long green wooden boxes, squarish brown boxes, smaller rectangular metal containers and some sort of trolley apparatus. There was little doubt about the contents. More care was taken in getting the other two crates off.

Over the weekend the crates remained under Rafiq's mango tree, the broken one still open, but all well covered with tarpaulins.

On Tuesday afternoon Rafiq drove into Lautoka where he met a man called Saheed at a travel office. Saheed was asked to come out to Rafiq's place to fix the broken crate, as he was a skilled woodworker.

When he arrived that night he saw Rafiq and a man called Dean sitting under the mango tree, apparently waiting for him.

"Come and join us under the tree, we're waiting for Satendra to bring the truck," called out Rafiq.

As they chatted Saheed became suspicious about what had been in the crate he was to fix. "What's in the boxes?" he queried.

Rafiq looked cautiously over his shoulder as if to emphasise the sensitive nature of what he was about to say. "Guns and bullets," he said, breaking into a grin.

A while later Mohammed Kahan came walking up the drive. Nobody knew where he had been but Saheed wasted little time in asking him about the guns.

"They were brought to Fiji for the protection of the Indian people during civil disturbances," said Kahan, not venturing too much information to the man whose only role in the affair so far was that of carpenter.

With the help of the others Saheed took the two damaged crates away when Satendra arrived with his truck. It took about an hour and a half to patch the crates and return them. Then the green and brown boxes, the metal containers and the six trolleys were loaded back in, the lids resecured and the crates slung onto the back of Satendra's truck. Kahan checked the crates one last time and the men covered them with a heavy, dark tarpaulin.

It was Satendra's job to disappear into the night with the crates on the back of his truck, taking the whole shipment to a safer overnight storage place, and to return with them the next night.

It had been a long day so Rafiq invited the three remaining men into his home for a late night meal of fish curry, dahl, roti and spicy condiments.

When their meal was over, Dean produced a large canvas bag. He opened it to reveal six rifles and an ammunition box. This was the used machinery — AK 47 assault rifles, not the latest in military hardware, but effective enough to keep an army on its toes.

4

CHAPTER TWO

WHO DARES TO CHALLENGE:

MAY 15 1988: It was cold and damp as I headed towards the Air New Zealand boarding gate at Auckland International Airport, bound for Rotuma via Fiji on TE 04. It was a trip that would bring about experiences I would feel compelled to write about.

After two coups, Brigadier Sitiveni Rabuka, (pronounced Rambuka), was still presiding over a military-cum-civilian government. A religious zealot doubling as a military dictator.

What the hell was I doing, off to Fiji at this particular time?

Some opportunities knock but once in a lifetime, to recognise that time and have the courage to act, despite the odds, is to accept a challenge. A chance to engage the military strongman from Fiji was such an opportunity. No holiday for me this time in Fiji. The real situation was tense. The general mood was one of fear and concern. Yet for the tourists who went to Nadi and then to the western islands, Fiji remained a holiday haven.

Suva, the capital, the heart of intrigue and politics, on the other hand, had a significant smattering of Fijian extremists — the Taukei, 'land movement people.' They posed an undefinable threat to the capital merely by their presence. This group claimed all the land, they claimed parliament and had faith in the only sanctioned religion — Christianity. They had effected media censorship and Sunday bans, a devastated economy and a holiday trade dashed by coups. Fiji, the way nobody wanted it.

The drama as each Fijian moment unfolded, like a black moth emerging from its cocoon, was an experience of fear and exhilaration. But the impression that 'fair play in action' since the

5

military takeover had disenfranchised all Indians raised my dander and a fighting instinct in me.

Defending seven Rotuman chiefs, charged by the Fiji Director of Public Prosecutions with the crime of sedition, was right up my alley as a criminal barrister in a Commonwealth country. It was alleged the men had held a meeting at Juju on the island of Rotuma with the seditious intent of declaring Rotuma independent of the recently established Republic of Fiji, and further, that they had wanted to declare allegiance to the Queen of England, under whose care and guidance Rotuma had existed for over 100 years.

It seemed ironic. People were being charged and arrested for something far less serious than what Sitiveni Rabuka was twice pardoned for. My wildly imaginative defence lawyer's mind seized on the witness scenario in which another defence lawyer would call his witness, and I would cross examine none other than Brigadier Sitiveni Ligamamada Rabuka, OBE (Order of the British Empire) Minister for Home Affairs, Commander of the Security Forces and Minister charged with the responsibility of military security, on his official record of allegiance to the Queen of England.

I would base the cross examination on his blow-by-blow book, *NO OTHER WAY* written after the coup and which I had bought and read in Fiji during my March holiday. Maybe my revolutionary thoughts of university years gone by in Calgary, Canada, had begun to return. Was it possible that dreams of adventure and revolution in the South Seas had been crystalised by a few lines in the *New Zealand Herald:* "Seven Rotuman chiefs arrested."

For four of the past five years I had practised at the New Zealand Criminal bar in an ongoing love/hate relationship with two High Court judges who had presided over my first two criminal rape trials five years earlier.

My fight with these two judicial officers was to affect my relationship with the whole of the judiciary. I made each and every judge a part of the adversarial system. Almost every decision, ruling or comment they made, I challenged. But my last remaining challenge by way of a High Court judge with who I didn't get along had dissolved when His Honour commented favourably on my skills and ability in front of an Auckland High Court jury.

This conquest achieved, life became a bit anti-climactic. Rid of my last nemesis, I began to look hard for a new challenge. Three days later I picked up the Saturday *New Zealand Herald* and began to read, "Seven Rotuman . . ."

In his book Rabuka makes reference to the Queen and Commonwealth no less than 27 times. I was confident as a lawyer that, given the opportunity, my skill at cross-examination would ultimately allow me to hoist a captive and possibly hostile witness by his own petard. Sedition for preaching loyalty to the Queen should surely be defensible.

It is always easier to have your treason pardoned by the new president of a new republic if you control the guns. Sedition in Fiji carries a rather light maximum penalty, two years jail for a first offence and three for a subsequent offence. Punishment for treason against the Queen of England and the Commonwealth was and still is, death by execution. Within this web of intrigue I hoped to help defend the seven. Now I was flying back into the South Seas, enticed by the thought of such a challenge.

Rotuma is a luxuriant fish-shaped volcanic island some 400 miles northwest of the main island of Fiji. Rotumans are Polynesians, as distinct from the Melanesian Fijians. Whalers, traders, and missionaries exploited the island and its people for labour and copra back in the early 1800s. The traders also introduced alcohol and men long in need of a female companion.

At first my role in the Fiji-Rotuma sedition matter was to be that of an outside observer. I didn't think I could be admitted to the Fiji High Court at such short notice. My trip began with that one inch story clipped from the newspaper on Saturday: Sunday night I was in Fiji.

Tourist Beginnings: March '88

I had been to Fiji with my family earlier in the year for the March Easter break, 10 months after the first coup. We stayed in Korolevu, halfway between Suva on the east coast and Nadi on the sunnier west. One day during a tropical rainstorm, my wife Philippa and I rented an air conditioned Avis car from a local Hindu businessman. There was nothing strange about that; Indians run 80 percent of the business in Fiji. They are fundamental to a healthy and vibrant Fijian economy.

We left our children Kate, four, and Joshua, six, in the care of a Fijian nanny. Stereo blasting and air conditioner blowing we drove into Suva to browse and to take a look at the Fiji High Court. My wife reminded me I was on holiday, but she had understood that I really wanted to see the court.

Philippa knows me. As my friend and partner, wife and lover, she has been wonderfully tolerant of my trials, travels and tales over the 10 years we have lived together, married the last eight. As a reformed alcoholic turned workaholic, striving ever onwards and upwards, I've been sometimes hard to slow down and often difficult to live with.

I convinced Philippa that a trial in a Fiji court would be an exciting new adventure. A robbery trial was in progress in the older Number One court with its polished wooden walls and slow moving overhead fan circulating the humid tropical air.

Three Fijians stood charged with robbing a taxi driver. Their defence: the Indian driver was a receiver of stolen goods who had refused to pay for goods delivered. None of the accused had legal representation. Legal aid payments by the Fijian government to criminal barristers were relatively unheard of except in serious cases such as murder or treason. Few could afford to pay a private fee, so many people appeared in Fijian Court without representation.

This trial was taking place before Justice Dan Fatiaki, a 38-year-old Rotuman, who graduated from Auckland University Law school in 1978 just as I started my first of five rather event-filled years towards a law degree.

The judge sat and listened with some delight as the more mature defendant named Joe, cross examined the police officer in charge with a gusto that could only come from one who had experienced life on both sides of the law. It later transpired that Joe was an ex-police officer previously dismissed for criminal offending.

At the 11.30 morning tea break I popped into the barristers' locker room where — surprise — I walked right into the three accused discussing their strategy for the closing addresses. Joe saw me first and responded with a big Fijian smile that reminded me of a crocodile. Introductions over, the three beamed like sailors stranded on a deserted island finding a life boat loaded with provisions as I casually informed them I was a criminal lawyer from New Zealand on a family holiday. In their eyes they suddenly had a secret weapon to bring them back from the crevasse they had hovered over in the prisoners' dock all morning.

After a brief lesson about the onus of proof being on the Crown, the burden of proof being beyond reasonable doubt and some comment about lies not being evidence of guilt, the four of us marched back into Court. It was time for the closing addresses to the judge and three lay assessors picked at random from the civil service list to assist the judge on findings of fact. Although the assessors might render a finding of guilty or not guilty, the verdict is not binding on the Judge.

An unexpected bonus — fun — returning to the court to watch these budding barristers-behind-bars plead for their freedom. Sitting on the wooden church-like pew behind the Court bar I seethed with a frustrated desire to leap to my feet and launch into the case, but I had not been admitted to the Fiji bar and could not yet practise. The thrill in the Fiji High Court was the same as in the court rooms at home, inexplicable unless you have actually been bitten by the law bug; a driving force that can push me, as a lawyer, to great expectations. Like an actor I longed for another leading role.

Disappointment. The judge adjourned the trial after the defence's closing addresses to give his summing up speech to the assessors the following Monday, four days away.

At first I thought this move was deliberate because I was sitting in the court. Earlier the clerk had asked me when I was leaving town. I thought at the time it was a strange question, but on reflection have reconsidered. Judge Fatiaki had been most fair in his proceedings the whole morning, on occasion asking very probing and at times very telling questions of the police officer in charge of the case.

The prosecutor, a young Indian by the name of Babu Singh, declined to give a closing address for the Crown case. Chatting at

9

the end of the day in his office it became apparent that few of the prosecutor's staff remained, most had left for greener and perhaps safer pastures overseas. Babu seemed drained of any fight. The first coup had been a kick in the guts, but the second was a knockdown, if not a knockout, at least in the short term.

After the trial finished for the week I roamed the sandstone corridors surrounding the courts in the old government buildings. The cobblestone walkways were about eight feet wide, they had big supporting beams, and open unglazed windows let in the tropical rain, sun and wind.

Down the long hall and around the corner was the Public Prosecutor's office, where all prosecutions originate. The Public Prosecutor in Fiji is ultimately responsible for deciding who and when to prosecute, what charge or charges to lay and under which act or decree. This is a practice, in principle encouraged by Westminster-type parliaments, to ensure integrity and independence between politicians and prosecuting authorities.

In Fiji the principle of an independent prosecutor would seem to be clouded by the fact the DPP (Director of Public Prosecutions), Captain Isikeli Mataitoga, and the acting DPP, Major John Semisi, are both commissioned officers of the Royal Fijian Army, appointed personally by Brigadier Sitiveni Rabuka.

When I enquired of the chief clerk about the possibility of being admitted on a temporary basis as a barrister for a trial or two in Fiji, my suggestion was met with encouragement, even glee. After the second coup all the New Zealand High Court judges who previously sat as judges in the Fiji Court of Appeal, including Sir Graham Speight, returned home, none of them prepared to swear allegiance to a Republic created at the barrel of a gun. In a letter to the Governor General Mr Justice Speight said: "To put the matter as bluntly as possible, we wish to advise that unless we are assured that no attempt will be made to alter the Constitution other than by lawful means, we would not be available for any further service to Fiji.

When my new-found friend, the chief clerk, asked, in a whispered tone, "Would you like to be a High Court judge in Fiji for $38,000 a year?" I politely declined with the sort of impish grin that

10

my four-year-old daughter Kate could make. It was obvious that the New Zealand judicial flavour was sadly missed. Couldn't you just see it now. "Mr Justice Harder, of the Fiji High Court."

I entertained the possibility of coming back later in the year to do a murder trial on government legal aid. The idea of island hopping from court room to court room, adventure after adventure, had a certain appeal. The fanciful thought of travel through the South Pacific tickled me, but it would not be lucrative. I will not quote the paltry sum paid to a lawyer under legal aid Fiji-style so as not to embarrass my good friends practising or drinking at the New Zealand bar.

The possibility of doing a murder trial in tropical Fiji seemed an effective way to get a return-paid working holiday in a South Pacific paradise. I was determined, if possible, to take the chance. As it turned out, I was to return sooner than expected but not for a murder trial. Politics intervened.

Back For Business: May 15

My blue sports Walkman tapedeck lay on my lap as I settled into 47a, the window seat in the no smoking compartment of economy class. It was six years since I quit smoking — it was one of the hardest things I have ever had to do. The overriding nicotine addiction I developed from smoking four and five packs of Pall Mall menthol cigarettes a day over many years was difficult to beat.

My therapy was mixing a repulsive brew of water and cigarette butts in a large glass jar and leaving the foul concoction on the coffee table. It was enough to put me off tobacco for a long time. Even that briefest mention by the stewardess . . . "Window seat, Row 47, no smoking section" was enough to rekindle memories of the vile therapy.

As the jet taxied out onto the rain covered Auckland International runway I listened to my own headphones and my forever Fijian music tapes purchased during our March holiday. I was in Fiji mode. My wife was pleased I was heading back to the land of the golden sun, to the everyday greeting "Bula, bula," (a common Fijian term meaning "health and hello").

It was Philippa's fervent wish that I replace my worn Seru Serevi

11

and Friends music tape with something different before returning home. She was tired of hearing the same tunes. Perhaps she was even prepared to send me off to Fiji just to change tapes.

My heart began to race as the plane accelerated. The blood pumped through my veins as if adrenalin had been injected and my imagination ran wild. As the aircraft accelerated through its rush of power towards cruising speed that initial adrenalin buzz wore off.

Pushing the arms up on the two empty seats beside me I stretched out for a bit of slumber, eyes shut tight in an effort to switch off. But still the thoughts ran wild. Would my Indian guide show up in time to meet me on my arrival at Nausori Airport? Was this really a revolution? I did not really expect trouble as I flew into town to help Tongan-Fijian lawyer Tevita Fa prepare for the coming sedition trial, but I was not sure.

I am one of those blessed, or tortured persons — depending on how you perceive it — who has a racing mind. My lateral thinking brain was firing like an IBM mainframe computer.

I will always remember that spot on Parnell's Ayr Street hill, by the Auckland Grammar Old Boys Club driveway entrance, where the Rabuka battle plan began to ferment in my head. I was out on my usual late morning jog. By the time I had run up Shore Road, along Portland Road and up the hill to my home in Eastbourne Road, Remuera, a definite formula had entered my mind. Afterwards when people asked how I became involved in the Rotuma case in the first place, I always answered: "I just plain ran into it."

My plan was simple. I would contact the local representative of the Rotuman Chiefs in Auckland. As soon as I got home I would telephone the *Auckland Star* newspaper to get his name and number.

Rotuman Kava Auckland Style

By mid-Saturday afternoon after my run I was drinking Kava with 'His Royal Highness', Gagaj Sau Lagfatmaro at his suburban headquarters in Auckland. The Gagaj had adopted his royal name and title about six years before when he was made head of the Molmahao clan. In Auckland some Rotumans accuse him of pretensions beyond his due status. He was formerly Henry Gibson.

12

Kava is a mild narcotic from the root of the yaqona plant. Traditionally it is powdered by heavy pounding. The crushed root is then wrapped in muslin cloth and filtered with clear water. More commonly a couple of bags of premium brand Waka Kava are washed and rinsed by the nearest pair of hands to the kava bowl.

This Rotuman kava ceremony was impressive. A special cup of kava was first prepared for Gagaj Sau with a labourious routine of chants and traditional talk. The end result was the same however. It was a browny dishwatery type of liquid served in the communal kava cup made from half a coconut shell.

Kava is an acquired taste. Not being about to drink alcohol, if for no other reason than fear of the consequences, I had a few cups of grog. The taste was something between liquid sawdust and a dentist's local anaesthetic. Definitely an acquired taste.

My offer of free legal services, excepting expenses, to defend his followers was accepted. I had decided to go to Rotuma and defend the "seditious seven."

The Gagaj saw the jurisdictional question of the sedition charges against his men as a political issue. It seemed from the passion with which the Gagaj spoke of his cause that guns could soon replace the existing diplomatic attempts to find a solution. I saw it as a preliminary defence point for the seven accused.

The little piece in the paper said the seven chiefs had been charged with sedition for declaring allegiance to the Queen. It was this that gave the case such a high degree of appeal. From what I had read and seen, Fijians, including Rabuka, were perhaps more in love with the Queen of England than the British themselves.

Where ever you went in Fiji you saw the Queen's picture. Royal birthdays were celebrated and the High Court at Suva still displayed the Royal Crest over the Judge's bench. It was obvious from reading *NO OTHER WAY* by Sitiveni Rabuka, that he too had a profound desire to be loved and respected by the Queen of the Commonwealth. His Order of the British Empire is a source of continuing pride. A lesser mortal such as Lester Piggot, of racing and tax fraud fame, was stripped of a similar Queen's Honour without notice in 1988.

Rabuka has twice been pardoned for treason by the now

President of the Republic of Fiji, Sir Penaia Ganilau. Ratu Sir Penaia was the Governor General, appointed by the Queen, at the time that Rabuka went along with his gang of 10 and arrested her members of Parliament at gunpoint.

Ratu Sir Penaia pardoned Rabuka the first time for treason on Saturday May 23, 1987, only one week after the first coup. Nobody said whether he acted on his own initiative or whether the Queen sanctioned the pardon.

The distance and time display on the extra in-flight video screen said that the plane was one hour and 15 minutes out of Nadi. The stewardess was poking me awake for an early breakfast. The sweet smell of pancakes with maple syrup and whipped cream and sausages wafted through the cabin. A bowl containing a variety of different fruit pieces on my tray reminded me of some mouthwatering photographs I had been shown by Gagaj of Rotuman oranges, pineapple and papaya. Remembering the picture made me want to get to Rotuma as fast as possible.

As the plan stood, I was to meet a Fiji lawyer named Tevita Fa, who was currently handling the case. A reporter — Mesake Koroi of the *Fiji Times* — was to join us at six o'clock on the Wednesday morning, a day and a half away. We were to meet at Sun Pacific Airline charters at Nasouri Airport, outside Suva.

By sheer coincidence, I had met an Indian lawyer named Anand Singh at the home of Gagaj Sau Lagfatmaro in Whenuapai. He had come from Lautoka, in Fiji, to attend to some personal affairs. I was to become much more involved with Singh later in a way I could not anticipate at that stage at Whenuapai. The two told me about Fa, a Fijian lawyer of Tongan extraction, who would be my instructing solicitor.

I tried to picture Fa as I sat in the Gagaj's living room sipping his Rotuman kava. There were some rather tall tales about Fa. He was described as an unusual, short, solid man and a heavy drinker. Fa had been the Ombudsman in Fiji, then a magistrate, leaving his post, it was rumoured, because of the dreaded drink.

My vision of Tevita Fa was of a Richard Burton-like figure, a bottle of bourbon on a dilapidated office desk and a pack of Players filter forever clutched in hand or stuffed in his shirt sleeve pocket,

14

truly a stereotype of a South Seas lawyer if there ever was such a person. As the plane passed the three-quarter mark, I wondered if Fa would resent an outsider being foisted upon him by 'His Royal Highness', Gagaj Sau Lagfatmaro, King of the Molmahao clan of Rotuma.

From The Bottle To The Bar

When I decided to take the plunge and head for Fiji to defend the Rotuman chiefs, I had to move fast. I tried to call the president of the Auckland District Law Society, Judith Potter, at home, urgently needing a letter from the law society stating that I was a "person of good character and a fit and proper person to be admitted to the Fiji High Court."

This was no simple request. Fear and trepidation rose as I recalled the law society refusing to give me a certificate of good character when I first applied for admission to the New Zealand bar some seven years before.

My admission was opposed for a variety of reasons. Not the least of them was my involvement with an organisation called Strike-Free. This anti-union group did not go down very well with the law society, as was evidenced by the questions asked by the council members hearing my application. Then there was the fact that I was still drinking heavily. Before coming under the guidance of Alcoholics Anonymous I was much louder and more abrasive than I am now. These factors, couple with a $50 fine for practising law without a licence in Alberta — I had put my name at the bottom of an affidavit as the person who had prepared the document — counted against me.

That fight for acceptance to the New Zealand bar struggled through the High Court at Auckland and ended up 18 months later before the Court of Appeal in Wellington, New Zealand. Peter Hillyer, Queen's Counsel, and now a High Court judge offered to help me with my case on appeal. When I asked him how much his fee would be, he told me, "Don't worry, you will be able to afford it." In the end he asked for no money and paid his own plane and hotel expenses connected to my case in the Court of Appeal.

The appeal was dismissed, but not for want of effort by my

lawyer. In return for his declaring no charge he required that I one day do the same for someone else in need. This undertaking to my senior barrister was about to be completed as I took on Rabuka and the Rotuman seven.

But, inside every cloud, they say, is a silver lining. Although my appeal to the Court of Appeal was not allowed, the court added a non-binding comment about there being room for different types of persons within the profession. This helpful snippet supported by my two years' participation with Alcoholics Anonymous and sufficient votes from council members saw me finally storm the inner sanctum of the bar.

Alcohol was the millstone around my neck. I used to drink to be merry, drink when I was sad, mad, bad or for any other excuse. I used to drink just to make my problems go away. Whatever you call it, for whatever reason you take it, for some of us alcohol is a non negotiable issue. The old saying with us alcoholics is that those afflicted are no more than one drink away from disaster.

I began to drink when I was very young becoming a teenage alcoholic in the early 60s. I doubt that any one thought it possible. Alcohol was never the instigator of my wild younger life but it was definitely an inhibitor to reasoned actions.

Violence in critical situations and in relationships hindered my growth in those younger years. A blackout as a 17-year-old after having walked three miles to the Fountain Bleu Hotel in St. Jean, Quebec, just outside my boot camp training barracks, was the first signal that booze and I were going to have a problem. Being on the sauce continuously tends to mould your thought process in a very narrow path, restricting rational thought and considered decisions.

After my experience in the military came to an early end because of my desire to drink, came two years work on the Canadian prairies installing microwave communciations equipment. Month on month we lived in hotels and motels across the country. My work mates and I had little else to do but party and drink. We did both to excess.

Joining Alcoholics Anonymous in June 1982 gave me the strength and courage to take one day at a time to conquer my addiction.

I am to this day most appreciative of Auckland barrister Colin Nicholson, Queen's Counsel, for it was he who opened the door to my admission as a barrister at law in 1983. He knew my predicament.

The Court of Appeal had turned down my appeal against the law society's refusal to give me a certificate of good character. Without that piece of paper I would never practise. But I convinced Colin Nicholson that I was worthy of a second look in the door.

Nicholson made an eloquent plea on my behalf. I had written a letter to the council which was really a plea in mitigation. Somebody on the council made a comment that "If Harder can make a case for himself like that, then maybe it is time to give him a go in court." The vote went my way and Nicholson did me the courtesy of a phone call halfway through the meeting to give me the good news.

My Saturday night search for someone on the Auckland Law Society to help with a letter in support of my good character proceeded without success. There was no answer at the president's home, and no joy with the secretary of the society. But the vice-president Colin Nicholson QC was home and he listened fairly to my plea for a letter before acknowledging that he thought I was entitled to such testimonial. But he said I would have to track somebody down with a key to get into the law society building if I wanted to take the letter with me to Fiji.

I did not get my letter before leaving for Fiji. Thank goodness for facsimile machines, my wife and Joan Bowring, den mother of the Auckland District Law Society, for making sure the document followed me to Suva.

When the Jumbo Jet stopped at Nadi Airport, I stood in line with my fellow passengers for some minutes before the doors were opened, eager to step off into the tropics. For some unknown reason I had dressed in my black pin-striped suit; I guess I wanted to look the part. The suit had been made to measure in Suva during my last holiday.

The Chinese gentleman who runs the South Seas Tailor Shop has such skill and ability, no thinking visitor to Suva should miss out on his services if they have three days and $300 for some quality apparel.

As I stepped from the plane walkway a wave of hot air struck me. Was this Fiji or had I strayed too close to a blast furnace. As the minutes went by in the customs queue my temperature quickly rose inside my impeccably made winter suit. Why hadn't I taken my wife's advice and worn some lighter clothes?

It was early, early morning, the airport abuzz with a trickle of tourists coming in and a flood of Indians pouring out. Security was tight. Fijian army and private Fijian security guards checked the luggage coming and going. Around us labourers who had worked through the night completed a concrete pour. The Indian workers took turns pushing wheelbarrow loads of concrete up a ramp.

The rush to complete an additional wing to the Fiji International Airport was on. Where the new tourists were to come from I was not sure. Tourism will not return to the heady days of previous years until Military Dictator Rabuka retires from the army and returns to his village. And tourism may never return to Fiji if a hand grenade explodes in one Fiji hotel or island resort.

As I left the luggage turnstile, jacket and vest now draped over my arm, sweat dripping from my face, I explained to the native Fijian immigration officer that I was intending to be admitted to the High Court of Fiji in relation to the Rotuma sedition case. I don't think he understood my English very well. The copy of the book *NO OTHER WAY*, Rabuka's inside story on the Fiji coups, in my briefcase attracted more attention than any other item in my bag. The guard had not read it. "No, we can't afford to buy books like this in Fiji," he said.

Once outside the immigration barrier I was besieged with offers of help from Indian taxi drivers. The high pitched chatter of competitors for the fare went on till I indicated I wanted to go to the Gateway Hotel. Cries of "No, no, try another better hotel," in hopes of a longer trip petered out when I said I had paid reservations.

At the entrance to the Gateway, across the road from the Nadi airport, I met Big Dan the hotel doorman, a person of distinguished features; six foot tall with a leathery cracked face, obviously weathered by many years of tropical sun and wind.

After a dinner of raw fish and salad, I was invited by my Fijian friend to come down to the taxi shack at the back of the hotel for a bit of kava. It was a little wooden hut with open windows, more like a shelter from the rain and wind. We sat in a circle, seven Indian drivers, one Fijian, and myself decked out with my walkman and new Fijian tape — "Mela in Rabual".

One Indian taxi driver was making short work of a chicken, using a great big Chinese meat cleaver and an old board. The meat was for a curry he was cooking outside the hut in a battered aluminium pot on a piece of corrugated iron over a smoking wood fire.

A dollar to the keeper for a bag of fresh kava to toss into the community bowl was my first order. Eyes lit up and conversation began to run. Seldom, though, did the boys discuss the current situation in Fiji. The Brigadier was mentioned in whispers. They did not speak out and say what was really on their minds unless they trusted you.

My stated purpose for being in Fiji, to represent the Rotumans charged with sedition by Rabuka's boys, and my attitude towards these poor citizens, was soon sufficient to displace any fears the men may have harboured when I first sat down.

Things were bad. Tourism was crawling along. Decent taxi fares were a thing of the past. Stories of poverty and open begging for tips to make ends meet were commonplace. Tales of suppression, of fear, and when all alone, of loathing for what Rabuka had done to Fiji spilled out over the kava bowl.

I quickly became known as the "ginger lawyer", needing a swig of ginger ale from my bottle after each cup of kava to wash away the taste. The camaraderie among this little band and its interaction with me was satisfying yet sad, because soon I would fly off and they would have to go back to their days of minimal fares, even smaller tips and fewer trips.

What a hell of a way to go. No time for family, no time for rest. Lost souls kicked from pillar to post, struggling to make ends meet on subsistence wages in a devastated tourist mecca. Tourism to this day has the potential to lift Fiji out of its economic woes: all citizens,

19

be they Fijian Indians, commonly referred to in the street as "visitors", or the indigenous Fijians, often referred to by Rabuka as "God's children" would benefit from a boom in Fiji's tourism.

Commuting To Work In Suva: May 15

Having slept little of the night I woke early and went for a run in the sugar cane-covered countryside. After eating breakfast by the pool I took a taxi to the airport. The flight to Suva, the capital of Fiji, took 25 minutes.

As the plane began to descend I wondered if I would have a reception party. My stomach began to churn. To my surprise I was neither checked nor stopped. Creeping paranoia — would the security forces meet me at the hotel?

At Nausori Airport just northeast of Suva the Gagaj Sau Lagfatmaro's personal representative, Mr Shanti Lal, met me. Shanti is a friendly little fellow, ever willing to help or please, a real gentleman in difficult times. A short, slight Fiji Indian, he is one of that rare breed to whom loyalty to friends is of the first order. That this trusty friend came to my aid when he did was fortunate, because I was worn out from the stress of my paranoid mental gymnastics. Shanti picked up my bags and placed them in his white Ford Econovan, a vehicle, like most others in Suva, lacking regular maintenance. I remember Shanti Lal as a pleasant little man. But looks were deceptive, he was a karate expert, allegedly trained by the Gagaj.

At $100 a night the Suva Travelodge tariff was a bit higher than expected in a town crying out for tourists. But in the no smoking section, room 261, its long balcony overlooking the sea, was a pleasant place to be. After a day of relaxing in and about the swimming pool I showered, changed into my dressing gown, and called room service for dinner. It was time to settle down to some preparatory legal work. "Bula bula" and a $2 tip for the smiling face who brought my dinner guaranteed a 5.00 a.m. wake-up call.

A hearty knock, knock ended my deep sleep with a start. The trip to the airport was smooth. Nothing much stirred in the almost chill tropical dawn. But for the third time in 36 hours an Indian taxi driver wanted to know how hard it was to immigrate to New

Zealand. This one also wanted to pay me $200 to track down his alcoholic wife — last known address somewhere in Mangere, Auckland five years ago — in the hope she might be able to help him get to New Zealand.

CHAPTER THREE

ON A WING AND THIN AIR:

MAY 16: At 5.45 a.m. the sun was nowhere to be seen. There were only flickering fluorescent tubes over the ticket counter to light the way.

Tevita Fa and the *Fiji Times* reporter Mesake Koroi met me near the tarmac gate. We shook hands and embraced. It was like we were old-time friends, and if we were not now, then we surely would be by the end of the day. Fa was much as I had imagined, nearly the perfect cliche. Shortish, bearded, sunken green eyes with that special Tongan sparkle. He had an exceedingly fat stomach and a smouldering filter cigarette constantly dangling from his lips. He was swathed in a green kimono type skirt stretched around his bulging middle; brown leather sandals, unstrapped, on his feet.

Mesake Koroi was a Fijian of extremely pleasant nature, an educated man who obviously liked his job. But it was soon apparent that the limitations of living under a military dictatorship with heavy press censorship were exacting a toll on this spirited journalist.

The flight to Rotuma in our silver-and-red twin engined charter plane would take two hours according to our pilot. He sat alone in the front seat. Tevita Fa and I sat behind him with Mesake behind the two of us. By the time we were about an hour and a quarter out, flying through light cloud cluttered with the odd storm, there was a golden sunrise slowly developing in the distance. Suddenly our bird in the sky plunged through the air like a rock in a vacuum.

My left hand clawed Tevita Fa's forearm. His left hand froze on his seat. Our right hands clung to the roof straps like sap on a tree.

Fa's arm and his chair probably still bear marks to this day. My life passed before me. I thought of my long struggle to succeed as a lawyer, and my wife and children waiting for days at Auckland Airport for the flight that would never come.

I was dead certain that it was only a matter of time before the blue seas swallowed us. Whatever our religious beliefs prior to this, you can be assured we were religious men before our battle with gravity was won. I could not see what the affable Mesake Koroi was doing in the back seat but I am very glad he missed his breakfast.

My heart was racing like a runaway wheel. It seemed certain the wings would tear from the body of the plane, like the dried wings of a dragon fly. But just then a very cool and courageous pilot found some light air.

As if our prayers had been answered from the heavens above, like waking from a childhood falling dream, we swooped back up into the sky. In life, some experiences one never forgets. This was one of them. A bond had been forged between three people which will no doubt last three lifetimes.

Thereafter I proceeded to direct the pilot around the clouds in the better interests of all of us hoping that this would prevent any repeat down-drafts. At least my layman aviator's instructions made me feel a bit more secure, even if they irked the pilot.

One's heart can only take so much. Two and quarter hours out and no land in sight, we started to really worry. Ten more minutes ticked by as we all recalled the two hour estimated flying time from Suva to Rotuma.

Two and a half hours crept up on the clock as I began to have visions of flying around the South Pacific, nowhere to land, with our fuel gauge edging towards empty. Then, just as the robust Tongan and I looked into each other's eyes for the second time with the certain knowledge that death was inevitable, the plane suddenly passed over a large split granite outcrop in the sea off the north tip of Rotuma.

We swept over the fish-shaped tropical island covered in coconuts and thick jungle with a green grass carpet laid out below for the plane. Our feelings of relief were so strong, it was as if we had never before felt so alive.

23

Rotuma was first recorded by the western world when Captain Edwards called there in 1791 while searching for the mutineers of the Bounty. From a distance of 10 miles out to sea, Rotuma appears undulating, hilly and densely wooded, the greatest elevation being near the centre of the island, where Suelhof attains an elevation of 840 feet. It is probably little changed from when Captain Edwards first saw it from the decks of his ship Pandora. Certainly as we approached there were no vast signs of modern civilization.

Rotuma is an island pretty much unto itself. Some 400 miles north of Fiji's main island of Viti Levu, it is not part of any major chain and its people, more Polynesian than Melanesian, are not closely tied in tradition or blood with any other Pacific peoples. They speak their own, distinct, language.

The island only became part of Fiji through colonial administrative convenience. The island was to have been included in the annexation of Fiji in 1874 but was left out because of a blunder in the paperwork. In July 1879 the island's chiefs sent a letter to Queen Victoria asking for annexation.

Being so far away from the mainstream, Rotuma remained substantially unmodified. A few castaways and, in later years, whalers and traders introduced a slight European influence, but far less than in most other parts of the South Pacific.

A steady stream of Rotumans have left their island for work and adventure in Fiji proper. Now there are only about 3500 people on Rotuma and far more Rotumans living in Fiji, where many have prospered.

But among those left on Rotuma a large number are unhappy over Rabuka's move to declare Fiji a republic and cut ties with the Commonwealth.

Their dissatisfaction grew into a partial rebellion which saw a group of them defiantly raise the Union Jack on a public flagpole.

To their horror the administrative officer appointed by Fiji showed his outrage by firing several shots at the flag.

Instead of treating the incident as some bizarre anachronistic joke the military fathers of Fiji sent troops to the island to quell the disturbances. They arrested and charged eight chiefs with sedition.

But the man who had sown the seeds of rebellion, the somewhat eccentric Gagaj Sau Lagfatmaro, who describes himself as a martial arts professor, was safe in his family home at Whenuapai on the outskirts of Auckland.

Six years ago Henry Gibson was appointed head of the Molmahao clan from which he is descended. But instead of returning to the island to lead his subjects, he remained in Auckland with his European wife and two children.

His most valid claim to fame would appear to be a string of martial arts schools he has started in the South Pacific.

As the plane taxied to the field station situated off to the left of the airfield, I looked down the runway to the vast green expanse of jungle. Green vines and creepers dominated the view.

The building was made of concrete block with a flush toilet and running water. It was a pleasant surprise. Painted lemon yellow, it stood out against the background of glittering emerald green. A wind sock blew lightly in the breeze coming off the South Pacific Ocean.

A small group of locals gathered to greet the three of us as we got down, each of us being careful not to step on the fragile leading edge of the wing of the plane. We had to fly home later that day. A red Daihatsu pick-up truck was parked by the gasoline pump near the landing strip.

A woman called Akeneta met us. Her South Seas beauty was accentuated by long flowing ebony-black hair lying over her left shoulder. She wore blue Levi jeans with a light blue silk top which seemed to highlight her green eyes; a refreshing and pleasant presence after our recent fears in the sky. Akeneta was a local schoolteacher married to one of the seven chiefs arrested by the Fiji Military Forces the previous week. The army had arrived on the island by military aircraft using the same airstrip that we had just touched down on.

She-devils In Paradise

From the air as we approached, I had seen a navy gunboat moored at the far end of the old Rotuma wharf, which had been built many years ago for the local copra dealers and island traders. The vessel reminded me of the PT-109 Torpedo gunboat which nearly took the life of John F. Kennedy when sunk in a similar tropical island paradise during the Second World War.

The rumour was that the boat would take the men back to Suva after the court case. Whether this implied the Government knew what the Chief Magistrate Apaitia Seru was likely to decide when the question of bail arose later in the day, I was not sure.

I climbed into the back of the truck with Mesake. Tevita, or Fa, as I had begun to call him, was invited into the front passenger seat for the journey. Mesake and I had to sit on the spare tyre, loose on the tray of the truck. Fa, on the other hand, enjoyed the comforts of a foam covered seat as we wound our way through the thick jungle. But out in the fresh air we had an uninterrupted view of the vast array of colourful tropical flowers, among them beautiful red, white and purple orchids.

Akeneta drove our taxi over the crumbling roads like a she-devil. Sand from the sea shore had been mixed with bags of cement years ago to make two parallel strips for vehicle wheels to run on. Without the concrete strips the heavy rain which often falls would make the road impassable. But the salt content of the sand had diminished the binding power of the concrete over the years and the edge of the tracks had begun to crumble, crack and wear down from the pressure of vehicles and tropical weather.

At the government station we jumped down from the truck to stretch our muscle-cramped legs. I had not felt such cramps since I ran the mile in 4:29 as a personal best some 22 years ago when I was at air force boot camp in Quebec. Fiji in June 1988 had many of the overtones of Quebec in the late 1960s and early 70s. If you were Anglo-Saxon and English speaking and had the nerve to walk into a French shop at that time in Quebec's history you were likely to be sneered at, ignored or asked to leave and never, but never, spoken to in English.

Born and raised in Canada, I had not liked those experiences of being treated as an outsider in my own country. Twenty years later, after terrorist attacks and political murders, Quebec has settled down and reached a level of tolerance. Special legislation dealing with culture, laws and lands now allows French and English speaking Canadians to live together in relative harmony.

As we stretched our legs, I became aware of a growing number of people closing in on us. The families of the seven arrested chiefs came forward to thank us for coming. Cool slices of oranges, the fruit Rotuma is famous for, were offered to us for refreshment.

As Fa and I entered the interview room, normally used as a school kitchen in the concrete block building we were greeted by a sea of hands. Freddy Emose and Afasio Mua, two of the arrested chiefs, stepped forward and thanked Fa and I for coming. Ian Crocker, a foxy old Rotuman, watched on with his one good eye. We sat on the bench top and I began to take down some details, writing with the Parker pen bought cheaply after haggling in Suva. Hiagi Apoa spoke of being arrested.

Every one wanted bail. As a criminal lawyer I understood their desire for freedom. Being in custody is no fun. Jail bars and concrete floors are not very comforting. We discussed our plans and shared confidences. One of the men brought out a tray of cool oranges.

Fa suggested we go outside for a moment and look about. Around the corner of the building Fa and I came across a grass field as big as two rugby fields. The far end of the field was bordered with drooping orange trees, to the east was the school. On the south side facing the sea was a grand old covered platform made of finished timber framing and planks now warping in the weather. The stand had a tattered Union Jack flapping in the wind. A number of locals sheltered under the roof from the sun. A senior military officer, possibly a major, stood off in the shadows watching me walk across the grass. I stared at him for a moment trying hard to not to betray any feelings.

Fa wandered over to talk to the Director of Public Prosecutions, Isikeli Mataitoga, about the case. I felt like a real outsider and hung back. When Isikeli saw me he turned and walked straight up to me shaking hands and talking like an old friend. If I met him at law school in Auckland, I didn't remember him now. I was about to ask him had we met before when the Chief Acting Magistrate for Fiji, Apaitia Seru, walked up to me, clasped both my hands and greeted me most warmly.

"Is this the famous Christopher Harder of the Tramways Union injunction case?" he asked. It seemed the notoriety from my strike breaking past would never let me go. Magistrate Seru smiled with a knowing grin to Army Captain and prosecutor Mataitoga. I blushed. Thinking back to those days now tends to send shivers up my back and make my cheek muscles twitch.

Striking Back And Paying For It

The Tramways Union injunction happened in Auckland while I was studying at Auckland. University seemed to have an effect on me: it didn't matter whether it was Calgary or Auckland, a devilish spirit arose in me at times during my student days.

I was living in Mission Bay with my previous wife. We had a 12-month-old son Justin. While I attended Law School she worked. On the days I had classes I took Justin to the University daycare centre. Not having a car, I had to rely on public transport; I needed the buses.

I remember lying on the floor of our rented home. My head up against the radio speaker in the living room. A Radio 'i' news bulletin screamed in my ear. "Henry Stubbs, Secretary of the Tramways Union, has confirmed that the buses will not be running in downtown Auckland tomorrow. Radio 'i' News has contacted industrial law lecturer Bill Hodge who confirmed that the bus drivers were required to give 14 days notice of strike action by law."

This was to be the third rolling strike of an on-going campaign for more benefits by the bus drivers. They had momentum and would not stop on their own.

Earlier that day in a legal studies class at University I had been given a copy of an English High Court case called Gouriet v Post Office Workers Union. The British Union had banned all mail and telephone calls from South Africa because of Africa's apartheid policy. Gouriet applied to the court for an injunction to stop the interference with the Queen's mail. After protracted argument the London Judge ruled that Gouriet had sufficient legal standing to bring his claim. He won his case and the union was ordered to stop the strike.

My request for a similar restraining order in New Zealand, adopting the same principles of law and legal standing as Mr Gouriet was, to my, surprise successful. The granting of the injunction brought me the wrath of the left wing of the New Zealand trade union movement.

I had been working part time at the Kiwi Hotel in Symonds Street, Auckland as a barman. When the news got out that I had been successful in my court case, the private bar where I was working was flooded with Socialist Unity Party members asking for double measure drinks from the top shelf. The only catch was that these left-leaning patrons would not be served by me. About 50 people clambered into the room waiting to be served at the bar. But none would drink unless somebody other than Christopher Harder would serve them. Two hours and many words later I was walking down the road looking for a new job.

The successful court action brought the national press to my front door. The telephone never stopped ringing. Cameramen and TV crews waited outside our house. The news media went wild with the case. A sort of David bringing the Union Goliath to heel.

When the Union refused to obey the court injunction my lawyer Dr. Rodney Harrison and I took them back to court; a good fight. Here was a small group of persons inconveniencing the whole of the city. A lot of people seemed to get in behind me. It seemed a whole segment of the population had just been waiting to have a real go at a union. It didn't matter which union. Any old union would do. With a toe in the door the right wing was off with a vengence.

The trial Judge Mr Justice Chilwell ordered the Union to pay $412 towards my costs. When the sheriff went to collect the money from the union's bank all the money had gone. It was rumoured that the union secretary had taken all the funds out of the bank moments before the sheriff arived with his charging order requiring the bank to freeze the bus drivers' funds until they paid the costs. I was determined to get my money from the Tramways Union. It was a matter of principle: they lost, they pay.

The special union fund that was set up to fight this right wing rebel was the key to their undoing. I had a cheque for $10 mailed to the Tramways Union fighting fund by a friend. Five days later I had his returned cheque and the location of the new bank account. Six days later I had my $412 and some new enemies for life.

Queen Elizabeth Barracks: Suva 9:00 a.m.

I later found out that the Fiji military forces had kept me under surveillance: "Christopher Harder, N.Z. lawyer, is staying at the Travelodge Hotel, room 261. He is booked in for five days. Ate dinner in room. Has wake up call at five o'clock for six o'clock flight to Rotuma. Sent by Henry Gibson." concluded a brief surveillance report. When this information was handed to Lieutenant Colonel Jioji (George) Konrote he had erupted.

"Why was I not informed of this report sooner?" he bellowed.

"The report only arrived shortly before you came in sir. The duty officer brought it in," the Corporal replied.

Colonel Konrote was a man of short temper. Like most Rotumans his skin was lighter than the very dark Fijian tones. His receding hair line left a bald patch on the top of his head. He was the number two man in the Fiji military.

I had been told Konrote was an unreasonable, arrogant man with a vested interest in Rotuma remaining part of Fiji. Obviously he and his Rotuman colleagues in the army did not wish to have outsiders interfere with what can only be described as good career opportunities for themselves in the military. The job is known to have some perks.

Konrote simply had no time for outsiders who interfered with the internal runnings of Rotuma. Henry Gibson was a traitor in the eyes of the Colonel and anybody sent to Rotuma by Gibson would be treated as such.

"If Gibson ever comes back to Fiji," yelled Konrote, "I will personally execute him!" The Colonel had his fists clenched as he pounded the desk. He was angry, mad but loyal like a dog to the Brigadier.

"Arrest the two of them. Fa and Harder," yelled the voice through the half opened door.

Konrote continued to rave. "I will not have either of those communists on my island. You tell the Major I want them arrested and taken off the island. My people will not stand for such interference. I expect a report by noon, do you understand me? Fa is history. Outsiders dabble at their own peril. Arrest them and take them off the island."

The radio telephone crackled with static as the Corporal tried to confirm that the Colonel's orders had been carried out. In the Rotuma post office communications room the operator called back to the Corporal in Suva." Wait, I will send somebody across the field to the Major."

The Major was walking on the soccer field by the old celebration platform. Chief Magistrate Seru interrupted. "They can't do any real harm. Leave him be. Tell Colonel Konrote I advise against any such action."

The magistrate had remembered me from his time in New Zealand which coincided with the highly publicised Tramways Union case. He saw me as a public spirited lawyer, and felt it would be counter-productive to arrest me.

At the same time neither Fa nor I realised how close we had come to being arrested. It was not until much later that a friendly soldier told me about Konrote's outburst.

Under the 1927 Rotuma Act of Fiji, the Fiji Chief Magistrate was required to sit as a magistrate on the island of Rotuma to hear the criminal charges of sedition against the seven. When the Chief Magistrate returned to the make-shift court after considering the question of jurisdiction that had been raised, His Honour betrayed no indication of what that decision might be.

In defence of the seven Rotumans, Tevita Fa argued that after the coups Rotuma ceased to come under the Fiji Government's discretion. He said Rabuka's coups and declaration of a Republic in Fiji had abrogated the Constitution of Fiji under which the Rotuma Act was listed. As such Rotuma was no longer part of Fiji and the islanders should be able to decide for themselves. Fa had told this unusual court that the two coups in Fiji were executed to further the interests of the Fijian race politically, economically and socially. Rotuma was never a colony of Fiji, but had been a colony of Great Britian administered by Fiji.

The Director of Public Prosecutions, Mr Isikeli Mataitoga, countered with the argument that Decree No. 5 had reactivated all other legislation including the Rotuma Act. Mataitoga also claimed that the Rotuma Council had expressed the wish to remain with Fiji

31

and it was likely Rotuma would be represented in Fiji's Parliament in the new constitution.

The court was again called to order. Along with the prisoners everybody in the room stood up. All the windows of the school room were open. Villagers from across the island stood outside and listened. This court hearing was the biggest thing to happen on Rotuma since the Fiji Military Forces had sent soldiers to the island to eradicate wild pigs.

This pig hunt episode began two months after the second coup, and only days after the second military government turned control over to a civilian administration headed by former Prime Minister, Ratu Sir Kamisese Mara. The people of Rotuma thought the exercise had more to do with the army asserting control over the island than pest control.

For this event in the schoolroom, the locals were hanging in the windows, lying on the floor and standing near the door; small groups gathered on the grass outside while succesive members took turns coming into the court to listen, then going back to report to the group while someone else took their place.

All the while the army major supervising the proceedings stood watching in the wings. I was told there were soldiers armed with loaded M16 rifles on the island but that they were being kept out of sight during our stay. The magistrate began to read his decision from hand written notes. As he started speaking I noticed two young Rotuman women staring at me. One pointed and giggled while the other blushed. I turned back to listen to the magistrate as he paused to wipe his brow of sweat. Fa was gazing at the ceiling contemplating our next move as the Chief Magistrate ordered "that a serious question of law arose in relation to the question of jurisdiction, such that the matter should be referred to the High Court of Fiji for final determination."

Out of the corner of my eye I saw the two young women trying hard to get my attention. I looked straight back and struggled not to smile.

As the decision was concluded Fa proceeded to make a formal application for bail. The accused would appear for trial should they be bailed, he submitted, all seven lived in Juju, a small village about three miles up island from the government station. It is the home of the Molmahao. Bail was denied and ultimately the seven were taken to Suva in the gun boat.

Rotuma has seven provinces and Molmahao is one of the clans in one of these provinces. Each province has its own group of chiefs in a parochial system.

As we said goodbye to the seven I could see tears in the eyes of Afiosa. I badly wanted to assure him that his leader the Gagaj was coming, but in my heart I knew it was not true. As I turned to walk away he shook my hand firmly. He asked us to do what we could so they might all return home to their families soon.

Mesake and I climbed back onto the truck as Fa climbed into the front seat. This time we went in the opposite direction, heading into the heart of the island. The road to Juju was long and winding. The same sidewalk tracks snaked through the jungle and along the sandy sea shore lined with coconut palms.

Empty houses dotted the foreshore. Concrete houses were often built on the beachfront above the high water mark. Like the roads the houses also cracked and crumbled in time. When the house finally deteriorated too badly, the members of the household just moved out and built another house in the same fashion, next door. The old house was then stripped of internal fittings for the new building.

All along the waterfront youths meandered aimlessly near the road. Very young girls played with and even nursed small babies. Most people wore a cloth sulu wrapped around their waist, and all were barefoot. Some western dress had been imported from Fiji, including the ubiquitous faded blue denim jeans.

With not a cloud in the sky this ride was much more pleasant than the trip from airport to court. We could see the seascape and the waves breaking on the rocks out on the point. An outrigger canoe, three quarters submerged in the water, was bobbing up and down like a discarded log. Ripe coconuts, fallen from their own weight or shaken free by the wind from the multitude of trees, lay scattered along the way.

On the flat by the shore the concrete strips on the roads disappeared. No doubt the main purpose of the roads was to get vehicles up and over the knolls and hills in the wet season. As we approached Juju the people began to take more notice of us. It was not very often that a six foot two inch palagi (white person) came to the village. The truck swung to the right off the road and the wheels skidded to a stop in the dust.

The three of us slowly climbed out of the truck. We were shown through a garden littered with bones and shell. A goat bleated as we passed by and a kitten skittered under the verandah of a little house. I stepped around the mud puddle by the communal water tap. Three young teenagers, with a wicked looking knife, were busy removing the skin from steaming taro, obviously just out of an oven.

Everyone had a cane knife in Fiji just as they did on Rotuma. A more offensive weapon you could not find, yet there was no law against them. The big knife is a crucial implement in field and bushwork.

Food For Cultural Thought

We walked around the house to a large thatch-covered construction built on eight big posts shaved from old coconut trees. The floor of the building was covered in sand which had just been raked smooth by a young man with a wisk broom. We took our shoes off and walked in.

I was a bit uncertain of what was expected, but watched Fa for a lead. A large number of mats were laid out on the ground by four teenage girls. The mats were obviously handwoven and of the best quality. An older woman came into the room and unfolded a huge piece of orange silk, which she laid over the mats with a practised flick and a shake of her arms.

The rest of the clan stood around the outer posts and watched. Then the elders came into the feasting room and stood with an old man who had been number eight of the men charged with sedition but had his charge dropped because of his age. Colonel Konrote knew there was no capital to be gained in jailing an old man. Even traitors had soft spots, I thought to myself.

We were invited to sit cross legged in the centre of the silk. Fa sat in the middle, I sat on the left and Mesake moved to the right. Then

34

three young maidens entered and knelt before us. One of them began to fan my face with a hand-made fan. The second one put a lei of flowers and sandalwood pieces around my neck. Then the third nubile young woman splashed perfume on my temples, the top of my head and then the nape of my neck. Another came in with peeled and sliced oranges to eat. She placed a piece on my tongue. Each of us was given a fish, a piece of goat, a leg of lamb and a pot of corned beef plus mounds of taros, yams and a big bowl of salt.

If I had not eaten in a week I might have been able to handle a fraction of what had been placed before me. I thanked the elders for their hospitality and told the gathering I would hand on their blessings and thanks to their Gagaj Sau Lagfatmaro on my return to Auckland.

I picked at the mountain of corned beef and pulled at the lamb. The tall, cool glasses of chilled orange juice left me wondering how they had been able to make the juice so cold.

The wives of the men in jail each spoke of their appreciation for our coming. Akeneta spoke out for all to hear that the girls wanted Fa and I to stay for the night. Every person in the room giggled. The old lady across the floor from me put her hand over her mouth and chin as she turned her head away so nobody could see her laugh. I looked at Fa with the certain knowledge that if he and I did not get off the island before dark there could be an international legal scandal.

The food left over from the feast was presented to us again at the truck, along with five loaves of steaming hot bread, as we readied ourselves to leave this absolute paradise before nightfall. Fa and I looked at each other again for a long moment but agreed we had work to do on the case on our return to the main island. There was not an hour to spare. Fa fixed me with that wicked Tongan glint in his eye and said, "Christopher, do not despair, the jurisdiction question will surely fail and we will be obliged to return to Rotuma again for the trial."

The Gagja had promised us a bure to sleep in, down by the sea on our return to the island. Rotuman hospitality was hard to beat.

The quality of the houses and the display of some wealth by way of a car or bike parked in the front yard was more frequent as we

35

moved closer to the government station. Our travels took us full loop back past the playing field and school on our way to the airport. Enroute to the plane I noticed for the first time that the roadside bush was filled with massive green orange trees dripping with camouflaged fruit.

On the way a gaggle of girls waved their hands in the wonderful slow Polynesian way. I wondered if I would come back to Rotuma sometime in the future.

At the airfield the locals presented us with three huge thatched leaf baskets of oranges. We had to weigh the oranges to see if we could carry them on board. After two men dragged the produce onto the scales it was decided that one full basket and some of the fruit from the second would have to be left. The rest was shoved into the nose of the aeroplane.

As dusk was fast approaching the pilot started up the motors and got ready to taxi out to the grass strip. The people were waving goodbye as a woman ran up to me with two letters to mail for her on my return to New Zealand. One was to the Prime Minister of New Zealand pleading for help for her people. The other letter was addressed to Gagaj Sau Lagfatmaro begging for his return.

The plane picked up speed as we chased down the runway, up, up and away as the pilot banked to the left and the island disappeared behind us.

For over an hour and a half we flew blind into the dark. The only lights we could see were the amber flashing light on the wings and the reflection of the red tail beacon on the plane's belly. A brief down draft shook the plane. For a moment our thoughts raced back to the morning flight. Rain smacked on the windscreen as the pilot struggled to determine our location in relation to Suva radio tower beacon. Fa was fast asleep on my left, snoring like a horse.

Mesake was desperately trying to write the Rotuma court story of the day under a small dim overhead light. As we began our descent towards the Suva runway, I saw the direction lights flash on like a guiding arrow in the dark. Two thousand feet and slowing, descending until the altimeter showed 900 feet. The wings on the plane dipped then levelled as our descent continued. At 90 feet I could see the reflection of the navigation lights on the rainswept tarseal.

Thump, thummmp, the wheels bumped and slipped on the wet, and we were down. I sighed as the pilot applied the brakes and reduced speed, then turned the nose of the craft towards the tower block and passenger terminal. As the plane came to a stop, and the propellers spun down, a considerate young man ran out to the plane to hand each of us an old golf type umbrella to fend off the tropical rains lashing the airport.

We were met by the loyal Shanti Lal, who drove Fa and me to the hotel. Mesake took a taxi, he was in a rush to finish his story and submit it before the night's deadline. We agreed to meet again soon and promised to keep in touch.

It had been a long day. I was dead tired as we arrived back at the hotel. Fa went home after a quick drink in the downstairs bar. I went into the dining room, but changed my mind, a quick dip in the pool might soak out some of the tiredness.

I swam a few lengths then exhaled and slowly sank to the bottom of the pool, lying there totally relaxed. Suddenly my lungs began to burn. As if I might never breathe again, my feet propelled me up through the water in a desperate rush to gasp fresh air . . . flash back to my previous trip in March when my family and I had holidayed at Korolevu.

I had been snorkeling in about three feet of water, but being totally submerged could not really tell how deep I was. I had just pushed off from a piece of coral and was gliding, peacefully, my body fully extended, when suddenly out from beneath some seaweed slipped a black and white striped coral snake, the most poisonous reptile of the Pacific. Only snakes rate higher on my list of things to avoid in life than claustrophobic enclosures. My fins pumped the water like my feet had sprouted wings. My head broke the surface with my heart full of fear, I thrashed, crawled, then ran from the sea . . . and then I was back in the pool at the hotel, breathing fast, speeding, ready to eat . . . and then to sleep.

The *Fiji Times* slid under my door about 6.15 in the morning. I was normally awake at six, long conditioned to early rising by our two young children. "FIJI HAS NO POWER OVER ROTUMA" read the headline to the story about yesterday's Rotuma case. Missing were the words ". . . said defence lawyer." But it was too late to change things. Army officers are early risers too; by now Rabuka and his henchmen would have seen what no doubt appeared to them as Tevita Fa and upstart Kiwi lawyer Christopher Harder challenging their authority.

I could just see the reaction down at the Queen Elizabeth barracks: the Brigadier grimacing as he read the headline. 'FIJI POWERLESS OVER ROTUMA.'

"That paper will pay dearly for this. I want our people into the *Times* office now. Find out who was responsible for the story. Put Mesake Koroi on the list. I want security people in that office from now on. If this Indian editor thinks he can play games with me, then he's got a thing or two to learn about living in Fiji and so has Mr Koroi." Sitiveni Rabuka was worried that his fellow Fijians were concerned about public perception. Was Rabuka in charge or were the courts dictating to the Judas?

Konrote was simply embarrassed. To those who just read the newspaper story headline it might appear that the Gagaj, Henry Gibson, had scored a point or two. Konrote and Rabuka relied on each other. Both were terribly concerned about losing face. In Fiji, face is a priority, especially to military men.

About 7,000 Rotumans live and work in Fiji, many with the civil service and a significant number in the army. The secretary to the Chief Registrar was the sister-in-law of one of the arrested Rotuman chiefs. Wages earned in Fiji make up most of the money spent on Rotuma. Aside from some government jobs for the teachers and the postmaster, the locals subsist on root crops, mixed with fresh fish, coconuts and fruit. As second in command of the Fiji Army, Konrote's status among his fellow Rotumans was normally high. The *Fiji Times* article was not going to go down well with the Colonel.

38

CHAPTER FOUR

SUVA DAY TWO:

MAY 17: As soon as the shops were open I was off to a computer store down the road from the hotel. It was run by a petite young Chinese woman called Marnie who was trying desperately hard to sell quality computers, mostly to business minded Indians. She was a fast and efficient typist and I could rely on her for confidentiality.

I quickly prepared a motion to be filed in the High Court seeking an urgent hearing date for the Rotuma jurisdiction argument. A memorandum was prepared spelling out the chiefs' grievances. The submissions to the High Court were brief and to the point: because of Rabuka's coup, Fiji had no power over Rotuma. As I walked out of the computer shop, papers in hand, I called a cab.

In Fiji one hails a cab for just about any trip in town. The cars are mostly owned and driven by local Indians, the fares are cheap and the service plentiful. Walking in that humidity can quickly sap one's strength.

Fa's office was behind the old Government buildings. In the phone book his number was listed with the Alliance Party; Fiji phone books take even longer than New Zealand directories to catch up with people. He had quit his job as Alliance treasurer long ago after finding out how confused were the finances of the party which had ruled Fiji for the past 17 years.

Fa's brown sulu (Fijian male dress) was wrapped tightly about his stomach. Whatever anybody said about Fa, you surely had to admire his courage. He had taken Lady Mara, wife of the Fijian Prime Minister, to task for her handling of hundreds of thousands of dollars of land lease monies paid by the owners of the Fijian Hotel for ground rent.

The Fijian Hotel, situated near Sigatoka, half way between Suva and Nadi, was built on a 105 acre private island called Yanuca. It is the most complete resort along the coral coast, and the hotel paid big money to the local Fijians for its exclusive site.

Fa threatened legal action when he discovered that Lady Mara was the only member of the company formed to look after the ground rent money and that the articles of the company authorised her to pay any honorarium she chose to give herself.

He threatened to prosecute this high priestess if she did not stop her naughty ways. Lady Mara's husband, Prime Minister Kamisese Mara, never forgave Fa. Like myself and the left wing of the Labour Party in New Zealand, he had made an enemy for life.

Tevita Fa now had about as much in common with Mara and the Alliance Party as I did with the New Zealand Chief Justice's annual tea party. The accidental humour of the telephone listing is in stark contrast to what Brigadier Rabuka said in his book, *NO OTHER WAY*; Fa's pending political appointment under Dr Bavadra's newly elected Coalition Government was one of the last straws that pursuaded Rabuka to mount his first coup.

To get to Fa's second floor office you climb a set of old, rickety stairs. The wallpaper is tattered and torn, the reception room floor covered in linoleum laid over the electrical extension cords and telephone line; a one-phone office. In Fiji you are fortunate indeed to have a telephone.

Della, Fa's office secretary, greeted me with her normal, "Hello, Mr Christopher." Della is a Fijian woman not scared of hard work. While in Suva I frequently telephoned the office looking for the elusive Fa only to find loyal Della working away at all times of the day and night, including the weekends.

After exchanging pleasantries and giving Della a brief rundown on Rotuma, I was ushered into Fa's office. I explained the motion I had prepared for filing in the High Court that day. Della still used an old Underwood manual typewriter. I was thankful to have my IBM-equipped Marnie down the road.

The papers requested an urgent hearing date on the Rotuma

jurisdiction question. A memorandum explaining the grievance of the Molmahao clan that lead up to the application was also prepared. The memorandum was a bold statement of the clans' claim to independence for Rotuma.

Into The Inner Circle

I decided to file my papers for admission before I left. The motion asked for the right to practice as a lawyer on a temporary basis for the Rotuma sedition case only. I got Tevita Fa to sign an affidavit outlining the need for an outside lawyer. His statement read: "I am informed that Mr Christopher Harder has specialised knowledge in constitutional and criminal law and research abilities which will be of assistance to me in this matter." Fa was aware of my able reseach assistant, Ms Karen Soich, who has assisted me over the years giving my submissions an extra polish.

The other truth of the matter was things needed to be said in the Rotuma case that might be safer said by an outsider. Fiji authorities wouldn't be stupid enough to arrest a foreign national lawyer just doing a job, would they?

I walked up the stairs to the first floor of the Government Building, like a regular in the corridors — I almost felt at home. Quite a relaxed atmosphere exists between the magistrates and the lawyers appearing after a case. But during the times I sat in on the odd case I was astonished to hear how harshly one arrogant and punitive judge spoke to two local Indian lawyers.

The rudeness of this particular Sri Lankan judge reminded me of a scuffle I had with a local Auckland judge. The judge had only recently been transferred to Auckland. He was sitting in the old Number One court in Kitchener Street in downtown Auckland where most people were waiting for the wrecking ball to dash down the limestone walls built over a century before.

I appeared in front of the Judge for the first time on behalf of a client in a drugs case in late 1987. As my client was called to the prisoners' dock, I stood up to address the court. "May it please your Honour, Christopher Harder, barrister, appearing on behalf of the prisoner."

The Judge looked up over his glasses and bellowed "Is that a hyphenated name?"

I looked at him, paused and then said, "I beg your pardon?"

"Is that a hyphenated name?" he roared back from his perch in the sky, for all to hear.

I hesitated for a moment, looking around the court to see the reaction. Everybody stood still. You could hear a pin drop. The court room felt so electric it almost crackled. I quietly put my papers on the table and replied courteously, "No, Sir, that is my first and last name."

"I am not interested in your first name," he snapped back.

My blood was beginning to boil. Here I was being super polite, bowing in a traditional show of respect, calling his Honour sir, and he was bellowing like a stuck walrus. I began to see red. Who did this rude old bastard think he was, I said to myself.

"Excuse me sir," I replied, "I would like to see your Honour in chambers, please!"

"You may speak to me in open court Mr Harder," he replied.

"No sir," I said. The court was full of lawyers. Policeman were everywhere and the press benches were over flowing.

"I wish to see your honour in chambers now, sir." My request was one that his Honour ignored at his own instant peril.

I had heard my share of rude judges; no more I thought. A young lawyer sitting beside me looked up in utter amazement. Kiwi lawyers did not normally stand up to judicial figures in this sort of fashion. I could think of a handful — flamboyant criminal barrister Peter Williams QC, Kevin Ryan and Michael Bungay QC.

Anger began to rise in my chest. I was sure the judge could see what was coming. "I would like to see your Honour in chambers, now." I repeated.

With that the Judge declared the court as chambers and said, "Go ahead Mr Harder, what is it you wish to say?"

"No Sir," I replied, "I require the court to be cleared,." Chambers hearings were normally a private matter between the Judge, prosecutor and the defence lawyer.

By this time the Judge realized he had bitten off more than he could chew. "Clear, the court," he ordered. "Clear the court," he repeated.

I stood my ground standing silently at the bar table waiting for the moment. My chest began to tighten. A blast was welling up inside me like no judge had ever experienced before. As the last member of the gallery left the court I began to speak.

Like a cane field fire in Fiji the word would spread. Don't trifle with Harder if you don't want a fight. If this Sri Lankan judge sitting in the magistrates court in the Fiji Government building had spoken to me as he had just addressed a couple of local lawyers, he would have remembered my unhyphenated name for a long time to come.

Some rough justice had, on occasion, no doubt slipped by in the Fiji Magistrates Court.

There was an incessant chatter of Indian and English about the court, overhead fans slowly moved the muggy Fiji air about the room. It had been a long time since the dust had been cleaned from the blades.

Three Indian policeman stood in the court. A couple of Fijians lounged on the back row court seat waiting for their friend. One young Indian boy of about 16 displayed marks and bruising on his face and arms consistent with a savage beating from someone. I watched him as he sat down beside me. I never got the chance to ask him how he had suffered such abuse. One minute he was behind me, the next moment he was gone.

Then as I walked down the corridor towards the chief clerk of the court I saw the shaped Fiji-afro hair cut of my friend Rusiate walking away from me. " Hey, Rusiate," I called out. Everybody turned around. I could read their minds. I knew what they must be thinking. Who was this loud voiced person with the funny accent?

Rusiate heard me. He turned and walked back up the passageway with a warm Fijian smile as he approached. " How are you Mr Christopher?" he inquired.

"I have my papers in my brief case for filing," I said. This was my second black briefcase in a year. The one before had been destroyed in the dynamite bombing of my mint 1972 two-door pillarless Mercedes coupe.

Never let it be said that a lawyer specialising in criminal work does not earn his dough. My car was bombed because somebody was offended that he had been asked to pay a $1,500 fee still outstanding to my friend Peter Williams, who had specialised in criminal law for over 30 years. This person had been discharged by a High Court Judge from a criminal charge on the basis that there was insufficient evidence to put him on trial in front of a jury.

Both Williams and I had made some comment to another person that the proper thing to do was to pay what was fairly owed. The result was that Williams' house was torched by an arsonist and destroyed in the middle of the night. The Williams' family narrowly missed being burned alive and the two culprits missed a murder charge by the ring of a door bell.

At my house a stick of dynamite was placed next to the just filled gas tank of my mint Mercedes. The intruders had boldly walked down my leaf covered driveway just before sun up one morning.

I guess the bombing goes with the job. No matter, you still never get used to it. My car was badly mangled in the blast and only a wall of wood saved my wife from being pierced by shrapnel. The car was not insured, it was sold for scrap. I bought another dog and I surrounded our home with alarms, lights, and gates. A seige mentality set in for a while, but as time passes the memories of that morning continue to fade from my consciousness, despite the $50,000 loss we suffered.

A similar type of seige mentality had set into Fiji, like dark storm clouds hovering overhead. Nobody wanted to play together. You couldn't run or ride your bike on a Sunday. It was more than a year after the first coup before family members were allowed to picnic together on a Sunday.

Seldom did people go out in Suva in the evening anymore. The streets were quiet and empty, the summer winds blowing bits and pieces of paper down the roads. A national mental depression had set in. A schizophrenia had spread through the country, there was nowhere to go to get away from it in Fiji. Everybody was affected.

The only place still fully alive in town was the Suva municipal market. There politics were forgotten, Indians brushed shoulders with their Fijian, Chinese and European brothers. Vendors from all walks of life jibed, jostled and cajoled each other amidst all their ware.

Fruit and vegetables of every local kind were available. Green leafy plants called bele and bhaji, along with tomatoes, eggplants, carrots, red hot chillies, capsicums, yams, tapioca and dalo covered the market floor. Fresh fruit, sliced melons showing red sugary flesh, mangoes, bananas, oranges and mandarins were on display; laid out in rows, stacked in neat piles. The level of chatter indicated a heart still beating in at least part of Suva.

Out behind the stalls, sometimes behind wire grills, sat Fijian and Indian men drinking grog (kava) and chatting with each other. It will no doubt take years for Fiji to regain its once thriving tourist industry now so savaged by one selfish act.

Most revolutions come about when the weak and the oppressed overthrow their oppressors. Here in Fiji the privileged overthrew the oppressed to protect themselves and the lifestyles they had become accustomed to. Ministers of the Crown, Fijian chiefs and military officers often drove around the countryside in flash new Mercedes.

Rabuka's seizing of power by the gun would only beget more guns, I thought. The Gagja had said somebody would try and shoot him. How would they do it? Rabuka had surrounded himself with a group of young soldiers from his home village. With them he felt safer yet he would not keep to a routine.

Colonel Gaddafi of Libya learned his lesson the hard way about sleeping in the same place all the time when United States jets attacked his village in the Libyan desert. Rabuka didn't talk much about the possiblity of his own assassination but it was known to occupy his mind from time to time.

Rabuka would not allow anybody to tell the press where he was going in advance, probably because he feared assassination. Some western countries quietly sanctioned 'termination with extreme prejudice,' a spy term used to describe state-sanctioned murder. How would Oliver North have dealt with this South Seas traitor?

The black leather brief case hung comfortably in my right hand. Rusiate stood to my left. Today he had on his black jacket and tie. That meant he was either just going to see the Chief Justice or he had just been. Rusiate never wore his tie and jacket if he could avoid it.

Normally his jacket and tie hung in the registry office on one of the file shelves. There were stacks and stacks of yet-to-be-actioned files; bulging at the seams, spilling out onto the floors, files were everywhere, piled on boxes and stuffed into empty seats.

My best guess suggested it would take four New Zealand judges at least 18 months to clear up the existing commercial, civil, criminal and appeals list. As Rusiate walked into the office I walked around to the dark oak counter, lovingly aged and worn smooth by many a hand and elbow over the years. There is something magnificent about natural wood enhanced with age.

I handed Rusiate my admission papers and a letter for the Chief Justice. The letter, dated May 18, 1988, addressed to the High Court Registrar, was written on my gold lettered special bond. I didn't want anybody to think I was running a second class operation. The letter spoke of my imminent return to New Zealand. It also made the point that I had no intention of becoming involved in any domestic politics.

He took the papers from me and disappeared up the winding stairs. I sat down on the outer railing on the first floor looking out onto the front lawn of the main Government building. A huge Jacaranda tree and a stone statue of Ratu Sir Lala Sukuna, a former Fijian statesman, occupied my view. I wondered if Rabuka would be remembered in granite when it was all over, or would he be stoned out of office?

As I looked out over the courtyard I heard Rusiate call out. "Are you ready to go up?" he said. With a surprised look on my face I said "Where? I just came over to deliver this letter to the Registrar to inform him that I don't intend to get involved in the local politics, but I would appreciate temporary admission from His Honour to do the Rotuma sedition case before I leave for home."

Sedition cases in the South Pacific involving the Queen of the Commonwealth were rare, this had to be a lawyer's dream.

Dressing For The Part

"I can't go now," I said to Rusiate, "I have no jacket or tie." I was a strong believer in always dressing my best and making sure my shoes were clean and polished.

"Here, wear my tie and jacket, I can borrow one from the office," he said and handed me a well worn black jacket and tie.

If I had any doubts about getting further involved in this bizarre case, based on a island little changed since the days of sandalwood traders and Pacific blackbirders, it was too late to back out now. Rusiate was delighted to have an outsider taking an interest in Fiji's justice system. With all of the foreign judges having fled to more balanced judicial pastures, the backlog in the courts was mounting and the highlights of previously learned courtroom battles were diminishing.

A number of Indian and Fijian men were standing around on the circular tiled floor of the lobby outside Rusiate's office waiting for their names to be called in the magistrates court next door.

I put on the jacket and tied the tie under my short sleeve shirt collar. I was hot and sweaty wondering exactly what was going on. A Fijian girl I had not see before walked past me as I dressed and wished me well. I wondered what she meant; she probably worked in Rusiate's office.

I watched her walk up the steps in front of me. Her long black hair fell over a tight fitting yellow dress with shoulder straps coupled together by two great big green plastic buttons. Her legs were long and lithe but she wore no shoes. The yellow dress showed off her dark skin like a prized sun tan. At the top of the stairs, she turned right and carried on up the stairs towards the Chief Justice's office.

Rusiate directed me straight ahead into the Chief Registrar's office where I was asked to sit for a minute. He went in the opposite door and closed it behind him. I sat down and talked to the Chief Registrar's secretary Teresa. She, like many Fiji civil servants, was from Rotuma.

Then, to my surprise, I found out that she was the sister of Akeneta, our she-devil driver in the red truck.

"Come in Mr Harder," said a voice. I looked up to see the Chief Registrar, Apisailome Matebalevu, more commonly referred to simply as Apisai. I had first met him back in March when I had

47

visited the court with my wife to see a criminal trial. On that occasion the two of us had talked of me coming back to Suva later in the year to do a local murder on legal aid.

He had his hand extended and a big grin on his face. "So you really want to do a case in Fiji," he said. I had tried to pull the jacket sleeves down. I felt like a man wearing a boy's clothes. Rusiate's garish, huge, wide tie must have looked absurd. Normally I would have gone back to the hotel and changed. But not every day am I invited upstairs into the Halls of Justice of a foreign land.

I operate by the golden rule of taking opportunity when it offers. I could be dead tomorrow; a heart attack, run over by a bus or blown up by a bomb while I sleep. Life is far to short to dawdle.

The Chief Registrar's office looked out towards the sea. His desk was cluttered with files and papers. On the wall behind was a picture of the Queen. It was obvious that he also had lots of work to do. I couldn't help but feel that the judicial system in Fiji was drowning in paper and there were no life rafts in sight.

After a brief chat about admission procedures I shook hands and left his office. Rusiate had meantime gone upstairs to the Chief Justice's office. When I walked out of the Registrar's office I ran straight into Anand Singh. There was a look of absolute surprise on his face, and no doubt mine, as he stopped to say hello and see what I was up to. Anand is by nature a very nervous chap, like a dog that had been beaten once too often. Next time he just might bite back, I thought to myself.

"What are you doing up here?" I asked him.

"I have come up to see my ex-partner Dan Fatiaki." Judge Fatiaki's chambers were on the same floor.

"Christopher, come and meet the Judge." I hestitated because I was waiting for Rusiate, the chief clerk, to come back from the Chief Justice's office.

"Only for a moment, I don't want to miss my appointment," I said. Anand indicated to me to follow him down the stone hallway. The sign on the door said 'Justice Fatiaki'. I recalled Rusiate's job offer and tried to imagine 'Justice Harder'.

Anand went in first and then I followed. Justice Dan was sitting behind his desk in a moderate office with law books lining the back wall of the office. Anand sat to one side, indicating for me to sit in the chair before the Judge.

Fatiaki was about my age. Having graduated from Auckland University Law School, I felt almost related to him. Fatiaki, a Rotuman by birth, rose from his chair to greet me warmly. But I felt rather uncomfortable. I was getting ready to do battle with Rabuka and Fiji over Rotuma. Sitting having a coffee with His Honour was an enjoyable respite. We reminisced over law school and 'Harder and the Tramways Union'. I was dogged by this most notorious case.

"And to what do we owe the pleasure of your company, Mr Harder?" said the Judge. I grimaced, I didn't think he would want to talk about the Rotuma seven sedition case. Anand could see my difficulty. "Christopher is here to do a case with Tevita Fa."

His Honour understood. Everybody in Fiji knew that Fa was involved in the case. It became apparent from looking at the case files in the office and from what His Honour was saying that the Fiji justice system was in deep strife. It would take years to sort out. Finishing my coffee, I thanked him and left his chambers.

Back at the main reception foyer I said goodbye to Anand and sat down on the ancient hardwood chair to await Rusiate's return. About a minute later he came into the room with a perplexed look on his face.

"I couldn't find you a few minutes ago. Where did you go?"

I was sure he knew where I had been but wanted to hear it from my own lips. "I was in seeing Mr Justice Fatiaki with Anand Singh," I said.

"Are all your papers filed?" he asked.

"Yes," I replied, "except that I do have a motion and memorandum to file on the question of Fiji's jurisdiction to hear criminal charges of sedition against a Rotuman."

Rusiate's eyes lit up. I could see his face flush. He became fidgety. "Oh it is very important that the Chief Justice see them right away," he said.

"Here is the original motion and the memorandum," I said. "I have copies for the DPP in my brief case. I'll serve them myself on my way out."

"No, no," said Rusiate. "We always serve the DPP with their copies of the papers. I will take these up to the Chief Justice now, you must wait here." I took my seat again.

Fifteen minutes later Rusiate came down the stairs. He didn't say anything about the papers. "The Chief Justice says we have to await the law society, okay? You can be admitted on the morning of the case." That seemed like a reasonable approach to the situation. I had already been told the date would be some time after June 18. Loads of time I thought.

As I walked down the stairs Rusiate leant over and whispered in my ear. "I think you better go home now, Mr Christopher."

I heard the words but the message was in the tone of the voice. Obviously the Chief Justice did not like the memorandum about Fiji. Maybe it was time to go home to Philippa and the kids for a while.

Back At My Desk: Late May

In New Zealand I was to prepare the legal argument on the Rotuma issue with constitutional law expert Professor Jock Brookfield, Dean of Auckland Law School. I had been back in Auckland getting into my local work. I had a good case load on hand, in fact, it was all over my desk. It is a solid oak desk, six foot by four, which I am very proud to own. I bought it from Charles Hutchinson, Queen's Counsel extraordinary. I draw a certain strength from sitting at Hutch's desk when I need to make a serious decision about something. Among the Auckland law fraternity he was known as "Mr Integrity."

Hutch is a spry English gentleman just retired from the law. Halfway through his career at the Inner bar in London he had changed direction and come to New Zealand. He sold me the desk and his law book shelves for $1,200, which as a struggling young lawyer I paid off over a period of time.

Everytime I had saved up a few hundred dollars I would take it over to Hutch, at his townhouse in Remuera and take time out to listen to some of his stories. He told many a good yarn, dating back to the First World War and he had some words of sound advice for a young barrister.

Many people have influenced my path in life, but it was Charles Hutchinson QC who taught me the importance of diplomacy at the bar of the court. And it was Hutch who guided me through the appeal of Mark William Stephens, previously convicted of being the notorious Parnell Panther rapist.

The two Stephens rape cases, conducted as my first two trials some six years before, had the most profound effect on me as a lawyer. Having struggled to get into the Law the Harder way, I was determined to throw myself into my work with full resolve.

An indecent assault case involving a young Maori boy and his uncle took me to Kaitaia, a small town 200 miles north of Auckland. One weekend shortly after my admission in June, 1983 I had to drive up north to obtain a statement from the complainant in the case.

I took a District Court stenographer with me to take down the statement in shorthand, type it up on a portable I had in the back of the car and have the document sworn immediately before a Justice of the Peace.

During the weekend she began to tell me an interesting story of how this fellow Stephens was going to be "fitted" for a number of rapes. In police and criminal circles "fitting" is the fabrication of evidence. He was suspected of a whole string of rapes, she said. The police knew Stephens was the culprit but they couldn't prove it. Justice Department staff mixed with the police at the breaks and over lunch during each court day. It was inevitable that bits and pieces of conversation would flow back down the line, especially over such a hot topic as the Parnell Panther.

But this hint of "fitting" challenged my sense of fairness. As I understood the concept in legal terms, every person was entitled to a fair trial with the barrister standing between the accused and the power of the state.

Although Mark William Stephens was charged with seven terrible rapes, he was still entitled to a fair trial. If the New Zealand system of justice is to function fairly then every effort must be made to ensure that those persons on the outer fringes of society have their civil rights protected.

Only if those on the edge are fairly treated can the rest of society have some faith that the system will work in an unbiased manner for them, God forbid if their turn should ever come before a court. Little did that court typist know what she was starting when she told me what she had heard from a policeman in a coffee room on the first floor of the Old District Court in Kitchener Street, downtown Auckland.

When I approached this young woman asking her to do some after hours secretarial work I was a non-entity in the law. I had only recently been admitted to the High Court, my admission moved by my friend Peter Williams before Mr Justice Casey. It had been a proud moment. I had no other orthodox achievement that I could hold up for the world to see. Justice Casey on ordering my admission, congratulated me on my long journey to the bar.

When I returned to Auckland from the trip up north with the stenographer I went to the Paremoremo Maximum Security Prison just outside Auckland and introduced myself to Mark William Stephens. He was a 24-year-old Maori with a shocking list of previous convictions for dishonesty, burglary and a minor assault on a policewoman.

Stephens was tall, about six foot, brown eyed; he had pronounced cheek bones, a gap between his upper front teeth and big lips. His ears were pierced and he normally wore two gold studs in his left ear. He looked mean with his plaited long hair.

He faced seven counts of rape from up and down the country. The case was to become the most frustrating of my career, although five rape charges were dismissed at the deposition hearings.

In particular Stephens was charged with the vicious assault of a prominent female television producer, Ms Robin Scholes. The attacker had climbed in through a window wearing a nylon stocking as a disguise and attacked Ms Scholes from behind.

The severity of the attack and the fact that neighbours heard the screams but did nothing to help was the turning point in public opinion which lead to the start of Neighbourhood Watch in New Zealand, a successful community vigilance network.

The jury pondered the evidence for six hours before it reached its verdict of guilty. Their decision followed the most spirited attack

I have ever made on an individual, either before or since. The scientist from the DSIR, (Department of Scientific and Industrial Research), Phillip Stanley Groom, had unknowingly set lose a tempest in me which consumed three and a half long years and probably took 10 years off my professional life at the bar.

The scientist gave misleading and false information about the length of a pair of New Balance running shoes which appeared to match a blood print left at the scene by the attacker after standing in his victim's blood. Sort of "if the shoe fits, wear it."

I wrote letters to the Solicitor General, the Attorney General, the Minister responsible for the DSIR, every person I could think of. The trial, in my view, had not been fair. A crucial and critical crown witness, the scientist, was caught out during my cross examination. He had yelled out in open court, "Hey, help me Mister, what's he up to?" to the prosecutor, who quickly manoeuvered an adjournment.

The Crown Prosecutor then spent 25 minutes alone in a locked room breaking the most fundamental rule of procedure; not talking to the witness when he or she is under cross examination. He was locked away with the scientist who had been caught out in my cross examination. Groom had lied about the matching print being made from a shoe while it was on the foot. I knew that an impression of the same length as the blood print could not be duplicated by the shoe produced in court if it was worn on a foot while the print was made, and so did he.

Only if you stretched the shoe by hand, bending the toe of the shoe to the top of the heel, holding it in that position and rolling it out, could you add sufficiently to the length of the forensic print, so that it might appear to match the bloodprint found at the scene of the crime.

The unsavoury taste left in my mouth by the first part of the trial was compounded when the trial judge refused to let me recall a Crown police witness. I wanted to further cross examine the police officer on a new matter introduced since he had given his evidence. He had not mentioned his role in making the "matching print." It was the last straw.

For the next three and a half years, I would not give an inch. I attacked prosecutors, policemen and judges like a fox terrier chasing rats. I challenged every bit of evidence. I corrected every judge who made a blunder. Scientific evidence was examined with a magnifying glass. I gave no quarter, asked no favours and showed no mercy until a Government Ministerial Tribunal, headed by Christchurch Queens Counsel Brian McClelland, completed a report with adverse findings against the scientist, prosecutor and trial judge involved in the Stephens Case. Only then did I, finally, begin to unwind.

In part the Groom Forensic Enquiry read: "Mr Groom had a responsibility to report all relevant findings, and to ignore this highly significant dissimilarity or discrepancy between the shoes and shoeprints, was a gross deficiency, which can be interpreted as highly misleading to the court."

Two pages further on in the report into the Stephens/Scholes case the conclusion reads: "Mr Groom made an unjustified assumption regarding the tread pattern of a shoeprint, and failed to present a full and honest account of his examinations in comparing the shoeprint at the scene to the shoes of the accused. He thus demonstrated an unacceptable bias towards the prosecution case, seriously jeopardising the impartial role of a DSIR forensic scientist. Mr Groom contradicted himself in cross examination, inviting an allegation of dishonesty, although a less serious alternative explanation is also possible."

"Mr Groom's laboratory notes were not up to minimum acceptable standards."

Meanwhile the New Zealand police had tried to discredit me in various ways. They tried to have me charged with a number of alleged wrongs including touting. Then they wanted me charged with conduct unbecoming a barrister for making adverse comment against the Australian police over the David Howard extradition to Australia. Howard was kept 66 days in police cells while he was sought by the Australian police for an alleged domestic house robbery.

The Auckland Law Society wasn't much better. I was charged with having sexual intercourse with a police witness. They charged me with over-charging, improper questioning, attempting to get my researcher Ms Karen Soich — previously refused a certificate of character — a benefit in the form of a letter from the police not opposing her admission, and other time consuming complaints.

One of the Stephens' trial Judges had also charged me with two counts of improper questioning in relation to the second Stephens case known as the "telephone cord rape." I had suggested that the telephone handpiece and attached coil were planted. Funny that, the picture taken at the scene by the police showed five and one half coils of lead attached to the handpiece. The one presented in court had seven and one half coils and was of a different shade. The prosecution's inference was that Stephens' knife had cut the telephone cord presented in the court, tying him to the scene of the crime. The evidence tended to show something else. The judge got very cross and angry with my insistence.

I began to wonder if everybody, from the High Court judges to the police, was trying to get me; the judiciary cast as the huntsmen, the police as the hounds and Christopher Harder the fox.

Eventually, but for one count of overcharging, for which I was censured, all the other charges were dismissed.

The tall poppy syndrome of hacking down those who stood out from the rest continued to wound the cream of the criminal bar in New Zealand. Rules of evidence were changed to catch some of those targeted by the Law Society. The concerted attack on Edward Poulter Leary, Eb to his friends, a great criminal barrister of his time, was a blemish on the system.

A search-and-destroy mentality was adopted by the Auckland District Law Society and two of its employees — a frumpy middle-aged complaints clerk named Ugenie Laracey, and ex-cop, now defense lawyer, Michael Levitt — appeared to have been engaged to destroy the criminal bar. It seemed as if criminal lawyers, with their more abrasive courtroom brawling style of defence were unacceptable to the old school network.

It was this attitude of the Society that had caused me to call the first meeting of the New Zealand Criminal Bar Association, in Auckland in 1985, to protect my back and my backside from further attack. Peter Williams was elected president of the new association. With a hiss and a roar off we went into our monthly meetings,

55

discussing, debating and dealing with matters of concern and interest to criminal lawyers.

The Stephens case did not end for me when the damning report of the ministerial enquiry was published. We took the case to the Appeal Court after I had gained permission from the Solicitor General to present the report as part of the appeal.

I had not long started my submissions to the appeal judges, using excerpts from the report, when Mr Justice Cook interrupted saying the judges had not read the document, they were not interested in the document, that they did not know the source of the document and that it had no weight whatsoever. The fact that the Solicitor General had said I could present the report did not help. His backing was not relevant and I was to proceed with my submission without reference to the report.

For the next hour I struggled to put a case using other material, but without the report the appeal had little chance, and I was battered from pillar to post. Finally I put my papers down on the desk and stood with my hands on my hips. I can vividly remember licking my lips, as my whole mouth had dried out from talking so long in such a frustrated state.

Then I let rip: "Gentlemen, you can be assured of one thing, if the report had been favourable to the scientist, the prosecutor and the judge you all would have wanted to read it."

Mr Justice Cook just about choked on his hanky. I can remember seeing Mr Justice Casey visibly gasp and off to one end of the bench Mr Justice Henry appeared to crack a small grin.

Straight after my comment Mr Justice Cook looked at the judges to his left, then those to the right and without further consultation said they would retire and read the report.

The next day they came back to say they had read it, noted the comments but would still have to exclude it from the appeal because of the rules of evidence.

But the incident gave me a lot of satisfaction. Now the judges knew where I was coming from and why I was so hostile.

Stephens never admitted to me that he had committed the crimes and most of the police case rested on the written records of a series of verbal interviews with him.

For four out of the last five years I have campaigned to have the police videotape their interviews. It is so easy for the odd rogue police officer to add a line or two to the evidence on someone whom they know is guilty but on whom they don't quite have enough hard evidence.

Unfortunately if this practice goes on it slowly creeps into the middle order of society, not just in dealings with the ratbags. Then mistakes happen and innocent people get convicted and society ends up with a Lindy Chamberlain-type situation.

After the hearing was finally over, and I had lost the case, the judges were standing around in the grand foyer of the Appeal Court chatting when I walked past. John Henry broke away from his colleagues, crossed the foyer and asked me if I was all right before shaking hands and wishing me well.

He seemed to understand. Afterwards I wondered if he had not been thinking of his own experiences as an advocate, and how hard it can sometimes be to present a fair case.

Back in 1981 as a Queens Counsel John Henry had been involved in a Commission of Inquiry looking into the circumstances of the conviction of Arthur Allen Thomas for the murder of David and Jeanette Crew of Pukekawa. Following a lengthy forensic inquiry by Dr James Sprott it was established that the cartridge case that had been "found" by the police and used as the critical evidence to convict Thomas was not manufactured until a date after the killing. The suggestion was that the bullet cartridge had been planted.

Henry, who was acting for the New Zealand Police Association, felt his clients were not receiving a fair hearing and he said so.

HENRY: May it please the Commission, Mr Fisher and I have conferred over the adjournment, and I wish to advise the Commission that we are not prepared to be treated as we feel we have been, or to remain involved in this inquiry in the way in which it is being conducted. We feel it is obvious that we as counsel can achieve nothing to ensure that the police are fairly heard, and accordingly we now withdraw.

CHAIRMAN: Are you suggesting they have not been fairly heard?

HENRY: I am suggesting sir that we feel we can do nothing to ensure . . .

CHAIRMAN: Are you suggesting they have not been fairly heard?

HENRY: I am saying nothing more than I have.

Desk Bound Day Dreaming

Murder, rape and robbery in New Zealand all seemed somewhat mundane as I pieced together a defence with Tevita Fa for the "seditious seven." My mind kept flying off to Fiji. I remembered scuba diving on my March holiday, out with a commercial dive crew off the Coral Coast just past Koralevu. They knew where to go for breath-taking action and scenery.

We crossed the breakers in a long boat of near Captain Cook vintage. Our group of four was escorted by three professionally trained Fijian divers. As a beginner I had my own guide Joe Simi.

We each sat on the edge of the boat with our backs to the water. My stomach began to churn as I tried to throw myself backwards into the unknown tropical sea. When the 15-year-old, Brooke Shields-looking member of our group, pushed off the boat with youthful vigour, I knew it was time to go. Splash, into the sparkling water I went, rolling over and to my surprise floating upright and breathing through my air apparatus with ease.

The leader then pulled me backwards down the anchor rope into a different world. As clear as polished glass the sparkling sea showed off a multitude of angel fish floating by my face. As we approached a coral shelf about 40 feet down I could see schools of bright little red neons flashing in the sun's rays; Parrot fish showed off their banded stripes of black, blue and purple.

Suddenly my shepherd started to swim upwards at speed. He seemed distressed and looking around for something. He didn't signal any trouble, he just left.

I sat there in the middle of a strange underwater world wondering what the hell was going on and what I was expected to do. I couldn't call anybody. I didn't know where the dive boat was anchored, and my chaperone was fast fading into the distance, with only a trail of bubbles to indicate where he had gone. Scared and alone, my heart began to race and that addictive adrenalin began to flow. I began to take more air and deeper breaths.

Fighting panic I concentrated on the sound of the air coming through my regulator and listened and watched the air bubbles escape and rise to the surface as I exhaled. I tried to use my buoyancy compensator to take me up 10 feet so that I could see over the fish covered coral reef to where the rest of the group should be.

I began to float upwards; awkwardly because with air in my compensator vest I was no longer in control. Suddenly I froze — over my right shoulder was a school of about 300 four to five foot barracuda slowly cruising by and blocking my way to safety. I pressed the release button on the compensator to dump some air and halt my upward drift. But no air came out and I kept moving toward the unpredictable barracuda.

A tug on my foot almost gave me a heart attack. Above was impending trouble with the barracuda but now there was a frighteningly immediate problem. I didn't know what had touched me. I couldn't see anything except clear bright water. What had touched me could not have disappeared so quickly. I started to sense real trouble in the split second as I feared the worst. It took a second or two to register on my conscious mind that whatever it was had to be behind me.

My pulse was racing, my face was taut as my mind began to interpret the worst case scenario on the limited information it held. What was nudging my leg? I turned to face my destiny and my mask lens was filled with a big, grinning Fijian giving the thumb and finger circle for OK.

It was Joe Simi back like nothing had happened. He adjusted my release valve from behind and forced out the problem air stuck in my buoyancy jacket. Again I felt a tug on my arm as Joe pointed to the right. A gigantic sea turtle was floundering near the surface. I could see by the air gauge and my clock that it was time to go up. Fifty feet and 50 minutes was not bad for a first dive. We approached the turtle from behind, its flippers slowly fanning the water as if it was finding it difficult to keep balance. It would have been five feet across the shell.

Joe put his right hand on the rim of the turtle's back, then indicated with his left hand that I should join him. As I approached the turtle I could gauge by my own efforts that it was making some speed. I put a hand on the shell, trying to stay out of the way of the flipper as the turtle moved on. Suddenly I was able to stick my head above the sea and, like a submarine periscope zeroing in on the long boat, the turtle taxied us home. As the huge rotund reptile swam past our tender, we let go and pushed off towards the anchor line.

Time To Act: June 13

I had been back in New Zealand since the end of May. It was now June 13. Uncertainty was in the air over Fiji. There were different messages from different people. No action appeared to have been taken on my application for admission to the Fiji High Court although the papers had been filed for some time.

My affidavit attesting to my practice as a barrister for five years in New Zealand had been lodged along with my letter from Ms Joane Bowring of the Auckland District Law Society.

May 16, 1988
TO WHOM IT MAY CONCERN

I hereby certify that CHRISTOPHER LLOYD HARDER was admitted as a barrister and solicitor of the High Court of New Zealand at Auckland on May 20, 1983, and has practised as a barrister sole since May 31, 1983, his current certificate being issued on February 19, 1988, and expiring on January 31, 1989.

I am not aware of any reason why CHRSITOPHER LLOYD HARDER should not be admitted in the Supreme Court of Fiji.

J.B. Bowring (Miss)
for Executive Director

Tevita Fa had also sworn an affidavit in support of my admission. The effort it took to get such simple documents together was at times very frustrating.

The formal motion was a prayer for temporary admission, asking to be allowed in to defend the seven Rotumans charged with sedition. I had to get the information and make things happen using an inadequate phone system between New Zealand and Fiji or go back to Fiji.

Telephoning Fiji was difficult most of the time, and almost impossible during the day unless you put the fax machine on automatic dial. I had been told only 24 telephone lines connected the Republic of Fiji to the outside world now. Before the coup there were approximately 500. The Fiji telephone lines were monitored 24 hours a day, by eavesdroppers fluent in both Fijian and Hindi. Talking about the sedition to Fa on the telephone was neither safe nor practicable. Frequently calls would be cut off.

However, I could never quite follow the reasoning behind this. You would have thought that those ordering this gross invasion of one's privacy would have had the brains to tape those calls, not cut them off.

Landlines laid on the seabed further complicated communications by making Fiji a very expensive place to telephone, such lines also affect both the quality and cost of communication by fax. Satellite telephone systems are not likely to be introduced until Fiji normalises and until its economy recovers sufficiently to pay for them. I was staggered by the size of my Fijian telephone bill, phone and fax transmissions through this period cost me $3,875.00.

Information was the most valuable commodity you could possess in the turbulent Fiji political climate. The problem was differentiating between fact and rumour. Operating without information is like walking into court without having read the file, very dangerous.

Correct information and communication are vital to solving any problem. In Fiji it appears that information and communication are not properly coordinated by Rabuka's staff advisers. The result is that decisions are made without consideration of future implications. This style of law making, by decreeing away more than half of the former statutes, is more like instant gratification than measured progress.

The military members in cabinet apparently just listen while the civilian appointees grapple with the real problems. The officers then go away to their barracks and no doubt discuss matters among themselves. The only input they are known to have had within cabinet is to veto proposals put forward at previous meetings.

From the beginning of our very first trip to Fiji my wife and I noticed the sickness and poverty in Fiji. But by now I knew race relations had deteriorated to a lower ebb, igniting here and there into violence and bloodshed. Indians were suffering increased personal attacks.

The suicides of two young Indian women in the western districts caused concerns and rumours to run rife, the local police being accused of refusing to take any action over allegations that the girls had been raped by indigenous Fijians.

Yet almost all Fiji's magistrates are Indian, with training in New Zealand. A story from a responsible European, who had an Indian family in his circle of friends, told how their friends' 18-year-old son was now a vegetable because a Fijian man had rammed an umbrella end up his nose, piercing and permanently damaging his brain.

Racial discrimination was pouring from the very top of Government, flooding through the administration and even trickling down to the Fijian children. Continuously and with impunity children threw rocks onto their Indian neighbours' corrugated iron roofs. As a matter of regularity Fijian males treated Indians adversely by voice or violence.

In practise an Indian in Fiji now had no real rights and even fewer protections. Since then a decree has, in theory, made all equal under the law. But in reality none now have any real legal rights.

A phone call to my Auckland office from Tevita Fa added to my frustrations. The law society was probably not going to support me because I only had four years, 11 months and three weeks' service at the bar and not a full five years. Was this the letter of the law? It was time to make a personal appearance in Fiji. I checked the amount of credit on my Visa Card. Thank goodness for a good understanding with my bank.

If I got over the hurdle of the Fiji Law Society and through the maze of the High Court there was only one person who could stop my plans. I wrote a three page letter to Rabuka. The letter was openly faxed to the Brigadier to give him full warning and information about my intended visit.

I was never sure if Fa was pulling or pushing my application. He was probably under close scrutiny by the security forces, his track record included some unusual political moves, his traditional ties were at that time no doubt complicated. Perhaps it was not in his best interest as a lawyer to see me admitted to the bar.

At the time Fa had no known political affiliations. Well before the last election he had been given the job of trying to sort out the financial affairs of Ratu Sir Kamisese's Alliance party. But he quit the post in frustration when he found how tangled the finances were.

Recently there had been talk of him taking a position in the Bavadra government, something that seemed unlikely and certainly did not take place in the 33 days between the election and the insurrection.

Although not close Fa still has ties to Ratu Mara. He comes from the Vanuabalava in the Lau group of islands, where the Prime Minister's mother came from and is in some way related to him. However, there was at least a small amount of hostility between Mara and Fa. In his capacity as a lawyer Fa had represented a number of people in actions which were detrimental to the Mara dynasty.

There are not a lot of people in Fiji bold enough to engage aggressive legal services in these times. I had after all been somewhat foisted on Tevita Fa by the Gagaj Sau.

CHAPTER FIVE

BACK ON THE FIJI SHUFFLE:

JUNE 14: On Tuesday I flew back to Fiji. It was almost routine: blue Walkman on my lap, Fijian music easily, enchantingly restoring memories. The adrenalin buzzed as we gathered speed for takeoff. Soon I was on automatic pilot, speeding on a natural high from the anticipated challenge. Could I turn around the Fiji Law Society and persuade the Chief Justice of Fiji, Sir Timoci Tuivaga, I was a fit and proper person to be admitted to his High Court?

At Nadi International Airport this time I was dressed and ready. In light summer clothes I quickly moved through 10 deep immigration queues. I took out my Canadian passport and completed my Fiji immigration card as "barrister on visit". The back of the form said you could not practise a profession, or do research without a work permit.

The Fiji Law Society had advised me I did not require a work permit if I was not going to work more than 14 days. I had given the Minister of Home Affairs notice in writing that I intended to apply for a permit if the Fiji Law Society supported my application and the court admitted me to the bar. Anyway, I intended to see the Minister of Home Affairs before my admission, if possible.

My turn at the immigration desk was fast approaching. There was one person between me and the white line. Walk the line, here we go. My stomach fluttered just as it had during my first plea in mitigation at the Auckland District Court.

The person in front of me approached the immigration officer. I looked past him to the display board listing hotel names, rates,

64

phone numbers and special details. I was glad my turn was approaching, I was tired and ready for bed. The hotel where I was to stay advertised rooms at $78.00 a night. A lower rate than normal in the old peak tourist times.

The immigration officer looked up and nodded his head for me to move forward. He opened my passport, punched in my name, my passport number and flight details. I could see his finger move to push the enter button, as if in slow motion. Was he going to look up and yell "guard" when the screen revealed its details or would he just pass me by? One thing for sure, he wouldn't win the Mr Congeniality award for good public relations in 1988.

I stood on tiptoes and craned my neck to see the display screen. Flickering letters on the green glass. My mind racing faster than I could read. My thought process had always worked quicker than my reading skill allows. At times this is frustrating because it is difficult to slow the brain. Sometimes it is plain impossible. Then the words registered in my mind. "No Record of Notice."

A stifled sigh of relief, keep a straight face and keep on walking Harder, and remember to say 'thank you.' I picked up my passport and walked on through the gate. One more step towards my goal. At the bottom of the stairs leading into the main foyer two Fijian airport employees offered me a push cart.

The bag chain started to trundle out our luggage and people gathered around the track. The sign indicated it was Flight TE04 baggage. In reality it was a confused lottery. Surprise, my bags came through first and second, and out of the door I went to grab a cab. But as I rounded the corner I saw another table ominously marked "Customs and Security."

My pulse began to race as the guard took his time opening my suitcase, fingered through the clothes, looked briefly at the Rotuma folder of papers and then asking me to open my brief case — combination zero, zero, zero — easy to remember. In criminal law I have figures, names and facts thrown at me all the time and after a while the brain becomes like an over full computer floppy disc. My theory is not to overload myself with useless information, hence the triple zero.

"What is this?" asked the guard, holding up the whale's tooth from my bag.

"You can't have this, this is tabua." He was wrong, I could not take it *out* of the country, because tabua (whales' teeth) in Fiji are prohibited exports, not a prohibited *import*. Luckily the guard was sharp enough to understand.

Tabua is a strong traditional offering of peace or forgiveness in Fiji. Two bundles of kava roots and a tabua is supposed to be a symbol that makes it hard for people to turn you down, at least that was the way I understood things. I told the guard it was for the Brigadier. He stopped and looked at me, puzzled, as I showed him a sealed envelope from my chambers addressed to Rabuka, marked "To be delivered by hand."

For whatever reason the guard closed my briefcase, snapped the locks and handed it to me. Then he zipped up my bag and handed that to me carefully. Now I was armed with a loaded briefcase: Tabua, Rabuka here I come.

The tabua came from the Gagaj Sau Lagfatmaro, 'His Royal Highness', King of the Royal Molmahao clan of Rotuma, still living comfortably at Whenuapai, in Auckland. Whilst visiting the king and his wife Sandra, I had been told about the importance of the whale's tooth in Fijian tradition. At about the same instant the two of us had clicked on similar lines. I would present tabua and two bundles of kava root to the Brigadier. I had read that after the 1st coup Rabuka had made peace with the speaker of the arrested parliament with tabua and Kava.

A conscious effort had been made by the Gagaj to resolve the Rotuma issue by negotiation. My responsibility was the sedition court case. Rotuman politics was not my bag. His Royal Highness had signed a letter I had prepared for him to be sent to the *Fiji Times*. A letter from a very literate Fijian woman had also appeared in the paper. It described the former Henry Gibson, now the Gagaj, in rather unflattering terms.

A media circus with the Rotuma charges pending was, in my view, foolish. Hence the conciliatory approach in the letter, our faith being placed in the High Court of Fiji and the argument that would take place within those four walls. The letter on Gagaj Sau

Lagfatmaro's letterhead with his royal stamp was sent by bureau fax. We were taking a diplomatic and reasoned approach.

Dear Sir,

I have read the letter that was published in your newspaper two weeks ago about Rotuma and myself.

I do not accept the content of the correspondence. On the advice of New Zealand barrister Christopher Harder, I shall refrain from any comment of the Rotuma situation pending the forthcoming court case.

A situation has arisen. Differing views exist on the Rotuma issue. The matter is now before the High Court of Fiji. Eight men are charged with a criminal offence. Counsel from New Zealand and Fiji are endeavouring to protect the rights of these eight accused.

Every person charged with such an offence is entitled to a full, fair and prompt trial. The lawyers shall take every proper point in law. They shall test the strength of the Crown's evidence. They shall try to persuade the court to accept the defence submissions.

They shall act within the four walls of the Fiji High Court in accordance with the principles and ethics that stand true and fast in the Fiji High court at Suva.

The Royal Crest still sitting above the High Court benches gives the Court a majesty befitting the golden principles of English law.

A full hearing and a fair trial is all that any man can ask for in this day and age of learning to live together as good friends and neighbours.

Yours faithfully
H.R.H King Gagaj Sau Lagfatmaro
King of Royal Molmahao Clan
ROTUMA ISLANDA

The Customs officer having let me into the country with the whale's tooth, I headed for the Gateway Hotel, my previous haunt. The taxi boys at the Gateway were still drinking kava when I came down to the hut. "Hello, Mr Christopher." "Hey Ginger Lawyer," went the greetings.

A fresh bowl of kava and one of my friends asked if I was to do the gun case. "No, I'm here to do the Rotuma case." One of them said, "You should do the gun case, Mr Christopher."

The Guns Case

"Give me one of those cards with your rights, please. Last time you gave me one, my brother take it. He said he was going to show it to a policeman if he got stopped again."

On the back of my business card I had printed a list of five basic rights often abused by policemen. Even though the rights are based strictly on New Zealand law this chap was convinced such a card would be useful in keeping the local police off his back.

I pointed out to him that I didn't think he had any kind of rights in Fiji at the moment. This conversation was only eight days before Sitiveni Rabuka announced his draconian 1988 Internal Security Decree.

After an hour's discussion I went to bed and the boys worked through the night, waiting for a single fare.

On Wednesday I went for a long run down the road past the cane fields, killing time waiting for my 9.30 plane to Suva. I strode out to a natural high listening to good music. By noon I had arrived at Suva Travelodge for the second time in a month and the third time in 1988. Fiji had grown on me. I was besotted by the lifestyle, the friendly nature of the Fijian people, and the music. If you were white, were spending money and not talking about Rabuka — unless about the Methodist Church and Rabuka — you would have a very good holiday, except in Suva.

On arrival I contacted Rabuka's office by phone to try and make an appointment to see him. I was politely persistent, hoping I could persuade Rabuka's henchman to let me through the barrier that had been set up around the Brigadier. The tone of voice and how you said your words could often be the difference between winning and losing a client's case. Although telephones could be effective at times, a face to face approach was always the best.

Three times over the next 24 hours I spoke to his personal assistant, who identified himself as Jesse. I even tried to ask Cabinet Minister Apisai Tora to help with an appointment.

A politican, trade unionist and village head, Tora is best known for crossing the floor from the predominantly Indian National Federation Party to the mainly Fijian Alliance Party in 1979. A Muslim by faith, Tora was instrumental in setting up the Fiji Sugar Workers Union, the Building Workers Union and the now defunct Fiji Council of Trade Unions. He is also known to have had close ties with Moscow having made at least four trips there in 1977.

Tora has a record of convictions for involvement in trade union protests and was charged with sedition and arson. Rumours suggest Rabuka granted amnesty for people charged and convicted after the first coup on May 14 so that Tora could be pardoned. Surely he would have some clout with the Brigadier, but unfortunately for me Tora was on the other side of the island and would not be back for a week.

Next I went back to my hotel and returned a telephone message from Lautoka to call Anand Singh at his office. I had first met Singh in Auckland back in May at the Gagaj's Auckland hideaway. Anand and I discussed the Rotuma case then. Now in Fiji he asked me if I would like to come over to talk about the guns affair. I didn't have to think long. The gun case would be a real challenge.

On June 6 the Fiji police and military had detained 43 people in connection with a significant cache of Soviet made rifles, machine guns, hand grenades and ammunition.

The weapons were found on a number of cane farms near Nadi. The initial haul included 110 rocket launchers, five rocket propelled grenades, 93 AK 47 rifles, 10 light machine guns, four heavy machine guns, 72 bayonets, 105 steel helmets, 300 hand grenades and two drums of ammunition.

Australian police had alerted the Fiji authorities the week before. In Sydney they had found a container load of similar weapons ready for transhipment to Fiji. They quickly established that the container had originated in the South Yemen.

It was just what Rabuka and his military henchmen needed to justify a clampdown. Not only could they say it was subversive, treasonable and murderous to have imported such weapons to Fiji, but the origin of the weapons enabled them to trumpet a communist link.

Over the years since independence the Fijian authorities had developed deep anti-communist feelings. A populist revolt was unthinkable to the chiefly hierarchy. In addition hundreds of Fijian troops had spent long tours of duty with United Nations peacekeeping forces in the Middle East. There was little doubt that the Israelis had got through to these tough but politically immature troops.

When Australian police notified their Fiji counterparts of their suspicions the Fijians went to their task like hounds on a blood trail. They worked around the clock for a solid week before pouncing on a wide range of people considered potentially subversive.

The initial haul of 43 people included two former cabinet ministers of the deposed Bavadra Government, the former foreign Minister Krishna Datt and the Minister of Trade Industry and Tourism, Navin Maharaj.

When the dust settled from this amazing scene 21 people stood charged in relation to the gun running.

The one advantage Anand saw was that I was a lawyer from outside. The Security Police might follow him, force him off the road, slap him around if he stood up to them, but they wouldn't do that to a foreign national, not to a lawyer fighting only the case and not involved emotionally, politically or religiously. It would be just a good fight. I booked a flight to Nadi to see Anand Singh and discuss the case and my fee. My Sun Flower Airlines reservation was confirmed for noon the next day.

Security Decree Announced

Thursday, Day Two saw the world change for Fiji. I awoke to the phone ringing in my room. My wife was talking fast. She wanted to know if I was all right. Had anybody hurt me? I said no, I was all right. But what was the matter, what was she going on about? "Listen," she said, and read to me from the New *Zealand Herald*.

Fiji has decreed draconian new laws understood to include the death penalty for possession of firearms, and detention without charge for up to two years.

The laws are retrospective to March 1 this year, a move which will ensure that they apply to more than 20 people arrested in connection with large arms caches uncovered on June 6.

"Just a minute," I interrupted her, leaping naked out of bed and hurrying to the door to see if the *Fiji Times*, the only paper in Fiji, had arrived. I bent down and read the headline and first paragraph out loud as I picked it up. "Jesus Christ, is this guy crazy or what!" I called out. Back on the phone I calmed Philippa down. It was most unlike her; take it in your stride, had always been her motto. I was okay I assured her.

There was a delegation of Australian members of parliament in the hotel, visiting Fiji for talks on trade agreements, foreign aid, civil rights and now the security decree. They wouldn't arrest me as long as the Aussies were here, I said. I was more or less joking, but subsequently my words turned out to be entirely accurate. I told her to think about the dream house we had bought. Then I suggested a few things to keep her busy, as if she needed something to keep her busy. More than anything I tried hard not to betray the fear welling inside me as I heard what was in the *Herald*.

. . . reliable sources in Fiji said possession of illegal firearms would now be covered by a life sentence and possession in special military zones would attract the death sentence.

The only detail given in the official statement was the following list:
★ *"Prohibition of quasi military organisations and uniforms.*
★ *New powers of preventive detention.*
★ *Power to designate security areas.*
★ *Power to regulate subversive statements and publications.*
★ *Control of exhibitions and entertainments.*
★ *Additional powers of search and seizure and for the prevention of subversive activities.*
★ *Miscellaneous provisions pertaining to applicability of bail and police powers."*

Just being a legal activist in a foreign country was enough to make me scared. The decree allowed arrest, without charge or bail, for two years. The *Fiji Times* story was mild compared to the *Herald's*.

71

Dozens of people have been executed in Malaysia for illegal possession of firearms, while many more are held without trial for a variety of reasons.

In Auckland yesterday the sister of Lautoka lawyer Haroon Ali Shah who is being held without charge, apparently in connection with the arms seizures, said she was concerned for his saftey.

. . . Mrs Shah-Rasheed said her brother had taken a brief from five people charged in relation to the arms smuggling before he was arrested.

Another Lautoka lawyer, Mr Anand Singh, had taken up her brother's case, she said. If Mr Shah were not released soon Mr Singh would try to have him freed by a writ of habeus corpus.

. . . It is thought the Fijian laws are based on Malaysian legislation brought in as an anti-communist measure.

Long Distance Taxi

The Fijian woman behind the travel desk told me I could not get a plane because they were "otherwise occupied." I instantly thought the military was moving men for some purpose. But I had to see Anand Singh in Lautoka that day, clients with this amount of intrigue are fleeting at the best of times; here one minute, gone the next, like loose roofing in a hurricane.

Anand was not a criminal lawyer. His field of expertise was insurance, business and commercial. He was having a rough time. The security forces were leaning hard on him, his office and home had been broken into twice in the preceding week. Never before had it been broken into. He was representing six of those charged with the gun affair and needed a hand.

Criminal charges involving treason, sedition and gun running in the midst of a military coup, with a revolution waiting in the wings, are top line material for an emerging criminal barrister. The rights of the individual seemed to have been forgotten or lost in the two coups. It was only fair and proper for New Zealand judges to refuse to submit to Rabuka's authority and head for more stable surrounds but it was the duty of a barrister of the New Zealand and hopefully soon to be Fiji bar to challenge, to stand up and speak out about a situation that had the potential to create another fascist state, this one in the South Pacific.

Whatever the situation with the planes, I was determined to get to Lautoka that day. "Call me a cab, please," I said. "And please make sure that it is air conditioned and ask the driver to fill his tank up, thank you." She ordered the cab.

"We are driving to Lautoka." The woman behind the travel desk suddenly looked stunned and tried not to show any reaction to my countermove checkmate.

Half an hour later a robin-egg blue, air conditioned, diesel Toyota with soft lambskin seat covers arrived at the hotel. Masi the footman, opened the back door of my taxi, but I indicated the front seat so along the way I could talk to the Indian taxi driver. I had my Walkman wound up playing Nuka Vulvavula, Fijian vocal harmonies.

I had put my camera in my brief case, it might provoke the military. Others had been arrested for taking unauthorised photos. Buying postcards was safer and less hassle. Anyway I was simply a visiting lawyer, not a journalist or a spy.

As we pulled out of the hotel car park I saw my friendly Fijian sword seller. I didn't really think he was a sword seller at all. The day before walking toward town I had seen a man wave across the road to me. He acted like he knew me. He put his hand up, as if to say wait; I stopped and waited. The brown paper bag under his arm was a give away, I smelled a sword seller.

My sister-in-law Trisha had been to Fiji often. She told me about them and their patter designed to secure a $10 donation to a fictitious worthy cause, all for a piece of simply carved dakua, a local softwood.

As Trish had warned, the dialogue started. The sword seller was a middle-aged Fijian with two missing upper teeth. He was dressed in a multi-coloured shirt hanging over his scruffy pants and a pair of well-worn sandals. As he came level with me he was joined by another sword seller who didn't quite fit the image. He too had a Fijian shirt coloured orchid-purple, but something wasn't quite right — practising criminal law sharpens you to imposters.

The second man had a big grin, his teeth were clean and filled. His hair cut short-back and sides and his shoes well polished. "You British?" he asked before I had uttered a word. "Aussie?"

"No", I replied, "Kiwi," even though I am a Canadian citizen who has lived in New Zealand for 12 years and thinks of it as home after all that time.

"Oh, you know David Lange? "

"No, not everybody knows David Lange." Then he blew his cover.

"Oh, you must know my friend Henry Gibson in Auckland." Without replying I turned and walked away. They might have had some help from the Israelis, but their security intelligence people had certainly not been trained by the Mossad.

As we drove away past him beginning our car journey to Lautoka, I waved, with a grin on my face. Passing Nabua Prison in the taxi minutes later on our way out of Suva I wondered what it would be like to be a prisoner in Fiji.

What were the conditions and how did they treat them? I was not keen to find out. Jail has always been a deterrent to me. I like the feel of green grass between my toes. I enjoy playing with my kids and snuggling up to my wife in bed at night. No, jail was not for me, Fiji or no Fiji.

Passing the Fiji National Marketing Authority, where the fisheries building is, I leaned back on the headrest and closed my eyes. My mind wandered over the weapons case: 21 men had been arrested for involvement in the Lautoka arms shipment. The guns affair had a certain ring to it. Action, intrigue, and maybe a little adventure. My mind cast back, to another gun affair 20 years ago on the Canada/US border. And that time how close I had come to being part of an international gun smuggling incident.

The Ghost of Charles Manson

The driver of the black Chevy coming from the direction of the Stanley bypass whistled out the window with his two forefingers. A ride in a car full of hoons was the last thing I needed. The guy waving had shoulder length scraggly black hair and an acned, pitted face with piercing blue eyes, he wanted me to run to the car. The other figures in the car looked like Charlie Manson disciples.

Deep down I felt sick when the driver said, "Get in." One of the two back seat passengers opened the driver's side door, got out and invited me to sit in the middle. It was one of those situations in life where I wished I had been able to say 'no thank you.' I've never been able to rationally explain why I got into the vehicle. Those four were real mean dudes, they would not take no for an answer.

I had often read of people disappearing, gone from the face of the earth without trace. My mind ran back to the news of the murdered girl found the previous morning in the neighbouring state of Minnesota. The danger alarm in my head was going off like a string of hand grenades. For 300 miles sandwiched among four real live lowlifes I feared for my safety. I felt tied down, my body frozen, my mind trying to tell it to do something, but nothing happened.

As the Chevy drove up towards the US/Canada border crossing at Sweetgrass, Montana, I sat with that all-choked-up feeling, waiting for my lungs to burst. The customs officer waved us through. The Canadian border crossing was about 200 yards further on. Slowly we approached the guardhouse for our lane.

The immigration officer stepped down from the concrete walkway and looked into the car. I sat there as quiet as a mouse. When the guard asked me where I was from I told him the same lie I had given the police back in Stanley, I was travelling home from college on holiday through the United States.

For a long moment the guard looked at me, then flagged us through into Southern Alberta. Two hundred yards later I heard the sirens sound and the loudspeaker of a RCMP car approaching behind us crackle out its command, "Pull over . . ."

"Would you all please get out of the car one at a time," boomed a voice from the speaker on the car with the red flashing light. I could hear police radio chatter. A car door opened and somebody stepped down behind us. A voice rang out at the same time as a tapping on the right rear passenger window.

The person on my left was told to get out of the car one foot at a time with his hands to the front. Then the one on my right was ushered carefully out. Next the driver climbed out and turned to the rear of the car. The police vehicle was parked some 15 feet behind us with its headlights on high, shining on the driver of the Chevy.

75

From the middle of the back seat I slid out the passenger side with my luggage and stepped about 10 feet back into the dark, away from the car light. I heard: "RCMP, come to the back of your vehicle." [Royal Canadian Mounted Police]. I was feeling guilty as hell, having gone AWOL from the Canadian Air Force to hitchhike across Canada to see the Grey Cup Football game in Vancouver. My home town team, the British Columbia Lions were playing.

An RCMP officer, his gun holster flap undone, told the driver to open the boot. I moved ever so slightly and stretched to see what was in the trunk. From my spot in the shadows I saw the one I was mentally calling "Charlie" turn the chrome handle on the trunk and open it.

The RCMP patrol lights lit up the whole of the back of the Chevy. There in the headlights glistened a load of weapons. Shotguns, rifles, pistols and boxes upon boxes of ammunition. Slowly I backed away from the action. Picking up my bag I gathered pace and in the darkness fled down the road, heading for British Columbia, Vancouver, the 1966 Grey Cup and some friendly company.

. . . I snapped out of my flashback of 20 years ago when the Indian taxi driver broke into a loud string of curses. A cow was blocking the road. If we did not hurry we would not get to Lautoka with enough time to see the 21 being held on charges relating to the guns affair so that I could tell them what could be done for them and how much it would cost.

Lautoka was quite different from Suva. Hot, dry and much cleaner, the people were on the go: they were working, moving, not just milling around like lost souls. Lautoka is by the sea, with a substantial port. A mountain of wood chips was stockpiled ready for shipment. Even coming from British Columbia, a really big timber territory, I had never seen such a huge pile of wood. And there was no security, one match there would light a fire which would burn for years. Lautoka was still commercially thriving, even the market garden across from Anand's air conditioned office was being expanded.

The taxi stopped outside Anand's office on the main street. The shingle hung on the door still read Singh and Fatiaki, Barristers and

Solicitors, Lautoka. I knocked on the door. Not a soul was in sight. I tried to turn the knob on the glass door. I could see that nobody was at the reception desk and none of the lights were on.

From around the corner came a young Indian boy who opened the door. I introduced myself and asked for Mr Anand Singh. "He will be back soon," said the young boy. "Come sit in Mr Singh's office." I was sweltering in the hot sun. Thank goodness for the air conditioning in the taxi. In Anand's office the temperature was nice and cool too. I undid my jacket and took off my waistcoat.

Anand came into the room about five minutes later. He extended his hand and seemed genuinely glad to see me. I could tell he was nervous and scared though from the way he spoke and the way he shook my hand. I was simply enthused to be involved in such a potentially exciting case. The two of us discussed a variety of subjects about the case. Professional legal privilege prohibits me from discussing anything said by Singh to me about the case.

We discussed our fees and between the two of us we decided to charge an initial retainer. My share of the fees was to be about $7000. Having discussed the business of the case, we jumped into my waiting taxi and headed for the jail.

Inside Natabua Prison

Natabua Prison is situated on the outskirts of Lautoka, not too far from the Hospital. There are four long buildings in a row, mainly old army barracks converted into a prison in the late 1950s. The perimeter of the compound is surrounded with razor wire. Barbed wire scratches if you get entangled in it: razor wire slashes your flesh.

The long road leading up to the prison was barred by a metal boom. A guardhouse manned by two soldiers carrying M16 rifles confronted us. I identified myself as a New Zealand lawyer invited to see some of the "Arms Affair" men. I explained to the prison officer that I had been instructed by the man with me, lawyer Anand Singh, to represent some of the men who had been charged.

As the two of us walked down the red dirt road towards the main gate I noticed the eyes staring at us. Slowly every one in the compound, including the guards, turned to scrutinise the six foot two inch European and the Indian lawyer. At the compound gate I identified myself again as a lawyer from New Zealand.

The guns affair was big news in Fiji. It was obvious who we were coming to see. They seemed poor lost souls, Fijian and Indian alike. In this place the races were equal in their misery. They were just watching time go by. A daily diet of bread and tea for breakfast. Two slices of bread for lunch with gruel tea. Dinner, a choice of taro, bread and occasionally a piece of fresh meat.

Anand was nervous as we walked down the path. He was a sensitive fellow struggling to survive in a state where there was real oppression. He was depending on the cross-cultural link of his law firm "Singh and Fatiaki" to keep the military at bay. I was a reasonably high profile foreigner naive enough in local ways to think my tabua and Kava roots would help.

The Fatiaki of Fatiaki and Singh was no other than 38-year-old, recently appointed, Justice Dan Fatiaki — Rotuman islander, Auckland University law graduate and ex-partner of Anand Singh. Fatiaki graduated from Auckland in the same class as Tevita Fa. It was Fa who told 'Justice Dan' he had graduated ahead of him. He explained that Fa came alphabetically one before Fatiaki. Whether Fa was at an advantage from this familiarity or at a loss for having a foot in each camp, was sometimes hard to fathom.

Anand always felt that he was safe from ultimate arrest because of his former partner. In the same way I felt protected as a lawyer who was a foreign national. Although I considered myself a Kiwi, I had never taken out New Zealand citizenship. Somewhere in the back of my mind was a fear that someone in the present Labour Government might throw a spoke in the immigration machinery because of my past involvement with the anti-union "Strike Free" organisation.

It was a combination, my failure to meet this small challenge and laziness, that would soon make me wish I had applied for a passport years ago. When it came to diplomacy in Fiji I was legally a Canadian, not a New Zealander.

Strike Free
Strike Free was set up by myself and an Auckland baker who had

taken court action against a local union. Before I took out a High Court injunction against the bus drivers and their "Tramway Union" I had never before taken a stand, or any action, against any union. The publicity from the Tramways injunction was to follow me for years. My actions had made me either loved or loathed. Through an orchestrated attack on the trade union movement in 1978 and 1979 I was perceived as a right wing union basher and with it came a strange type of notoriety.

Strike Free was the result of a chance meeting between Tony Oric, the baker involved with the Drivers' Union, and myself at a bar and restaurant in Upper Symond Street, Auckland. I was bloated with liquor and my own self importance. Both of us were driven by alcoholic personalities. The media coverage that came with the bus strike injunction case had created a steamroller effect.

Every time industrial trouble erupted around the country I would get phone calls asking if I was going to do anything about this or that strike. Strike Free for me had nothing to do with politics. Strike Free was a good fight. I now think it was also destructive to the New Zealand social fabric and bad for the trade union movement. I was wrong.

Two of the eight prisoners the Fijian guards brought into the interview shack were represented by Fiji Indian criminal lawyer Sidiq Koya who had once nearly become Fiji's first Indian Prime Minister.

In 1977 the National Federation Party won 26 out of the 52 seats in a general election. Ratu Mara's alliance won 24 and two others went to independent candidates. But the Indian dominated NFP was bitterly split and unable to agree on choosing a leader. Four days after the election Governor General Ratu Sir Penaia Ganilau swore in Ratu Sir Kamisese Mara as Prime Minister, explaining that Mara had a majority in parliament who would support him as their leader. Now Ratu Sir Penaia was the President and Koya was a defence lawyer in the Republic of Fiji.

A solid diet of criminal law teaches you not to interfere with another man's clients. Fees, after all, are our bread and butter. I asked that Koya's clients be returned to their cells.My fees have been the subject of the wildest rumour. The man charged with trying to hijack an Air New Zealand jet at Nadi had apparently been charged $12,000 by Koya for an "all up" trial. It set a bench mark for future cases.

Contrary to rumours in New Zealand legal circles about my method of payment or quantum of fee, I do not have a hoard of Indian gold secreted under my floorboards.

As the prisoners came in Anand and I sat across the table from them. The middle of the table had a wooden divider about 18 inches high to stop things being passed between visitors and prisoners. Body contact was not allowed. The guard would see whoever dared to raise a hand over that height.

The first prisoner was a short fat little Indian named Rashid. I didn't have to ask how he had been treated. There was severe bruising to his face and eye. On his dark skin the brownish yellow bruises were unmistakable. He lifted his shirt and showed me swelling over his ribs and told me about being grabbed by the balls with great force and great pain. He had obviously been under considerable duress.

Speaking quickly in Hindi to Anand, his face contorted as he spoke, it was obvious that feelings of pain and anguish were pouring forth; but in a language I could not understand.

I chuckled, thinking of a story told by a former Indian Army officer I knew from university days in Canada. A British major had been posted to India. The new man, always well prepared for his next tour of duty, had taken Hindi lessons in Britain before leaving. The first time he addressed his Gurkha troops the ranks erupted in laughter. It seems the British major had learned to speak Hindi as a woman speaks the language. His London tutor had been a London madam. Even the most stony-faced soldiers cracked up as the major continued his feminine introduction. There was no chance that I could eavesdrop on the instructions Anand Singh was receiving. It was a local dialect and the messages were rapid. Anand listened, then quietly translated what the men had said. It was safer that way because by now the Fijian guards were close to hovering over us.

I told the men I would do the best I could for them. I understood how badly they wanted out of jail, having briefly seen inside police

80

cells in Canada when I failed to pay some parking fines and had to wait while friends brought money to bail me out.

From the looks of anguish and the obvious signs around me, being in jail was no fun. On the bright side Fiji's jails had fresh air, outdoor activity and warm sunshine to help pass the time of day. But such temporary distractions could not dispel the signs of their personal fears and national uncertainties.

Anand explained to them his reasons for hiring an outside lawyer who was not too close emotionally or politically to the whole problem. Our clients agreed and we shook hands. Now they were very apologetic for speaking Hindi in my presence. Sitting virtually on top of us were the four Fijian guards, one a woman.

At no stage did the accused make any comment about guns, like remand prisoners everywhere they were only interested in bail so that they could get out of jail.

As the two of us walked back past the prisoners' exercise yard we were treated to a unique sight. In loose unison, almost dance like, a detail of Fijian prisoners armed with the seemingly ever present cane knives, trimmed the lawn. Swish, swish . . . the steel blades of sharp, two foot long cane knives flashed in the sunlight. Standing at case watching them was a prison guard armed with a black wooden batten.

In the compound the prisoners were all shirtless. A few were playing leap frog, another group kicked a football while the remainder stood around and watched us. As we neared the exercise yard gate a senior officer approached me: "Mr Harder, have you been admitted to the High Court yet?"

"No," I explained I could not apply to the court until I had seen the accused. This inquisitorial approach from a prison officer suggested somebody in the administration was interested in my actions.

Applying Pressure

The Suva taxi driver took us to the hospital from the jail. Local criminal lawyer Haroon Shah was being detained by the police for unspecified reasons. Haroon, a Muslim, had been one of the 21 charged in the guns affair. He was initially denied bail by the local magistrate, as were the others. A subsequent application to the High Court for bail was successful, allowing Shah to be released. Within moments of his stepping free on bail he was rearrested, this time a trumped-up charge about paying a witness was the initial reason given by the authorities.

While in the police cells Haroon complained of feeling faint and having short sharp jabs of pain in his chest. This resulted in the Lautoka police, acting under instructions from the military, transferring him to the hospital where he was detained under guard.

Shah's original crime was alleged to have been to stand by when he knew some other person was going to commit a crime. In most civilised places such inaction is not recognised as crime. Every day somebody requires legal representation by a criminal lawyer when details of alleged criminal activity are discussed. Any excuse would have been good enough to arrest Shah. If it were not this complaint then they would probably have manufactured another false charge against this fighting lawyer.

We left him with the promise that we would try and arrange house arrest for him instead of jail. But my last words to Haroon Shah were, that as one lawyer speaking to another, I thought he had better batten down the hatches and get prepared for a bit of stormy weather and an extended stay. The writing was on the wall that Rabuka would not let him walk free. Nothing more could be done to help Shah today. I had to get admitted to the Fiji bar before I could effectively help anyone.

My priority was to get to see the secretary of the Fiji Law Society, Subash Parshotam. Without his support I had no hope of being admitted to the Fiji bar. Subash Parshotam worked from upstairs offices around the corner from Cummins Street, the busiest shopping area in Suva. The shops along this street are owned exclusively by Indian merchants. It was here most of the petrol bombings erupted during riots after the two coups. Shop windows were smashed and any Indians who walked through Cummins Street ran the risk of violent beatings.

The stairs up Subash's office were steep and rickety. At the top I went through a glass door to be greeted by a friendly young Indian woman. She went away, then returned to advise me that Mr Parshotam could not see me that week because he was very busy. With a big smile I explained to her that I had to see her boss. Would she please find a time and make a suitable appointment. I made it vividly clear that I intended to stay until I had seen him.

She went away again and soon returned to tell me that Mr Parshotam could see me for a few moments. I was ushered into his office and asked to sit down. Work may be on the decline in some Fiji law offices but the desk in front of me was piled high with files. Subash was simply a busy man with much to do, he could not afford a long distraction. On the wall was a degree from the University of Auckland.

Most lawyers in Fiji are trained in New Zealand.

At first we spoke in generalities. I explained my reason for insisting on seeing him. I needed a letter of support from his council if I was to practise on a temporary basis in the Fiji High Court. "I am sorry Mr Harder, but I don't think my council will support your application for the Rotuma case."

The Fiji Law Society had strict rules about outsiders coming in. The previous week an Australian QC named Steve Stanton had been refused admission because the society opposed his motion.

The Chief Justice had officially refused the request because Stanton faced a criminal charge in Australia. But it was widely believed that the Sydney barrister was advising Rabuka on constitutional matters. Stanton, who is Lebanese, spent time in Suva handling cases before the coup through contacts with former NFP leader Sidiq Koya and Vijay Parmanandam. In Australia he was known for his work with the right wing Sydney Liquor Trade Union.

Our discussion warmed to the subject of representing the Rotumans. Parshotam told me that he thought his council was still likely to oppose my temporary admission to the High Court. I had three cards to pay when I walked into his office. I tried to use my charm to get onto an equal footing in the formal and class structured world of Subash Parshotam.

The first major part of my argument was simple: the decree was a draconian measure that needed challenging, but because of its repressive nature it would surely make much more sense to have an outside lawyer arguing a sedition case. Slowly Subash was getting my message about Rotuma.

At what I hoped was the right time in this rather formal encounter I played my second card: I was going to act for six of the 21 people accused in the guns affair, that was if I could get admitted. Still up my sleeve was the third card, two letters from New Zealand High Court judge Sir Graham Speight saying I was a bonny fighter and a man for oppressive times.

As the conversation progressed I could see his frown soften and a twinkle come into his eyes, he was coming around. I asked him to reconsider my request and to discuss it on the phone with his colleagues so that we might resolve this minor matter as soon as possible.

I handed him the outline of a letter I wanted him to consider writing and sufficient copies to give to the other four council members of the law society remaining in Fiji. Since the coups about half of Fiji's 140 lawyers had left the country. Some had left as a precaution, others had fled for their own saftey or had left at the request of some unidentified person. The rumour was that the security forces put pressure on some members to go for extended holidays overseas. However, of the half dozen or so native Fijian lawyers none had left the country. Even now Indians completely dominated the legal system.

I left Subash Parshotam's office with quiet confidence, sure I had carried the day. Up Cummins Street I wandered through the crowd of mostly Indian people milling around on the sidewalks, clustered about shop doors. It was a hustlers' street. You could buy gold, diamonds and rubies, fish, lobster, crabs, colourful Indian cloth and lots and lots of junk. Despite the obvious lack of quality many people were still looking for bargains.

Tourists new to the street took care stepping off the footpath. The 18 inch curb was no doubt designed for some protection from rainy season flooding. Cummins Street is built on the edge of a tidal waterway running through the middle of Suva, like a small Venetian canal.

Back at the hotel I went for a swim. There was nothing else I could do. Anand had said he would call me by telephone after 6 p.m. but the phone never rang.

CHAPTER SIX

ALLIGATOR CLIPS, FRUSTRATION AND OBSERVATION

On Friday morning I thought I heard interference on the phone, as if somebody was opening and closing a circuit or shorting my line. I never liked talking on the phones in Suva, especially in a hotel with a switchboard. As I came down the steps towards the lobby I saw a Fijian hotel worker come around the corner with a civilian dressed in casual clothing. The civilian had on tan pants, leather sandals, and had tattoos on his arms. He held a telephone repairman's handset with alligator clips used for connecting to telephone terminals for testing. I looked at the pair with a cool stare as I walked past them to the manager. "Have you had any trouble with your telephone today?" I asked.

"No," he replied, "we have had no trouble today."

"How come I saw a repairman with a handset and alligator clips come out of the basement just after I was having trouble with my phone?"

"Oh. I am sorry Mr Harder, I am wrong. I do recall there was some kind of telephone trouble. I am sorry if it has bothered you." But it didn't really matter whether anybody was listening. I was doing my job, no more. The contents of my conversations were not criminal. At the time I made my complaint about the man with the clips, all my calls were going through the operator. Whoever was interested in my conversations would have a list of phone numbers identifying each call I made from the hotel.

After Rabuka had issued the Security Decree on Thursday there were incredibly wide-ranging grounds for arrest. There was no bail and no charge required for up to two years, with the right of detention for a further two years. The decree brought in retrospective laws with serious criminal sanctions of life imprisonment; 25 years jail the minimum for unlawful possession of a firearm; and the onus of proof was now on the accused to prove his innocence. Before the security decree came into force unregistered firearms carried a maximum sentence of two years imprisonment. I would put pen to paper or computer printer to my gold embossed letterhead.

I assumed the police had complete access to my room without my permission or knowledge. Whenever I went out I left a note on my briefcase reading: "Come in gentlemen, have a coffee or pour yourself a drink. My briefcase lock combination is zero, zero, zero. I am out for a short while. Please leave your name and number and I shall call you on my return. Thank you, Christopher Harder."

Earlier on Friday morning I had met three foreign visitors at the hotel poolside while sitting under a coconut palm in my swim,suit reading some papers on Rotuma. Our conversation began with lightweight topics, the weather, the hotel service. Really we wanted to talk about the decree and Rabuka. We agreed to meet at eight that evening next door at the Grand Hotel for dinner and kava.

Things were beginning to move, I thought, as I stood in the shower in my room with the lights out, the door closed and the cold tap on. As I began to cool off I adjusted the taps to relax under a stream of warm water and think about what was happening. There were some major hurdles to clear. The Chief Justice was one. The phone was ringing as I fumbled with a towel and bathroom door. "Hello . . . Hello Anand . . . very good . . . you confirm my instructions in relation to the guns affair. Good one my friend . . . just fax it to the hotel. You call Parshotum and explain .. . . thanks." I knew that Anand needed a hand. He would persuade Parshotum.

Half an hour later the phone rang again and a female Indian voice said, "Mr Harder, Mr Parshotum would like to speak to you. Please hold."

"Hello Christopher, Anand has spoken to me. We will support your admission for both of the cases. The letter addressed to the registrar of the High Court is ready for you to pick up any time.

Good luck. I'll call the court for the time of the admission motion. We can find you a wig and gown if one is needed." I thanked him and told him I looked forward to seeing him in court.

It was 11.45 a.m. I had until 1 p.m. to get the letter and the affidavit to the High Court registrar for filing. I hoped that the Chief Justice might deal with my admission motion that same afternoon since there was no apparent opposition to my application. The hotel security service flagged a cab and I urged the driver to greater speed on the way to pick up my papers from Subash and file them with the High Court before the 1 p.m. lunchbreak. Once the driver understood the court papers that needed filing in the High Court were part of the defence of the alleged gun runners he willingly sped through the streets.

I hoped my path would be easier with the Fiji Law Society's support. Four of the five available council members had voted for my admission. The one dissenting vote came from an instructing solicitor (also a law society council member) who had tried to engage the refused Australian Queen's Counsel.

I hurried to the High Court office reception. Outside the granite windowframe was a grass courtyard dotted with begonia bushes and coconut palms. About 100 yards away across the main road the Travelodge Hotel flew the Australian flag in recognition of the Aussie members of parliament who were testing the economic and political temperature of Fiji before making recommendations about future foreign aid. Rusiate came in and said, "Sorry Mr Christopher the Chief Justice has gone home early today. He is not well. We will call you Monday at your hotel."

Anand did not call that evening either. I became concerned for his well-being when I couldn't track him down by phone. In the past I had shown a knack for finding people all over the world. While I was attending law school I started a business called Document Services to search, locate and service people with documents world-wide. I have tracked down friend and foe through telephone systems around the world. This time I failed.

Later on, as arranged, I went next door to the Grand Hotel for dinner. Indeed, it must have been a majestic old place in its prime. Peeling white walls could not detract from its regal beauty. Winding wooden bannisters ran up the stairs and around the first balcony overlooking three sides of the impressive foyer. Crystal chandeliers hung majestically from the ceiling by golden plated chains. The Grand Pacific Hotel was opened in May 1914. Its balcony was where members of the Royal family had stood to make public addresses. The hotel was built by the Union Steamship Company for New Zealand and Canadian shipping service passengers.

As the four of us sat around the kava bowl outside by the pool one of my dinner mates, an ever alert Irishman pointed out that our group was under surveillance through a pair of binoculars on the second floor of the hotel. No prizes for guessing who was following my progress, but we had our meal and philosophical discussions regardless.

A Rare Crowd

On Saturday morning there was a charity fun run. I hadn't run 10k's for many a year and needed a little exercise. With my Walkman on and a pocketful of tapes I arrived at the start only to realise I'd forgotten to bring any money and had to jog back to the hotel for the 50 cent entry fee.

A crowd of about 1,000 had gathered for the run, no doubt the biggest authorised gathering of people in Suva since Taukei supporters had marched down the main street earlier in the month.

The Taukei now mainly consisted of dissidents who drifted together in reaction to the freshly elected Bavadra Government in early 1987.

One faction of the movement, led by former British Army regimental Sergeant Major Ratu Meli Vesikula, has now split away from the movement. Since October this year Ratu Meli has openly supported Bavadra's call for a return to democracy. He feels a sense of betrayal having fought Rabuka's battles on the streets, being rewarded with a post in an interim Government and then sacked at the hands of the two Knights Mara and Ganilau.

Bang! We were off. At first I kept a steady pace with the pack, but slowly the main group began to pass me as I loped along to Fijian tunes on my Walkman. A woman with a New Zealand embassy teeshirt was running beside me so we swapped short-winded conversation. Pam was on a two-year rotating assignment from Wellington, New Zealand.

I run for exercise and stimulation but I had not run this far in a long time. Adrenalin was being released into my system, like an invisible booster shot. But as I pounded along Cakabau Drive I could feel the muscles in my calves begin to stretch and hurt. It was going to be a long 10k's in this tropical heat. My chest began to burn as I began the long climb up the hill. The New Zealand Ambassador's house was pointed out by Pam, my running companion, a colonial style building covered in purple bougainvillea blooms.

As we ran Pam and I briefly discussed the purpose of my visit to Fiji. At the mention of the guns affair her expression tightened as if to say, "Hey mate, please don't involve me." I sensed that she must know more than she could properly let on.

Pam suggested I contact Mr Hill from the New Zealand Embassy for further help. She thought it would be worthwhile to register with the Embassy as a precaution should trouble arise. I did not, at the time, think things would get to that stage. It was obvious later that the guns affair was far more than just a criminal trial, it went deeper, to the very foundation of the troubled state in Fiji.

As the road began to wind down the coconut-lined drive towards the waterfront and home, my left knee twisted and a sharp pain shot up the inside of my kneecap. Slowed to a walk I tried to put the pressure at a different angle. I had to stop and rest then slowly begin to walk, almost hobbling, hoping I could run myself back into shape. But the pain became too much and I had to stop again. A small Fijian boy stood by the road spraying the runners with a garden hose, a bit further to a welcome drink table with juice set up. Along the tarseal and concrete road I hobbled, determined to finish, limp or no limp. I never got my placing but I finished, much nearer the end than the beginning of the pack.

After my tropical 10k's for charity I needed a few laps in the hotel pool to cool off and ease my aching legs. Taking a different route to my room up an outside staircase I met Mama. She was a middle-aged Fijian woman down on her luck, very religious, like all Fijians, believing in Jesus Christ and God. Mama, as she asked me to call her, said she would say prayers for me. She wanted to bring her teenage son along to see the Kiwi lawyer, so I invited her and the boy over for dinner on Wednesday. Their village was many miles out of Suva, she lived in the staff quarters but would get a message out to him.

"Hey Mama? Where does the Brigadier go to church?" I asked on an off chance. She didn't know but promised to find out.

I lay back on my bed listening to Fijian music and thinking about the possibility of getting to see Rabuka by going to see him at his church.

A while later Mama came back to the door. "Brigadier, he goes to Natabua Church on Sunday. It start at ten o'clock in the morning. You go and you see him and you pray," Mama told me."Brigadier, he Christian man, he would never hurt you, my son. God be with you. I will keep praying for you both."

Suva On The Sabbath

Sunday morning in Fiji and no morning newspapers. I woke early and lay in my bed looking at a copy of the original Security Decree. The 94 page document had been discreetly delivered to me late on Saturday night. I could not take notes, they were too dangerous to have in my possession and I was not allowed to photocopy it. But a quick read was enough to convince me. Then I delivered the evil document back to the desolate spot where I had been told to leave it and returned to my room to think.

I lit a cigarette out on the balcony overlooking the sea. Smoking again after all those years was maddening, but the tension on me, and all around had been exacerbated by the imposition of The Decree. People were genuinely scared. I was frustrated and angry that a law like this could be introduced in the middle of the game. What I had constantly to remember was that the rules were made by the person who held the most guns.

I have always carried a deep seated opposition to arbitrary authority imposed on individuals without consultation. In the late 1970s in Canada, the premier of Alberta, Peter Lougheed, had his government introduce a civil emergencies bill. It allowed any civil authority to enter any property at any time without notice and to take any property or supplies required by civil emergency staff.

This bill authorised the seizing of radios, blankets, food and guns without fear of liability or prosecution. Such an imposition on the rights of the individual did not sit well with me or a small group of my constituents whom I was representing as the provincial liberal candidate in the local university riding.

A significant group of Mormons lived within the riding. I had been approached by one, a young Mormon named Shelly Winter. Pretty and full of principle and spirit, it was very difficult to argue with this determined young woman. She took me home and introduced me to her family. We discussed the principle behind the Mormon practice of storing a year's supply of goods and provisions to cater for their family and relatives in times of need. This emergency bill really struck hard at Mormons who could be unfairly targeted because of their beliefs.

My protest on behalf of them was from a genuine feeling of strong opposition to this intrusion on one's rights and property. As a student activist at the University of Calgary my youthful ideals had blossomed into different displays of individualism.

The Conservative party was the government in Alberta with a significant majority in the provincial legislature.

Edmonton is the capital of Alberta but Calgary was the oil capital where Premier Peter Lougheed, always sensitive to the needs of his own Calgarians, had established a sort of local White House.

The Western Canadian attitude to the east of Canada was not very sympathetic. Eastern Canada had always been seen as the spoilt sister who got whatever she wanted because of her political influence. The energy and agriculture-rich west had missed out on many subsidies over the years. Now the east wanted the Federal Government to ensure that the price of Alberta crude oil did not rise to world standards as the effects of the Arab oil crisis began to take hold.

Premier Lougheed was holding an International press conference on his government's position. Outside the Premier's office was a huge oval desk used for major press conferences. Reporters in attire befitting the Premier's pressroom came up in the lift eight to 10 at a time. They melted among the businessmen operating the oil town's support structure.

I had decided to protest against the civil defence legislation by joining the media brigade in the Premier's office. I took blankets, tins of food, batteries and a radio. I had the blanket on my arm partly covering the supplies. It was my intention to present these emergency items to the Premier as a symbolic protest against the authoritarian legislation and consequent erosion of personal rights.

I walked out of the elevator with people all around me, went down the hall, and directly outside the conference room put the provisions on the floor. Then I took my black leather briefcase and walked into the conference room. I sat down among the buzzing pool of reporters who seemed eager to hear the Premier's stance on the price of Alberta crude.

The Premier's press secretary handed out copies of a release. Questions began to fly as the news hounds began to bay. The Premier was not even in the room yet. Slowly I slid out a batch of my own prepared news releases, decrying the contents of the emergency bill. One by one the reporters to my left began to receive a copy of my deceptive document.

By the time the Premier sat down the remaining copies from my bundle had reached his seat. Simultaneously a couple of reporters began to ask questions about this ring-in news release. The Premier let rip: "Jesus Christ, what the hell is going on here!" as his eyes and everybody else's roamed the room for the culprit. Before I could protest my body was hoisted from its comfortable leather chair and frog marched into the Premier's inner office.

Premier Lougheed was frothing at the mouth, obviously restraining himself from physically venting his anger on me. He yelled, "If you have any complaint to make about the emergency bill, you take it up with your local MP, don't come in here and try to hijack my press conference." With those stern words I left his office under escort, feeling I had made an appropriate protest.

If Rabuka didn't watch out he'd be in for some of the same. At about eight o'clock I phoned the receptionist and asked her to arrange a permit for a taxi to Natabua Church for me. "I need to be there for ten o'clock or maybe five to ten."

The curtains were open and the morning sun shone throught the coconut palms and the mango outside my room, down onto the carpet and the foot of the bed. Shaved, showered and dressed in my best court suit I headed off for a fruit breakfast. Two cups of freshly brewed coffee later I called for a taxi.

A short Indian called Mohammed was the driver of my special permit taxi. With virtually no traffic on the roads on Sunday we arrived at the Natabua Methodist Church with time to spare.

The name had a strong ring to it. Methodist. My grandfather had been a lay minister during the depression years in Swift Current, Saskatchewan. It was ironic that I, Christopher Harder, with family ties to the Methodist Church, was today coming to hear lay minister Rabuka preach to his flock.

When I arrived hardly a soul was around. A few inquisitive, ebony complexioned Fijian children, dressed in their Sunday best, walked around the corner of the church to see this tall, white, stranger. Everybody had on their Sunday best. White skirts and mostly bare feet for the boys. The girls had hair combed and sparkling from grandmothers' brushing. Smiles and grins shone on the little ones' faces and I smiled back. Behind me nervous chatter accompanied by childish giggles indicated a following.

I took out my camera and got the children to line up by the lali at the front of the church. The lali is a big wooden drum shaped a bit like a half built dugout canoe. When beaten with two wooden sticks it booms out summoning the congregation to worship. Different rhythms signal different messages, including prayers of guidance and thanks. After taking several snaps of the children and church I went inside to pray.

I had gone through the church procedure with Mama the day before. I would enter through the great big arch of the barn-like structure designed to stand firm in storms and to hold many people. Inside the church I would take a seat in the back pew.

On Sunday I sat down and bowed my head in a moment's silent prayer. I prayed to God that things would work out, I didn't specify exactly how I wanted things to happen, just that everything should work out alright. Many times before I had talked to God, when I was really worried or scared. Throughout my life I have prayed to

94

God for help and guidance. Although prayer has at times given me strength, God has never spoken to me in the way Rabuka had described receiving divine messages.

In God We Trust

Slowly the church began to fill. Slowly the elders walked down between the pews.

The rest of the people sat in the main body of the church. A Fijian woman I had met outside came over to me and invited me to the front pew. It was reserved for special guests, she said, and sat down beside me. She was the Sunday school teacher and would be pleased to sit beside me and explain what was going on. I picked up a song book. I had asked Mama about the words. She told me no problem everyone had a prayer book. What she forgot to tell me was that the words were Fijian, not English. I improvised as best I could delaying my words a fraction to blend under the magnificent, full bodied, several part harmony of a Fijian hymnfest. For some reason I had thought the sermon would be Fijian and the singing in English.

The first lay minister rose to the pulpit to welcome the congregation in Fijian. The Sunday school teacher both translated and commentated for me. Before church my religious guide had asked me my name. I said I was a lawyer from New Zealand and had a chuckle telling her about my lay minister grandfather.

The sermon was about charity to one's neighbour. Strange that, since my guide had proudly told me that Natabua Village was all Fijian. No other races were allowed to live in the village community.

The only other lay preacher was not Brigadier Rabuka. He apologised for the two ordained ministers being late, they now had to walk to church. Vehicle travel was prohibitied on Sundays without special permission. But I had heard that lay preacher Rabuka always got dropped off by a military or security services car. The Brigadier was never late for church.

"Onward Christian Soldiers" flowed from 30 golden voices at the front of the church, "marching as to war", the words boomed on. I joined in to sing in English in the best voice I could muster, occasionally looking around ever so slightly to see if Rabuka had showed.

95

Then in Fijian, with broken English additions, the church information officer announced how pleased the congregation was to have with them New Zealand lawyer Christopher Harder, whose grandfather in Canada used to be a lay Methodist minister. He said that we might have a language barrier at present but that we were spiritually all together.

If Rabuka did not already know that I was at his church sitting in the front pew, he soon would. No further reference was made about the two empty chairs so obvious in the middle of the church. At the collection plate I put in a Fiji $20 bill, said thank you to the church people for having me in their house of worship and quietly exited through an open side archway. My Indian driver was waiting with his permit that allowed him to pick me up. I was worried he would not be there when I had come out. Mama said the service would last about an hour, starting at ten o'clock. When I left the church it was eleven thirty.

I met Mama coming out of my room. She had just changed my towels and made the bed. Her eyes beamed when she saw me come to the door. "No Brigadier at Natabua today," I said to her. A look of disappointment and sadness showed on her face. She could not understand. She did not know of the different roles being played out in the guns affair.

Mama started to talk, then stopped, like a child puzzling over something it cannot quite understand, then she blurted out,"But I know he was going to be there. I telephoned his home on the Saturday." Only then did I fully understand the two empty chairs.

Committed To Protest

I began to write my letter of protest to the Fiji Solicitor General and cabinet late that Sunday afternoon. This protest had to have an effect. Our five clients faced life imprisonment if their gun charges, which had a maximum penalty of two years jail, were replaced by charges under the retroactive Security Decree. Under the Decree the gun charges penalty was life in prison with no chance of parole for a minimum of 25 years.

The words began to flow from my pen as I thought of Rabuka's folly. But I was not going to deliver it until I had been admitted to

96

the Fiji bar. It just meant I'd be prepared to move fast when the time came.

I took the rough draft of the Amnesty request to the computer typist down the road from the hotel. My stomach tightened as I began to appreciate how firm a line I had really taken in the letter. This was Fiji, there had been two military coups, democracy, freedom of speech and many common laws had disappeared. On the other hand the letter had a number of positive suggestions to place before the cabinet and Solicitor General for consideration. Smart men don't ignore a good suggestion out of hand.

Many, many years ago I had a similar tight sick feeling in my stomach. I remember sitting outside the Housing Corporation Building in Edmonton, Alberta. It was two in the morning in the Artic cold of an Alberta winter. The car was warm, the engine was running as I watched for the police or uninvited strangers. James Lansky, recently sacked from a top job with the provincial government's housing agency was inside obtaining information for me about a Housing Corporation scandal involving $2.2 million on forged signatures, a crooked lawyer and the distribution of hundreds of thousands of dollars in brown paper bags at the Fontain Bleu Hotel in Montreal, Quebec.

Each morning during the past week in Fiji I had tried to contact Rabuka as soon as the business day began. But each time I had got no further than the desk officer at the Queen Elizabeth Barracks. In addition I tried other indirect ways of getting to see him. At the Fiji Travel Bureau I had hoped to see the director but ended up talking to a man related to the permanent undersecretary for Home Affairs. He was distressed to see that I had addressed my letter requesting a work permit directly to the Brigadier instead of to the undersecretary who officially looked after permits. He asked me why I had not written to the undersecretary? I told him that in the eyes of the world, Rabuka was top dog. Despite the pretence of there being a civilian government the reaction of this man from the tourist bureau was telling.

To The Top For Results
Going straight to the top dog to solve a problem was standard

practice for me. I learnt young that you go to the top for action. I had parted company with the electronic firm I had worked for in the prairies and gone back to high school, aged 20, wanting to catch up on my twin brother and my best friend who were both about to start at Simon Fraser University. I tried to convince the Vancouver school board to let me in two-thirds through the school year in an attempt to catch up on three years of schooling in three months. I was laughed out of the office by an old battle-axe of an administrator.

Not to be beaten, or at least not easily, I decided to go back and see Mr Tady the principal of my old school, Argyle Secondary, in North Vancouver.

Five years before I had been kicked out of school by the then vice-principal, the same Mr Tady, for many anti-social and rebellious reasons. Now, I was knocking on the door of his new, progressive school.

A fair man, he welcomed me back. Had he not done so my chances of ever becoming a lawyer would have been about zero. I enrolled for day-school, night-school, afternoon tutoring and correspondence school so that I could try and do the three years in three months. Despite intricate timetable juggling I could not fit in grade 12 English or Maths, but having made significant steps in catching up my twin brother, I applied for admission to a local college.

However the principal of West Vancouver Community College only allowed me to enrol on the condition that I did my missing grade 12 courses. Considering what I had done in three months at high school I thought this extra requirement was unfair and excessive. Refusing to give ground I challenged the principal's authority and elected to take the matter to a different forum. I booked a flight to Victoria, the seat of provincial government in British Columbia. I recall the secretary for the Minister of Education, Donald Brothers, saying, "I am sorry Mr Harder, but you cannot see the Minister without an appointment. He is a busy man."

With timing just like you see in the movies, a man walked out of Mr Brothers' office and asked the secretary for a file. Dressed in a grey pinstripe suit I turned to him, extended my hand and said, " My name is Chris Harder Mr Brothers, I am awfully sorry to have to bother you today, but I have a serious problem and only you can help me solve it." He looked at his secretary who standing with her mouth open and said, "Come in Mr Harder."

He had a few minutes to spare before his next appointment and quickly got to the root of my problem. The minister picked up his telephone and got the principal of my college on the line. "Hello this is Donald Brothers, the Minister of Education, I have one of your pupils in my office who says," and then he broke off in mid-sentence, obviously having been interrupted.

"Well, yes," said Brothers, "How did you guess it could be Mr Harder?" Pause. "Well, I am telling you that he does not have to do those two courses, do you understand me?" From that day I realised that most obstacles in my path through life could either be moved or avoided. It was a matter of looking forever forward, never back. Now the man at the top I needed to see was Rabuka.

Desperate For News

Throughout Monday I tried to get news of what was happening on the political front, and in particular what was going on in the guns affair case at Lautoka. Hardly any telephones were working, neither of the radio stations mentioned guns or the decree in any of their news bulletins and I still couldn't get hold of Anand.

With no reply to several calls to Anand's office and his home I began to wonder if the lawyers over in the west were being hassled.

Thirsting for news I waited until one o'clock the next morning and took a taxi to the *Fiji Times* printing factory so that I could get a copy hot off the press.

I felt sick when I got back to the hotel and read the story about the lawyers pushing for bail. I knew the writing was on the wall, anybody granted bail would be rearrested under the security decree where they could be held for two years without bail, without charge or they could be recharged under the Arms Section of the Security Act which automatically made them liable to life imprisonment, 25 years minimum.

The onus of proof normally on the Crown to prove a case beyond reasonable doubt before a person was convicted of a criminal offence had been removed. Now the accused had to prove his innocence. It was blatant. It had been announced in the court in Lautoka on the appearance the day before I arrived that they would put the guns affair people under the decree.

One probably has to know what it's like to be arrested and put in a cell to understand why when somebody is picked up by an authority the number one thing they want is bail. It was all the gun clients wanted and, no doubt, the lawyers were following their instructions. But it was probably a situation that called for strong advice from senior counsel that bail was inappropriate at this stage.

The Fijian authorities were holding an enquiry into the guns affair. It would have been appropriate in Australia or New Zealand courts to give them 30 days to finish their enquiries before suspects were released on bail. There was a fear that our clients could be put under the decree because of the efforts of the others. I sat down to prepare a release indicating that Anand Singh and I would be withdrawing our applications for bail on behalf of our clients at next Monday's bail hearing. And then I turned off the lights and tried to go to sleep but it wasn't easy, my mind was speeding through this adventure. All manner of options whirred about my brain as I tried to come to grips with one of the most exciting cases I was ever likely to be involved with. Working on a gun running case amidst a coup d'etat in the tropics had the appeal needed to keep my lust for life alive.

First thing Tuesday morning I dived into the refreshing water of the hotel pool. It was quiet and desolate. Not a soul was around the pool. By seven the sun was shining through the palm trees as I floated under the water, drifting towards the deep end. I was excited, nervous . . . scared. But I was feeling proud as I climbed out of the pool and headed back to my room for what would be the turning point of my adventure, or so I thought. Would I be admitted to the High Court of Fiji today?

My black tie with small white spots contrasted with the white shirt and suit, charcoal with ebony pinstripes. My black leather loafers had a respectable but not startling shine. My grandfather, the one from Saskatchewan, had always told me how important it was to have clean shoes. The first thing most people saw when they looked at you was your shoes because people tended to look down. He thought that if you wore clean, polished shoes it would make a good initial impression. It was something I had always remembered.

CHAPTER SEVEN

GETTING THE NOD

Rusiate handed the file to the Chief Justice who flicked through the papers only slightly slower than a bank teller thumbing notes and said, "Mr Harder, I find that you are a fit and proper person to be admitted to the High Court of Fiji in relation to the Rotuma case." And there he stopped.

I waited for him to utter the words "and gun case" but nothing happened. Then Fa, Subash and Rusiate exploded in unison "and the gun case."

His Honour looked puzzled, paused and then began to leaf through the papers, obviously unaware that I had made a formal application to appear in both cases.

"Your Honour it's in paragraph four of Mr Harder's affidavit and the letter I signed from the law society also makes reference to the gun case and the Rotuma case," said Subash.

"Why did it take the law society so long to come back? Why has this taken so long?" the Chief Justice asked.

This was not the time to say anything. I sat silently.

Subash defended himself: "The court registrar has to this day never sent me a copy of the application to the law society." He told the Chief Justice that it was only because I had faxed a copy of all the documents to him that he now had a copy of them in court.

Rusiate looked nervous and flustered until, finally, at the bottom of the pile, the Chief Justice found my arms affair documents. He looked straight up at me, with a judge's learned look of knowledge and experience . . . "and the gun case".

My heart rate leapt and skin tingled, I had just cleared hurdle number two.

I stood and bowed to His Honour as he rose and returned the courtesy to a new member of the bar. He turned and left for his chambers. Fa, Subash, Rusiate and I walked out onto the balcony overlooking the vast Government buildings courtyard; a giant horseshoe facing the Travelodge and the shores of Suva. Three or four freighters sat at anchor inside the reef, waiting berths at the wharves. Another was slowly steaming towards the western side of the port. As we stood on the balconies a seagull flew over and squawked. I flashed back to my home town, Vancouver, and the seashore. Everything else was vastly different but the seagulls looked the same. Fa and Subash congratulated me. It was like a mini-graduation. They were very warm, considerate and pleased. "Now, now you are admitted. Now you can go for it," Fa said. "Now you can go and fight them."

Up until this time Fa had been holding me back, a restraining force, advising me of the Fijian ways and customs. We didn't agree on everything. Some of it was tactics and some of it was just style. Experience had taught me there was a certain way to win a case, but here we were not playing by the ordinary rules of court.

On the Rotuma side there was what really amounted to political dissent lead by a band of unsophisticated Rotumans bound together more by the Gagaj Sau Lagfatmaro's karate school than anything else. They respected, even adored, their Gagaj. The case was punishable by a maximum of two years imprisonment; hardly the most serious of sentences. Two of the nine originally charged with sedition had their charges dropped because of their old age. The others ranged between 35 and 60 and at first glance were not what you would expect in the vanguard of a revolution. On the Chief Justice's balcony I told Fa that I was going to send a letter.

"Okay you can do that now, you are admitted. You can go fight."

I think he held some respect for me in that I would go and say what had to be said, he understood as a lawyer. He is a strong character and, in most instances, able to divorce politics and emotions from the case of the day. He could, if well instructed, push

103

the Rotuma constitution issue quite properly, quite ethically, for his client the Gagaj Sau Lagfatmaro.

My clients were the seven Juju Chiefs charged with the criminal offence of sedition. I made it clear to Fa that my job was to defend the sedition case, pointing out that the jurisdiction question was a valid issue but not one that would predominate.

On the other hand the Gagaj wanted the case to go to the World Court. Fa was keen, should he be properly compensated, to put the case on that world stage but he had first to exhaust all the domestic channels. Having raised the question in the Magistrate's Court and taken it on referral to the High Court where the Chief Justice confirmed Fiji's jurisdiction over Rotuma, Fa had yet to argue the matter in the Court of Appeal which would finally open the door for the World Court in the Hague.

I thanked these two loyal soldiers for their assistance, without their support I would not have been admitted. It was a tremendous display of teamwork in very difficult circumstances. It gave me a confidence to push towards the remaining hurdle, to fairly defend the arms clients in the Lautoka Court. I now needed Rabuka's okay. Along with the rest of the world I knew that in a military dictatorship it is the man who holds the guns who pulls the strings. Rabuka controlled the army. If he didn't want somebody somewhere, they would somehow be removed. Recognising this, I continued to try to see the Brigadier. My biggest concern was that he should not think I'd pulled a fast one on him.

When I wrote my June 14 letter telling him that I was coming to Fiji and why, I had thought the letter out carefully, not wanting to mislead or say anything that was not absolutely correct. I had operated on a principle used in court. My evidence in court has to stand the test of cross-examination; if I have good evidence I don't mind telling the prosecution about the strength of my case in advance because I know it will stand that test of time and cross-examination.

I had written to Rabuka in a similar vein. My letter told him I was coming to do the Rotuma case and that he had nothing to fear, and that his Government had nothing to fear from a properly conducted criminal case. I made no mention of the guns affair because I was not involved in it. On June 14 there had been no suggestion I would be engaged for the guns affair. I'd be a liar if I didn't say that the possibility had crossed my mind but I didn't see any chance of it happening so quickly.

The opening came when Anand suggested in a telephone link between Lautoka and Suva that he would like a hand. From then I pursued the case with vigour. I'm a criminal lawyer who likes an exciting case. Sometimes you do a court case for the fee, sometimes you do it just because you like the case or sometimes you think there's a principle at stake. This situation was mainly a combination of the last two. There would be a reasonable fee. On the other hand fees were secondary. You couldn't get Fiji money out of the country.

Embarrassing The Boss

I called Rabuka's bodyguard Jesse again, urgently trying to see him because I wanted to tell him I had become involved in the gun case. I still regret not leaving a message with Jesse telling him why I required to see his boss.

On Tuesday I got no response from the Minister of Home Affairs, Sitiveni Rabuka. I called the Tourist Bureau and spoke to the under secretary's cousin. He wasn't available, so I asked for him to call me back. Twice more on the Tuesday afternoon I phoned, without luck.

After the admission ceremony I'd gone back to my hotel room changed into my swimming trunks and cruised about the pool on a personal high. Progress was highly satisfactory. Here I was practising law in a beautiful South Seas republic. Time and again memories of youthful revolutionary zeal flooded back as I sat down to analyse the situation as it was developing; trying to calculate moves and counter-moves where the five accused would get out of jail — whether on bail, found not guilty or released through plea bargaining, or even pardoned because of a change of Government, it didn't matter. Men were sitting in jail and I would do my best to see that they got out.

I walked into my hotel room still dripping wet from the pool, picked up a towel and began to dry my hair and face. I dropped the towel and stomped on it so the water didn't soak into the carpet. The phone rang, two rings. Normally I pick up my phone on two rings if I am near it; three rings if I am outside. Prompt communication is crucial to a winning case.

"Hello, yes, Christopher Harder speaking. Mesake, how are you my friend? . . . Yes, yes I was admitted before the Chief Justice this morning. Tevita Fa moved the motion. Subash Parshotum, he confirmed and the law society supported. Initially he only did it for the Rotuma case but by that stage he had concluded that I was a fit and proper person and he didn't have much room to manoeuvre, he had to let me in on the gun case or it would have seemed political . . . Yeah, I'll be here for half an hour. Call-over."

I hung up considering what I would say to the media. You were limited to what could be said in Fiji. Press censorship was very real. The newspaper office was closely monitored by military security people. Now that I was admitted and the amnesty letter was about to be delivered it was probably time to crystalise the situation in the public's mind.

Throughout my public career I had found the newspaper a helpful companion in defending individual clients. It is a perfect medium for reporting exciting cases and difficult defended cases that have some public appeal. It is also a way to bring pressure on officialdom when injustices need righting. Like the case of David Howard who was held in police cells for 66 days while they argued about his extradition to Australia on a robbery charge.

Without the media, in particular Philip English of the *New Zealand Herald*, I doubt that a commission of enquiry ever would have been held into the "Parnell Panther" stretched footprint case. They had followed my career from the very first day back in 1978 when I had appeared for the first time in a New Zealand paper, a front page picture of me holding my 15-month-old son Justin, during the Tramways dispute.

The *Herald* followed my career throughout Strike Free. I have always had a relatively charmed life with the media, learning early that if you want co-operation or assistance from the media on a particular case then it has to be an interesting issue with some public appeal. They were often not particularly interested in one-off issues and definitely not in bullshit. Dealing with the media one had to be impeccably accurate. They could make or break a person. Lying to the media or to the court could ruin a career.

Three knocks at the door and I turned the handle to be greeted by a person I didn't recognise holding a camera.

"Is Mesake Koroi here?"

"No, he just called and said he was on his way. Come in, come in."

"I'm Joe the photographer from the *Fiji Times*. I'm just waiting for Mesake."

"I'm not really dressed for a photograph. If you want to take a photograph you'll have to wait till I change."

I was a believer in always presenting myself in formal attire. Otherwise a photograph would be taken that might later be regretted. In the Tramways case many years ago my photograph was taken in an open-neck shirt with a tartan jacket and my hair in some sheepish looking fashion. It was a horrible picture but it was difficult to do anything about it because that was the only picture they had and they kept using it.

When my car was bombed a picture was taken of me having just woken up, with uncombed hair. I looked very bedraggled. After that if a newspaper wanted to run a picture of me, I decided I would get a good one taken and send it to them. Finally I had a private photographer take some decent pictures which I sent to the different papers asking them to please update their files.

I put on my suit pants, dried my hair and ran a comb through it, put on my vest, tie and dark blue leather shoes. Mesake suddenly appeared in the part open door with his big grin. "How are you Christopher?"

Mesake and I were now like old chums who had known each other for years. It was good to see him.

He came in. "So you've been admitted to the Fiji High Court, what do you do now?"

"Well, I've got this letter here that I'm about to deliver to the Solicitor General which is likely to ruffle a few feathers," I said. "But I think it's got to be done and I think the suggestions of the amnesty and leaving them under the two-year maximum penalty charge is fair and reasonable. At least they'll have to have a good hard think about it."

"I want to get your picture for the story. We'll do a little piece. I've got a space reserved on, I think it's page two," said Mesake. "Hey what's with the tabua?"

"I've got that for Rabuka," I said. "I figured if I'm going to stay here I'd better see him and make peace. If I don't, it's going to be difficult. I've tried to see him probably seven times in the last six days. I've gone through Apisai Tora's office through the Tourist Bureau, I've tried through his office as the Minister of Home Affairs, through his personal bodyguard and through Major Mataitine. I asked them all to call back and say yes or no, and if they weren't interested just to say no and I wouldn't bother them, but I never had the courtesy of a reply, so I'm just waiting here. Waiting to see Rabuka," I chuckled, "And I'm not quite sure what's going to happen in the next scenario."

"Well, pick up the kava and tabua and we'll shoot a picture."

"Do you think anybody would get upset at that?" I asked.

"It's traditional, it's Fijian. You come here as a professional and you're coming to make a Fijian offering and I don't think anybody can fault you for that."

Everything else had been tried and failed. This way I'd be sure to get his attention. It could force him into having to see me and take the steam out of things a bit. It might just be the catalyst we needed.

Joe had me hold the kava and tabua about waist high. I tried to keep a serious face as the cameraman snapped away, the seashell print on the wall featuring in the background was identical to one we had in our bathroom back in Auckland. I had bought it in a Remuera printshop thinking it was an original.

I thanked the cameraman and told Mesake the letters would be delivered to the Solicitor General within the half hour. Then I would just come back to my hotel and wait. I chuckled, he grinned and walked out the door.

I picked up the typed letter and at the front desk asked the receptionist to photocopy it for me. The Fijian woman took the document and walked out to a larger complex where the telephone operators and office manager worked.

She returned with a "Sorry Mr Harder but the photocopy machine is not working."

I didn't want to challenge her, feeling empathy for the Fijian staff who sometimes asked me to join them after hours when they sang, danced and drank kava. I felt comfortable with the average Fijian person. On those social occasions we didn't speak much of Rabuka but it wasn't a secret that I was acting for some of the accused in the guns affair and the Rotuma case. I was a lawyer. I was there doing a job.

CHAPTER EIGHT

SOME THOUGHTS FOR CABINET

I hurriedly took a taxi. The road was quite busy. It was approaching noon and there was all manner of hustle and bustle. The daytime commercial traffic in Suva is quite congested. Taxis fly back and forth, trucks push and shove, here and there a forklift or tractor drives by while people meander down the sidewalks. In the daytime you wouldn't know there was a serious political crisis.

I burst into the computer shop, "Sorry Marnie, I won't bother you but a moment. Could you give me 21 copies please and good copies, they're going to the cabinet." I wondered if Marnie really appreciated what she had been engaged in. I presumed she took the professional approach and would type anybody's letter if they paid for her time; just like a barrister acting for a person accused of a criminal offence.

"Have you got a brown envelope I could put them in?" She hunted around till she found a larger size envelope into which I placed the original and the 21 signed copies. I had the letters prepared, 'secretary of the law society' but Subash had not called me back. Before I could seal the envelope I had to call him.

"No, listen," he said, "You'd better hold onto the letter because I'm checking with my council. I had better get their support before I issue it under my name as secretary of the law society. There could be repercussions on people if I took that stand."

"It's imperative that we get this to the cabinet today," I pleaded. "The cabinet is still sitting. It will be sitting until 1 p.m. and then it adjourns for lunch. I don't know how long it goes for in the afternoon and there's always a possibility that it won't and, if this

110

letter's going to go and be dealt with, then it should get there within the hour. Subash are you prepared to, if I change the letter and take out 'secretary of the law society', are you prepared to sign it as an individual now, and I will deliver them to the cabinet before lunch?"

There was a pause of a couple of seconds before he answered. "Yes, yes I'm prepared to sign it as an individual. That's probably the wiser course."

"I'll have somebody bring the papers up to your office shortly. Could you sign each one individually? I think that it's better that we both sign in original ink even if we're signing copies. It will help show we've taken the time to think about what we're saying and that we mean what we're saying . . . thank you Subash."

"Marnie did another 21 copies without 'secretary to the law society'. I arrived at the High Court out of breath, having hustled taxi drivers and typists alike to get the letters signed, if not sealed. Now I was about to deliver.

The adrenalin was evident again as I climbed the stairways to the third floor and walked around to the far right hand corner of the Government building to the Solicitor General's office. I walked in and asked for the Solicitor or his personal assistant. A Fijian woman identified herself as the Solicitor General's personal assistant and offered to help.

"I have an envelope here with some documents that must, as a matter of national security, be placed before the cabinet before they rise from lunch."

The woman looked at the envelope.

"There is a copy in here for each cabinet Minister and it is imperative; it's written on the envelope — you can see there, 'Delivered by hand, must be delivered to the cabinet prior to 1 p.m. Matter of National security.' Do you understand that? I don't mean to be pushy or tell you what to do, but you must ensure that the documents go before the cabinet before they rise. Will you do that for me?"

She stood back, then she looked at me, "Yes Mr Harder, I will see that the cabinet gets these documents before 1 p.m."

"Thank you very much, I'll be back at my hotel room. If you call me as soon as you have any kind of response, I would be forever in

111

your debt. It's important that they read the letter." She smiled and I smiled back running my finger around my neck and pulling my sticky white shirt up off my damp skin. Getting anything done at speed in the tropics is hard, hot work. I looked forward to getting back to the hotel and having a swim.

Back at the hotel running the days events through my mind it suddenly occurred that I had been a bit rude in demanding that the letter be put before the Solicitor General and the cabinet without first attempting to get a personal appointment with the country's top law officer. I picked up the phone and dialled, asking for the woman who I had just delivered the 21 copies to.

There was a bit of confusion on the other end of the line and the person there asked me what I was referring to. "To my letter to the cabinet, the one suggesting an amnesty for anyone who surrenders weapons."

"Who is that speaking and where are you calling from?" asked the person on the other end of the line, suddenly taking on a strongly inquisitive air.

I spelt out my name, told them where I was staying and that I had just been admitted to the Fiji bar so that I could help defend six of the people accused in connection with the guns and could I get a message to the Solicitor General.

At that point the person on the other end explained that I had been talking to the Prime Minister's office and must have the wrong number, there only being one digit difference between the phone numbers of the two offices.

At the time I did not think too much of the mistake, but redialled the correct number in an effort to overcome my protocol slip up. But many times later on I wondered if that call to the PM's office had not had something to do with my being arrested the next day.

There was nothing more to do today. I had been admitted to the High Court of Fiji when the Chief Justice had ruled I was a fit and proper person. I now had a proper base to criticise the decree in an effort to dissuade cabinet from implementing some of the sections because of the dire consequences they could have on our clients.

It's a principle of criminal law that legislation is not retroactive unless specifically stated as such. Here it was spelt out. The onerous penalties applied from the first of March to encompass all those on the possession of firearms charges. As I lay by the poolside soaking up the sun and listening to my Fijian music, I read the latest *Time* magazine.

I looked up and saw a young woman of fair skin walk by the pool, pull her golden brown dress over her head and sit down in a black one-piece bathing suit to soak up the sun. In normal times such sights were part of daily life in Fiji, but now people looked up and counted the tourists in the hope more would soon return. I turned back to *Time* magazine and began reading the latest about the situation in Iraq and Iran. I thought about Iran, wondering what happened in their courts.

Back to matters at hand, I continued trying to make an appointment with the Brigadier. I had certainly passed the word around town that I was looking to see him as a matter of urgency over whether or not I needed a work permit. The 14-day visitor's visa limit on my working didn't matter from a practical point of view. I needed Rabuka's stamp of approval if I was to appear in court and have the independence needed to speak up on behalf of my clients without myself being arrested. I wanted to sell Rabuka on the fact that I was a criminal lawyer there to test the quality of the evidence and that he should not interfere.

I also wanted to size him up for possible cross-examination about allegiance to the Queen. It would be good to get a measure of him. As an attorney I had examined and cross-examined all manner of people. I should be able to size up Rabuka fairly quickly, but didn't think there was anything he could say that would change my opinion of him.

As a military dictator, as a religious and racist zealot, I saw him developing like a Mussolini of the South Pacific if he continued along his path. He was suggesting that 300,000 Hindus, and Muslims and Sihks should be converted to Christianity, a most profound objective indeed. But it really only tended to confirm a thought I had already had about the Rabuka family.

During the last six months a cousin of Sitiveni's had blown his brains out in the middle of a football field in Australia. Then there was the Magistrate Rabuka sitting in Suva and related to the

Brigadier. While sentencing a woman for a serious assault where jail should have been seriously considered he said, "Woman I will not send you to jail this time but if you ever come back before my court I will [expletive deleted] your arse."

It seems the magistrate, who was quite a drinker, had been out till all hours and had gone on the bench still affected by alcohol, where he suffered a black-out and this incident took place. The prosecutor was aghast at what had been uttered in court by Rabuka. He immediately offered to pull the rest of the court cases from the prosecution bench. The court was full of chattering Indian lawyers, the disbelief on their faces a strange combination of smirk and disgust. Immediately the court adjourned.

Shortly after, the Chief Justice contacted Magistrate Rabuka in his chambers and informed him that, he would have to step down. Rabuka, lost for words, pleaded "Please give me two hours," and hung up. The Chief Justice called to reiterate the absolute requirement that the magistrate step down from the bench in traditional fashion.

If I had not quit drinking alcohol when I did I might have been in jail now or struck off. An incident far less serious than this would end any lawyer's career in the New Zealand courts.

After the fight I had with two trial judges involved in the Stephens case I often imagined what would have happened had I walked up the hill from the Auckland High Court in Eden Crescent to the Hyatt Regency and consumed two or three double Canadian Club and Cokes before those encounters. No doubt in alcoholic hazes long past I'd have been capable of telling a judge to "take a flying leap." Survival at the bar would not have been possible had I been drinking.

Rabuka was about to lose his career because of alcohol. The native Fijian grog (kava) never seemed to have the aggressive, violent affect of alcohol. As a narcotic, kava tends to numb the body, leaving the brain alive and alert but the lower extremities, especially legs, feet and toes, almost dead. On occasion you may literally have to crawl home but never with the ill effects of alcohol. Kava is consumed daily at work, at home, at play; at any time with any excuse.

Brigadier Rabuka surprised the Chief Justice when he appeared at the door to his office. The judge was sitting in his over-stuffed leather chair as the Brigadier stormed into the room, striding about in his uniform with spit-polished boots, his strong Fijian features and big bushy moustache dominant. He jabbed his finger at the Chief Justice and yelled "You remember that I could have put an Indian in your chair," in a display of anger obviously related to the order to remove his cousin, Magistrate Rabuka. The Brigadier turned and left the halls of justice and today his cousin continues as a magistrate in Lautoka.

The afternoon was quiet in my room. I walked out onto the balcony and looked at the sea. The sun was shining warmly through a hole in the clouds. I sat quietly by the balcony rail on the lounge chair in casual shorts, my Walkman playing, drinking cold tonic water. I picked up the letter to the Solicitor General, reading and rereading it, trying to second guess what the response would be and how the argument might take place. Anything was on the cards. Subash had said jokingly when he signed the letter, "Well, if I get arrested you'll have to defend me."

And I replied, "yeah, unless I'm arrested, but they won't do that while the Australian MPs are in town."

At 10.30 on Wednesday morning, about half an hour after the Australians left the grand lobby of the Travelodge Hotel and headed for home via Nausori Airport outside of Suva, I was approached by a young Fijian. He wore casual clothes, tattoos visible on his hands and forearm. The tattoos were evidence of times gone past, idle times or perhaps temporary custody in Her Majesty's jails. Criminal lawyers notice these things. It never ceases to amaze me how people disfigure themselves with tattoos, almost totally destroying their chances of rehabilitation.

For the Fijian male with little to do at home, tattooing is a common show of strength and masculinity. The more crude form of tattoos are worn mostly by prison inmates. Many soldiers have tattoos from their home villages where Rabuka's men had recruited a large portion of the security forces.

In the air force 23 years ago I was about to put a tattoo of a tiger's head on my arm when my father persuaded me by long distance telephone that tattooing would lead to nothing but disaster.

Please Come With Me

The Fijian whispered quietly, it seemed he didn't want anybody to hear him. Nor did he want to come too close, as if he would be repelled by some kind of unseen force. Finally he got my attention by raising the level of his whisper, "Mr Harder," he said in a very soft voice, "Security forces, please come with me. My boss wants to speak with you."

I was stunned for a second. I had expected something like this might happen but was not prepared for it when it did. My heart began to thump and I could feel a cold rush come up my chest and down my forearms and the hair stood up on the back of my neck. I didn't have to close my eyes to imagine that I was being picked up by a Tonton Macoute type individual. His hair was cut short-back-and-sides and he wore sandals, an open-necked blue and white teeshirt hanging out of his casual pants. Shining white fingernails and glowing white teeth completed the image.

My moment of decision came and I didn't need to ask who his boss was. I had been wanting to talk to his boss for some time and if this was the only way I could get to him, so be it.

Standing there in my bathing trunks, nothing more than a towel in my hand he said "Come with me."

"I'll change," I said.

"No — you come now as you are."

"Like hell I will." I said. "I will get dressed before I come with you, do you understand?" and he stopped, looked at me and stepped back. I walked off without further consultation and headed towards the outer stairwell that goes up to the first floor.

My room was the first on the right by the corner looking out to the harbour and the sea beyond the fringing reef. I went into my room, picked up the phone and dialled the *Fiji Times* to get Mesake Koroi. He wasn't there, and I was scared I wouldn't get the chance to tell anybody what was happening. I wanted Mesake to call my wife in Auckland. As I had left the pool after speaking with the tattooed security man, I had stopped and asked an attractive blond woman sunbathing at the other end if she would write down my phone number and call my wife in Auckland if I wasn't back by one that afternoon.

On the way back from my room, dressed in my black court suit and holding the tabua and kava roots, I stopped by the woman and said, "No, would you phone that number now." Feelings told me that, despite the lack of warrant, I was being taken into custody and I wasn't sure how long I would be held. The guard asked me if I had seen Fa today.

"No, am I supposed to have?"

"Have you seen Fa today?" he paused, "You don't say anything to anybody, you just walk through the lobby and get into the vehicle."

I opened the bar door, pulled the glass handle and stepped into the lobby. Most eyes turned and watched as I walked through the entrance accompanied by my escort from the security services. Everybody knew where he was from and what was happening. It was no secret that I was involved in some controversial court cases.

The front desk staff were very polite as I gave them my key and asked if they would contact my wife. We then proceeded to march out the door to the four-wheel-drive Landrover that would take me away. The security guards permanently stationed at the hotel were very formal, very curt. It was clear that in the presence of other security force officers there would be no show of familiarity. They were doing their job and had no association with this guest who was being marched out the door by Rabuka's special force.

The vehicle was new and in tidy shape. I was placed in a back seat running at right angles to the driver's seat and asked to sit up the front. One of the security men, moved in behind me. The driver was told to drive around the Government building toward Fa's office. We stopped a 100 yards up the street from Fa's and one of the security men jogged up the road looking for my lawyer friend. I had taken the chance when I came through the lobby to go to the bar and buy a couple of packets of cigarettes. Now I undid one, lit up and inhaled deeply as we waited.

CHAPTER NINE

REALITY IN REVOLUTION

A deep draught of smoke, a rare occasion in my life when I was glad that cigarettes existed. Fa came out of his office and walked towards the four-wheel-drive. He was ushered in by another Tonton Macoutes looking individual who helped him up on the tail gate, Fa being a little overweight. As Fa sat down he turned and looked at me with those deep eyes that have so much expression; a glint of sunlight, a glint of humour and hope, a subtle hang-in-there message of confidence.

The man was trying hard to be brave. This wasn't the first time he had been arrested. On three or four other occasions Fa had been held in custody for short periods. Sometimes questions were asked but most times not. Many people arrested by the Fiji military are never questioned, just held then let go. It is simply a way of letting people know that the security forces are the real power. They can just invoke the name of the boss and accomplish whatever they wish throughout the countryside.

We looked at each other waiting for the truck to start up.

"Queen Elizabeth Barracks?" the driver asked with some hesitation. Yes, the Tontons replied and we drove away past the Government building and football field where we had begun our fun run on Saturday morning. As we went up the hill past the playing field I looked back on the hotel with a tinge of fear, not knowing exactly what was in store but knowing it was something out of the ordinary.

Our captors, all in civilian clothes, all security officers, spoke little. When they did speak it was in Fijian beyond my understanding. Fa endeavoured to converse in Fijian but was met with a wall of silence as the driver hurried on; left then right and down the hill and through a little Indian shopping centre, around a corner past a Fijian village. We came up to the main road by the Queen Elizabeth Army Barracks. As we went in the sun was shining brightly. We approached down the long driveway from the main road entrance, barbed wire on both sides of the road; up the hill and around the corner to a level entrance guarded by timber blocks and beams and concrete protrusions, no doubt designed to stop bomb laden vehicles from crashing into the barracks.

The four-wheel-drive stopped at a security bar, having driven around the obstruction block at the front. The driver climbed out and slammed the door. I sat there and my chest began to palpitate, cold sweat broke out on the palms of my hands. As we approached the guardhouse there were 20 soldiers practising rifle salutes, their shoulder-high hand action slapping the wood of the butts with a loud clap. Dressed in their green uniforms and spit polished boots, short, shorn fuzzy hair on most of them, these tidy looking recruits kept drilling as we were escorted into the guardhouse.

Inside we sat on chairs in the main office where Fa and I quietly shared a cigarette and a very brief conversation barely saying anything. What we did say was very quiet. There was mounting tension. I started to get trembles through my heart, spawned by emotions of fear and uncertainty; a desire to get back in control before my destiny was no longer in my own hands — too late for this round Christopher. But I knew deep down I would get out somehow.

We were put in a room 10 feet by eight feet, office windows looking out over the jungle to housing on the other side of the gulley. There was an old wooden desk in the middle of the room, well worn with years of doodles on it. The kava roots and tabua were put in the corner behind the desk. Fa and I were required to sit motionless for 20 minutes.

An officer came in and beckoned me into the doorway by the cells. There was a hallway about 35 feet long and four feet wide with five cells on one side. On the other side, side-arms, pistols and

M16 rifles were stored in one cell, the remaining four cells had their iron bars covered with grey army blankets.

The first prisoner I saw as I walked through the entrance to the jail cum-makeshift-armoury was an Indian in his fifties. He had no shirt, no shoes, just his pants. He looked defenceless, huddled in the corner of his tiny cell. He was obviously at a loss to understand his situation and not coping terribly well.

Second was a younger, chubby Indian standing up and looking proud but alone in his four foot by six foot cell. I knew the dimensions as eight hands by 11 hands until I got home and measured my hand span.

In front of cell number five we stopped. The short chain hooked around the iron bar in the gate was unlocked and the gate swung open. There it was, a bare concrete floor with a drain hole in the wall, white plaster walls smeared in blood where mosquitoes had sucked their victims' veins and paid with their feeble lives. The view from the window, if you were over six foot tall, was similar to that from the guardhouse overlooking the valley. The camp boundary had been cleared of all shrubbery and six foot rounds of barbed wire plus two fences around the perimeter stopped any nosey-parker from wandering accidentally into the barracks.

I sat down on the concrete floor in my suit, feeling hot and stuffy, took my jacket off and put it on the floor, and sat with my back against the corner to contemplate what was actually happening. Fa was taken from the guardhouse room and put into a cell further down the hall closer to the entrance, some two cells away from mine it sounded.

When I asked to go to the toilet I was taken back up the walkway. I saw Fa two cells down, sitting there in his sulu on a wooden chair, with his legs apart. His dark, hairy hands slapped his kneecaps as he stared straight ahead and concentrated on keeping his sanity in a situation which rivaled a John Wayne movie. Periodically the guards walked up and down the hall slapping their sides, zinging their rifles up, saying "Make my day" and pulling the trigger — CLICK — on an empty chamber; little boys with toy guns. It was especially unnerving when they pointed their rifles towards somebody in the cells.

The cell next to me was ordered open and the guards commenced to carry out gun after gun after gun. Obviously the cell was being used as an armoury, there were .22 rifles,.303 rifles, shotguns, double barrel shotguns, old long barrel shotguns, sawn off shotguns, home made guns, spearguns. Every imaginable kind of gun was slowly paraded out in front of me and taken to the front of the guardhouse where it was individually itemised, identified by number and name and classified in a register, then stacked on the floor by the outer wall of the guardroom.

Straight Flush For Sanity

I sat in the cell in fear of my response to being enclosed in such a small space because I am a claustrophobic, one of those people who cannot stand confined spaces. Struggling to retain my composure I settled into jail in Fiji. There was little to occupy me. A drainpipe with ants that crawled back and forth from the outside grass onto the concrete to pick at the rubbish that had washed from the floor and was trapped in the cracks was my main source of immediate interest. The ants worked industriously supplying their unseen colony with minute pieces of food from my floor. I lay on my stomach for a while with my jacket as a pillow for my elbows.

I began to slow down a bit and tried to occupy myself by following the individual ants as they climbed over pebble mountains in the concrete drain, their leader sitting on a larger rock. The frustration of sitting in a space so small was medieval. My inability to get up and walk around on the grass and stretch my legs, to go where I wanted when I wanted was compounded by not being able to pick up a telephone to resolve the problem or jump in a taxi and fix it directly.

It was a situation that could have affected my sanity, I'm sure, if I hadn't found a way to occupy my mind. The first step was to sit up straight, back against the wall, and begin to slow my breathing down in an attempt to meditate. Several times I had started studying a meditation tape in earlier years but had never practised enough so that I could meditate as a matter of course. Now by trying to slow my breathing and clear my mind I seemed to find some peace that allowed me to relax a little in this situation. But I could only use this technique for so long, it didn't fully compensate for the circumstances.

I took my black leather wallet out of my coat inner pocket and pulled out all the credit cards and their receipts. I looked at the cards and read all the details on the receipts over and over. There were four suits, Visa, Bankcard, Mastercard and Clubcard.

I began to add the numbers on the cards and receipts; 5, 8, 17, 36 . . . how long could I continue to dream up new ideas to occupy myself in a situation where I had no external control. I got to the end of the credit cards — 505, a number seared into my brain like a military dog tag.

I took my Visa receipts and folded them up into little triangles so that the receipt numbers faced the perpendicular of the triangle. I made two piles of five triangles and began to play poker with myself and then I began to play an imaginery game with Fa. We couldn't talk amongst ourselves. The guards had said no talking to one of the Indians in a loud enough and harsh enough voice for everybody to hear. It didn't take long to decide to obey such an order.

The closest I got to communicating with any of the people in the cellblock was to the man in the cell across from me and one up towards the armoury. Part of his grey blanket slipped from the bars so that I could see him and he could see me.

The day began to drag. Maybe things had got right out of hand. How would my wife settle on the new property that we had purchased unconditionally, with the sale deferred until the middle of September? I wasn't there, money wasn't coming in. If work wasn't being done, no money. There were problems. I wondered if my sickness and accident insurance covered me for being arrested in the course of duty outside New Zealand. It was a point I wanted to discuss with my insurance company.

How long would I be a guest of the Brigadier — a day, two days, a week, 28 days? On my understanding of the decree, based on a brief reading on Sunday, if they kept you for more than 48 hours they had to keep you for 28 days. I might just have to get down, grit my teeth and get into it because I wasn't going to let these bastards know that I was not looking forward to their company.

It was my one relief that they would allow me to go to the toilet pretty much when I wanted. I would yell out firmly "Hey Mister" or "Guard". I never yelled more than once, somebody would come and I would say, "Toilet", and they'd go back and get the key.

But it didn't matter how many times they tried they could never find the right key for my cell. First of all they locked it with an old lock. But as if I was a special prisoner, they got a brand new lock and a set of keys, put it on my chain and put the keys on a ring. They had so many rings of keys and none of them was properly labelled. They were forever bringing the wrong set or bringing the right set and not being able to put the key in the lock properly, or turning it too quickly in too big a rush.

It became a bit of a joke whenever they came to my cell. They would try and open it with one key and I would say "No, you're wrong, it's got to be a three key" and when they got the three key it wouldn't fit and they'd go on to another one. I'd say "No, *that* is the one." It became a sort of challenge to show them how to unlock my cell.

When they did finally find the right combination and let me out, I took great pleasure in stretching my legs, walking slowly down the cell corridor trying to take in as much as I could. On one occasion I saw Tevita and in the next cell I saw a figure I thought was Subash Parshotam sitting there in his pyjama bottoms, with no top and no glasses. But I wasn't sure because to me he looked like so many other Indians at first glance. I didn't really know his personality and characteristics and I was not sure it was him. At any rate he showed no recognition. He stared straight ahead.

If it was him he was probably saying, "You bastard, you got me into this." I walked out through the front entrance and around the corner and through the crews' bunkroom to get to the toilet.

Four Fijian soldiers were sitting on their bunks. One was spit polishing his boots with a tin of polish and a bit of rag. I stopped and complimented him on his spit shine. After watching him for a moment I asked if he could get some shoe polish and a piece of rag for me to do my shoes. I was desperate to find something to occupy my time. You never knew whether they were understanding you, whether they were simply ignoring you or if they were being polite and saying yes.

123

Even in the toilet with its urinal smell I savoured the few precious moments outside my cell. Looking through the unlocked bathroom window I considered the likelihood of a successful escape. I wanted out of the situation but wasn't confident about getting out of the army compound if I climbed out the window. For that matter perhaps the window was left open on purpose — temptation. Luckily I didn't, because a week later an Australian who had been picked up for questioning in a similar manner climbed out the very same window. He was quickly recaptured and quite severely beaten by the military forces.

Not being a great sports reader, I found it amusing to say the least that I spent 10 minutes sitting on the toilet reading the sports page of the *Fiji Times* I found there. I read and re-read a story about the Fijian boxer who had his first professional bout coming up.

Having taken my time in the toilet room I came out and proceeded to wash my hands with a bar of soap lying on the sinktop. I took off my glasses, splashed cold water on my face, washed behind my neck and around the front of my throat. I was desperate for some toothpaste and angry that I had not had the foresight to bring my toothbrush or tapedeck when I left the hotel under escort.

A leaf lying on the top of the bench caught my eye and I asked my guard what it was. It was a type of natural breath freshener he told me, so I began to chew it. The sap from the leaf left a hint of chlorophyll in my mouth, temporarily overcoming the taste of old socks.

I must have gone to the bathroom a dozen times my first day in jail. And every time I went through the barracks room I wondered if one of these Tonton Macoutes was going to "one-side" me, as they describe a king hit in Fiji.

Henry Gibson, the Gagaj, had told me that a Fijian could on the one hand be showing you all external signs of friendship but, the moment you weren't looking, two or three of them could "one-side" you. And when it was over they would be friends again. This thought was there whenever I walked through the barracks room but it was normally balanced by the sight of the young soldier sitting on his bed spit polishing a shoe.

Round And Round My Shoe

Not long after I had been locked up again a security man in civilian clothes came down to the cell and asked quietly, "You want some shoe polish, you want to buy some shoe polish?"

"Yes", I said thrusting my hand in my suitpocket and pulling out two $2 and two $1 notes. I put the money in my fist and as I passed it through the bars he slowly put his hand out as if having second thoughts about taking the money. Then he grabbed the notes, quickly squeezed them into a ball and shoved them into his pants. He gave me a black tin of shoe polish about two thirds used.

"Hey, you got a rag, please," I called as he went back down the alleyway. He returned with a white piece of flannel that I could use over my finger to rub the polish into the leather of my shoe. The funny thing about the shoe polish and the shoes was that after a while different unknown people began to come and check out what I was doing in my cell.

They saw me sitting on the floor, cross-legged, local style, with a shoe on my left hand and the white cloth wrapped around my right hand index finger as I rubbed the polish into the leather around and around in little circles, one section of a shoe at a time. I tried to squeeze my fingers deeper and deeper into the shoe so it didn't slide off while I applied polish to the side of the shoe. Gradually a thin film of black polish covered my dark blue shoes. Then I would spit carefully on the shoe and begin to rub with the cloth in a counter-clockwise motion, opposite to the way the polish was put on.

It was something to do, a simple, desperate therapy to keep my claustrophobia at bay. After hours of repeated polishing the leather began to shine and glisten like a work of art. Was I losing my mind, was I beginning to think like that simple shoe shining soldier who had sent me the polish? Or was the pride in my shining shoes a valid reward for accomplishment?

I sat there hour after hour after hour polishing until I could see my face in the shine that sparkled from the leather. Now when the security boys came to check me out their response was military. They stayed a respectable distance away. They seemed concerned. I wasn't quite sure if they thought they had driven me insane, or if

125

there was the possibility that I was military. It was many years before that I had learnt to polish shoes at bootcamp in Canada. Then as quickly as they came, all similar in appearance — casual shirt and pants, hushpuppies or running shoes — they went. During much of the polishing I sweated and shivered with fear of the unknown. I always liked to know what was going to happen. Normally I made things happen.

Was my arrest deliberate or had it just happened as part of my campaign to see Rabuka?

The Indian across from me and down one cell towards the armoury room could see me sitting on the floor reading the newspaper. By now they'd sent somebody to pick up my bag from the hotel and I'd been given the privilege of a *Fiji Times*. But the tension continued to rise because of the uncertainty of my situation. To occupy my time I began doing sit-ups in my suit.

By lying diagonally across the cell floor I could just straighten out enough to do sit ups, but my hands still touched the wall behind. I felt the muscles in the back of my knees strain, not having exercised like this for many years. Then the muscles in my stomach took their turn at feeling pain. Short of breath, I vowed not to smoke on my return to New Zealand; my children, having had it impressed on them that they should never smoke cigarettes, would not countenance such behaviour anyway.

I was trying to feel confident that I would ultimately return. At least I was being treated like a gentleman, everybody called me "Sir". When I got a headache the doctor came. But when he was asking me about my headache and where it hurt he was obviously also sizing me up and trying to get a handle on this mysterious man from New Zealand. "Here, take these." He handed me a little zip lock bag with "two disprin" recorded on the outside.

"If you have any more problems, don't hesitate to call," he said.

I apologised for getting him out when he was no doubt relaxing at home.

"That's not a problem, that's my job."

When the doctor left I was given a cup of very thick gruel-like tea, a dessert spoon and a bowl of bread with what looked like a slice of taro in it, not the most appealing of food. I had eaten breakfast but refused the bread and tea at lunch with my standard retort that I wouldn't eat until I saw Rabuka.

It was my own little show of defiance, of letting them know that I wasn't taking this lying down. I was determined to keep my cool, to not plead for any particular thing. I would ask once, if they responded fair enough, and if they didn't I treated it as a matter of little importance and went back to shining my shoes or practising push-ups . . . 24, 25, 26. I felt some pride as I pushed myself into physical exercise that I had not done in years.

Some time after supper had been offered, one of the security men came to my jail door and began to unlock the chain.

"Come with me." I stood up quickly and straightened my shirt and tie as best possible, grabbed my jacket, gave it a flick and put it on, beginning to feel a rush of excitement. Something was happening, was I going home, was I going back to the hotel, was I going to be questioned, or hang on a minute, was there something sinister about to happen.

Down the jail corridor we went. My heart fluttered as we passed the No.2 cell on my right. Tevita Fa had gone. My mind raced. Was he in a different part of the barracks where I could not hear what was going on? I had visions of Fa sitting on a chair being slapped and punched and poked by men with M16 rifles until he broke down in tears to answer their questioning.

I was worried that my friend was in trouble. We walked out the front of the guardhouse where in the dim light I saw six field guns with their barrelcaps on, parked in a neat row in the carport across from the watch-house. It was dark, the wind blowing softly from the north. A streetlight shining on the jacaranda blooming near the entrance gate gave me a sense of softness and warmth as I remembered that Philippa's favourite tree is a jacaranda.

But there was little time for thoughts of home; we were moving quickly towards a building. Fifty meters down the road I was taken up a concrete path past incredibly colourful flowers and marched into an office, a bare office with a plain desk, a chair for me to sit on in front of it. There were no mementos, papers, pictures, posters or signs. It was just an interview room. An officer who identified himself as Major Mataitene sat behind the desk with a piece of

127

paper between his thumbs, holding it up off the desk, looking at it, reading, writing, saying nothing, probably wanting me to offer an opening line. But I sat there.

"Are you a Canadian citizen or a New Zealand citizen?" he finally asked.

"I'm a Canadian citizen but a permanent resident in New Zealand."

"How long for?"

"Twelve years."

Then he paused and pondered for a moment. "You learned to spit polish in the military?"

For a moment I wanted to lie and deny that I had been in the military. It seemed any military connection would be held against me. "No, I learnt to spit polish from one of your men in the barracks." He looked up at me. "Yes I was in the air force," I admitted.

He had a file in front of him which looked like a report. I could not imagine what information might be on it. He looked up again and handed me the sheet of paper. "You'll be leaving on the next available flight," he said as I began to read the document: 'EXCLUSION ORDER'

INTERNAL SECURITY DECREE 1988
[Section 81 (1)]

EXCLUSION ORDER

WHEREAS Mr CHRISTOPHER HARDER of 32 Eastbourne Road, Remuera, Auckland, New Zealand has entered the country on 14th June 1988 as a visitor;

I, BRIGADIER-GENERAL SITIVENI LIGAMAMADA RABUKA, Minister for Home Affairs, Commander of the Security Forces and Minister charged with the responsibility of Internal Security, am satisfied that his continued presence would be dangerous to peace and good order in Fiji;

I, THEREFORE, in exercise of the powers conferred upon me by section 81 [1] of the Internal Security Decree 1988 Order that the said Mr CHRISTOPHER HARDER be excluded forthwith from Fiji.

Given under my hand this 22nd day of June, 1988.

signed S.Rabuka

[Brigadier-General Sitiveni Ligamamada Rabuka] Minister for Home Affairs, Commander of the Security Forces and Minister charged with the responsibility of Internal Security.

My first reaction was "does this mean my wife and I can't come back for holidays?" He looked up at me and smiled.

The major looked typically Fijian; distinctive facial features, a sharp Lloyd Bridges jaw, short curly hair like a brillo brush and sparkling strong white teeth the envy of any European. He rose from his desk and I thanked him. Then he turned, walked from his office and went outside. I heard talking; little conversation was held in English, it was obvious that they were talking in Fijian not only because it was their first language but it was also their way of keeping me in the dark. I heard words that were typically English that had been Fijianised or that didn't have an equivalent translation. From time to time I heard "passport . . . New Zealand . . . nine o'clock", pick up times and other distinctive words.

Death Threats

Back in my cell, my hopes of immediate freedom dashed, I reflected on the atmosphere in captivity and how it varied through the day. During the night it had been quiet. There were no sounds except for the slapping and smacking of mosquitoes. Next door to me in the No.7 cell, was a man whom I heard identified as Mohammed Rafiq. I met a prisoner at Lautoka the previous week by that name. Rafiq is a common Muslim name.

Everytime I went to the bathroom I deliberately checked my tabua and kava roots as I passed the guards' desk. I also briefly looked into the next door cell where the inhabitant was stretched out on the corridor floor in a similar position to me. His room seemed darker somehow. Was his window covered or did the cell just not get as much light as mine?

At times the atmosphere in the cells was simply a level of dull fear, at other times it was electric. One particular security force interrogator similarly tattooed to the rest had a terrible questioning technique. He made the Indian in the cell come to the bar and, in a most harsh voice, yelled: "I am only going to ask you this question once, I am a busy man. I haven't got time to waste. So you think when you answer it and you tell me."

He asked the Indian if he had discussed the Brigadier over lunch. The Indian stuttered and said "No" in a voice twinged with fear and concern.

"You are wrong, you lie. You are under the decree. If you don't tell the truth, you will be shot."

"But that's the truth, that's truth. I not talk about, I not talk about Rabuka. I say nothing about Rabuka. You are wrong. Whoever tell you, he's wrong."

"I'll be back," yelled the Fijian interrogator. "And when I come back I want you to tell the truth. I'll only ask you once. You think about that. I'm a busy man, I got no time to waste." And he turned and walked past my cell glancing down without saying a word to me. On his way out of the barracks he resumed yelling, "I'll be back, remember I'll be back."

But locked away in my tiny cell there was nothing I could do as this psychological interrogation went on around me. A fellow human was being subjected to extreme mental torment, having no idea how long he was going to be there, why he was really there, whether he would be charged or jailed or shot or beaten; these were all real possibilities for the Indian.

The Indians were divided. They were separated. They were all but naked. They were being treated no better than dogs and feared for their lives.

I watched as the lecturer from the university, Som Prakash, who had written the critique on the Rabuka book *NO OTHER WAY*, was marched past my cell, returning obviously from the toilet. He was barefooted wearing blue, typically Indian pyjama pants and no top;

a chubby man with a bit of a bulge for his probably 40 or 42 years of age. Yet he had a look of independence, a look of pride.

As he walked by I could see the film *Gandhi* and the scenes where he would continue to turn the other cheek and not be scared of the pain. He was a brave man. I later heard him being yelled at on Thursday morning as a guard stormed down between the cells with a metal rod in his hand. It was about three feet long, little more than a piece of thick wire with a sliding metal cap on one end. As he walked past my cell towards the professor's he yelled for another guard, "Open this gate. Quickly, quickly open it, open it!"

The second guard dropped the keys in his rush. They unlocked the cell and went in. 'Thwack, thwack' I heard twice. The only conclusion I could fairly draw was that he had gone in and beaten the lecturer with the rod because I heard the him cry out with pain but not utter a coherent word. They relocked his cell and the security man walked off into the main office.

After returning from Mataitene's office I had been put back into my cell and given the luxury of a foam rubber mattress, a pillow, and a blanket for the night. I tried to read the newspaper I had found in the bathroom and smuggled out, but I was getting tired of reading about boxing adventures in Fiji. I began to do some more sit-ups . . . 26, 27, pushing my body to 30 for a new alltime record. I reached 31 then gasping for breath lay back and began to analyse what was happening.

I remembered that the officer had told me that I could have a phone call to my wife when I got back to my cells. I summoned the guard and said, "I'd like to call my wife. The Major said that it would be all right." The chain of command had to be checked, nothing is done in the military unless somebody gives a specific order and an authorisation is made for that particular action. When it came to dealing with a foreign national prisoner, a well-known New Zealand lawyer, then everything had to be done by the book and everything was double checked at the very highest of ranks.

The military were trying to assess my involvement in the global picture. They were determined I would have no more involvement in the guns or Rotuma affairs.

Long Distance Assurance

I heard the phone ring. Every time I heard that phone ring I'd pray it was the operator putting through my call to Philippa. I longed to hear her voice. My heart cried because I knew the anguish she must be going through. But I also knew she was a tough cookie and would take things in her turn. About midnight I was roused from my mattress where I was trying to doze; my head under the blanket and the mosquitos, invisible in the night, buzzing around like a terrible drill trying to pierce my eardrums.

"Harder — phone call," the guard said as my door was unlocked. I got up and went out into the room, lit a cigarette and sat on the corner of the desk where the old style Bell-Edison black handpiece lay on the desk. I picked it up. "Hello, is that you Philippa?" I could hear the faint but distinct voice of my wife.

"Are you all right?"

"Yeah, I'm okay."

"Did they hurt you?"

"No they didn't hurt me, they've been very good, very polite. If I'm sick they get me a doctor. Everything's 'Sir'." Then it was my turn to ask how she was, and the children. "They said they'd put me on the next available flight."

"It's midnight here. Midnight in New Zealand . . ."

"Guard, my wife says there's a flight available at five this morning, Air New Zealand from Nadi. Is there a reason I can't take a taxi to the hotel, pick up my stuff and taxi over to Nadi, or maybe get a ride from your people from here down to the Travelodge and then I'll take a taxi? No disrespect, but if you don't want me here I don't really want to be here. I might as well just go back to New Zealand. I've got this order. It's signed by Brigadier Rabuka. I'm to be excluded forthwith."

I raised my voice and said, "Forthwith means now. And if there's a plane at five o'clock I would like to be on it. Now can you get a car here so I can get back to the hotel?"

"Yes, let me check," and he walked out of the office and disappeared into the darkness outside.

Could this be it, were they going to just let me go?

But the guard soon marched back out of the darkness, "Yes, when the car comes back."

"Well can I tell my wife that I'll be there, I'll be leaving on the five o'clock plane?"

"Yes," he said "everybody obeys the order of the Brigadier. Forthwith meaning now."

But it was not to be the end of the matter. I told Philippa I would be on the five o'clock plane. She was anxious to have me back. The excitement of getting ready to go somewhere began to build inside me. Things were developing nicely.

I hung up the phone, lit another cigarette and asked the Indian sergeant if I could remain outside the cells for a while, but the plain clothes security man was adamant. "No, no, you must wait in your cell." I went for another game of poker.

This was game three. I dealt the first card to the imaginary Fa. He got a four. My card was a five so I took a box of matches and split them in two and put 20 matches on each pile; 20 for Fa and 20 for me, and commenced to play for five cents a match. The value of the match didn't really matter, whoever won all the matches won the game.

After a while I became restless. The light from the main room only shone in a very small portion of my cell that allowed me to read the numbers on the poker cards fashioned from my Visa receipts. The cells had no internal lighting and no glass to keep the mosquitoes out at night. I stood up and pushed the gate open as far as it would go, as far as the chain allowed. "Guard," I yelled out in a firm voice.

I don't like to be constantly reminded of the time so had not been wearing a watch when arrested. It seemed about one o'clock. If I didn't go soon there was no way I would get to the hotel, pay my account and get onto the plane by five o'clock. It showed in my voice that I was keen to get away. But instead of a guard arriving to fumble with the keys and let me out, a new face, a dark and not too pleasant Fijian face, said "You stay the night."

He gestured towards the kava roots and tabua. "You want to see the Brigadier in the morning and make your presentation don't you?"

"Well that's what I came for. If he's prepared to see me, I guess the least I can do is stay the night." Philippa would not see me in the morning but it seemed I was going to meet Brigadier Sitiveni Rabuka. I would come eyeball to eyeball with this most unusual man.

But knowing I was to see Rabuka in the morning did not lighten the difficult time I was having in my cell. The claustrophobic conditions seemed to engulf me in the dark of the night. They had turned another light out and the only light visible now was a reflection in the hall from the main desk and fleeting moonlight from the cell window. How would I cope if they kept me for 28 days?

I began to worry about the mortgage again. How would my family live? What would Philippa have to do? Who would offer help? They were pressing concerns and kept reappearing in my mind. Soon they became too difficult to even consider because I couldn't deal with them; I couldn't help, I couldn't assist. To put them out of my mind I leaned back against the wall for more attempts at meditation.

I thought of Jeffery Wells, my comrade-in-arms at the Auckland District Court, as I struggled to meditate. I knew he'd say "Be cool bro', be cool." Jeffery, a Buddhist, had such a placid manner. I had seen him meditating yoga style many times and tried desperately to grasp some of that inner quiet. Several times I tried to lie down on the mattress and put the blanket over my head. My suit was hot and sticky and bulky in the wrong places and mosquitoes were abundant. You could swat and swish with the blanket, you could wait until the little bastards landed on your ear or pierced your cheek and then swat, but there was always another squadron buzzing about.

Failure At The Bar

A new guard came on at about two o'clock. He came down into the cell block and just stood and stared at me. I felt his stare, wondering what soldiers' gossip motivated his attention.

"You want a cup of tea?"

"Yeah, yes please." I had a foul tasting mouth and desperately needed something to take the taste away. Even a couple of spoonfuls of that syrupy tea would help.

I remember vividly the guard trying to pass the kidney-shaped aluminium pot through the bars. He was very careful not to spill tea over his new prisoner, but it was not that easy to squeeze the pot through.

At the thought of tea spilling, my mind cast back to early days in Calgary when I had won a part-time job as a barman. I had been desperate for some part-time work and approached the manager of the Royal Hotel. I upped my age to 21 and said I wanted stable, part-time employment.

It was a typical Calgary pub; black leather benches along the wall, furry tablecloths on round tables dotted about the room with quite comfortable black cushioned chairs. The bar was relatively quiet and not very well lit. It opened at 11.30 a.m. The barmaid in a gold dress and brown tartan belt walked past carrying a tray of nearly 20 beers on her left palm and forearm. I had told the manager a tall tale about previous experience in North Vancouver pubs and that it would be no sweat for me to take over the part-time morning shift. It fitted in well with my university timetable.

I was proud to have a good paying part-time job in difficult circumstances. The head barman handed me a tray, "Well, you might as well have a go," so I walked out and took an order for two draughts and a juice, went to the bar and called out "Two and a juice."

The tray was balanced quite firmly on my inner arm as I picked up the drinks, turned and looked out for my two customers. The man, obviously a local in for an early beer and hot-dog lunch, was conversing with an attractive blond woman in a wool dress, sort of an English look, but too much makeup. She had probably dropped out of the local typing pool for a beer with the boss.

A full tray was 18. I had at least 12 as I approached the table where the man had earlier ordered two draught and a juice. He had been my first customer so I was determined to serve this next round professionally, no mistakes. I took a beer from the right hand side of the tray and set it down on the table. Good. A second glass of draught from the right-hand side of the aluminium tray. Horror. I had forgotten one thing. Two from the right and, whoops, out of balance — beer and glasses flew over my first customer. Soaked in beer and a tomato juice I had been delivering, he was irate.

It was definitely a job for the bar manager. "Can I help you Sir, I'm awfully sorry. Let me help you and, I assure you we will have your suit drycleaned. I'm so sorry. He's just new on the job. He's just started today." He gave me the evil stare. Experience? North Vancouver? But he never uttered the words.

Our beer sodden ex-customer stormed out the door, and with a sigh of relief I turned and went sheepishly back to the counter. The next hour proceeded without event, except that my first customer came back in a different suit. Obviously he was a downtown apartment dweller. He sat down in the only available seats, in my section, and called for two more draught and a juice.

"Yes Sir," I apologised for the earlier incident. "I'm most sorry and I hope that you won't hold that against me. I endeavour not to repeat mistakes."

Awkwardly I headed off to the bar for his order and another part-tray of beer. I walked back gingerly, picking my feet up, I didn't want to stumble, or do anything as stupid as I had done before. Juice from the middle. One beer from the right. I began to put the beer on the table when, for the second time in a very short bartending career, my tray slipped and flung forward drenching the poor bastard again. I stepped back, absolutely shattered. The permanent ex-customer of this hotel was on his feet and raging.

I didn't have to wait for the manager to say "You're fired, get out of here!" There was no point arguing with the man. There was no point arguing the toss, game set match.

It was strange how this Fijian soldier trying to squeeze this aluminium pot through the bars reminded me of that situation. He was extra careful not to spill tea on the prisoner everybody called 'Sir' and for whom the doctor came on the run if he suggested he had a headache. Now I had some status.

"Thank you." I put the pot down against the wall and sipped at it a couple of times in the next hour.

Finally, fitfully, came sunrise at about 6.45 a.m. Roosters crowed down in the valley, birds and crickets warmed up for takeoff near my cell. In the tropics you get the chorus near the cool of dawn. Then small children started playing close by, probably barracks or staff families, and the odd shrill discussion over Fijian clotheslines followed.

When I stood on my tiptoes I could just see their hands on the clotheslines. I was keen to get a feel for the surrounding area. It also helped to occupy my time.

A bit later three young corporals and a lady chatting on the embankment near my cell window attracted my attention. The lady looked up and her eyes caught mine. Had I done something wrong? Should I not be staring? She said something to the boys who turned with a start. It was more appropriate to climb down back on the floor and practise sit-ups.

Three times they came and told me I would be going shortly. From their conversations, although they were in Fijian, I heard the words airport and passport mentioned several times and hoped that it meant I was finally going home. But locked in that cell it was soon back to occupying myself with Visa card receipts.

An unexpected bonus during the night had been finding the lunch receipt from the Hyatt, the hotel up by the High Court in Auckland. It had survived in the deep crevice of a suit coat pocket since I had taken my four-year-old daughter Kate out for what she called her "special court lunch" at least a month ago.

Philippa had dropped her off and we walked in hand up the street to the hotel restaurant.

"Good afternoon Mr Harder."

"Seat for two please."

"Non smoking?"

"Of course." And young Kate sat on her seat as proud as could be. Finding the receipt brought it flooding back . . . coke and chips, steak and coffee. I relived that lunch many times through the night. About the only other thought to recur so frequently that night had been cursing myself for not bringing my Walkman. I thought of the music sitting back in my room and how much more pleasant it would have been with it.

Let's Get Out Of Here

By around five o'clock on the Thursday I was fed-up. I was lying down trying to sleep, frustrated, annoyed. For the second time in two hours I had been told that I was going, only to be told that I wasn't going.

"Stuff this," I muttered and lay down on the mattress. Not knowing whether I was leaving, or just being told I was leaving, was getting to me. I could handle the situation for a little while more but the third time the guard rattled the door to draw my attention I sat up and barked, "Yes!"

"We go, we go now," he said.

"Just be a minute."

Before I could get up he shut the door and said, "Okay I come back."

Before I thought to protest the lock was back on and he had gone away. When I said a minute I meant second. He had taken me literally. "Hey guard," I yelled, "come here!" They were the first harsh words I had ushered and he came back quietly. He tipped his head slightly sideways and said "what's the matter?"

"Listen, this is the third time you've told me I'm going and I didn't go," I said. "You guys quit stuffing around. If you want me to stay, I'll stay. I'll go down on my mattress and I'll go to sleep. But if I'm going let's get the hell out of here and let's go now — no more, you're staying, you're going, you're staying, you're going. All right? I've had enough. Now open the gate and let's get out of here."

With that he unlocked the chain and took me outside to the Ford Falcon car the security forces were using that night. The same guards who had brought me up nodded in recognition, in the dusk they appeared in a more sedate mood than when we had arrived at the barracks. They weren't as aggressive. One waved, inviting me in. I sat in the middle, one on either side. Major Mataitene got in, this time he was driving. Another security man sat in the passenger seat.

As we began driving through the back roads of Suva, through the residential areas to stay away from the city's congested arterial traffic, I could see for sure that we were headed down towards the sea and the Travelodge. At last I was confident things were going

138

to get better. "You will be under house arrest," the Major said. "You will stay in your room until a flight is arranged, the next available flight. Who's got your passport?"

"I have Sir," said one, and my passport was handed to the Major who reached over as he drove and put it in the glovebox. They would have to sort out my passport and that would take a little time. I suspected they wanted to check where I had been in the last while. They would find that Fiji and Canada were my two main haunts outside Auckland; Canada for a week or two most every August and we had visited Fiji for Easter in March.

Approaching the Government buildings from the back we drove past Fa's office and I saw a light on. I asked if Fa was all right and I was told, for the first time, that he had been released the night before. As we drove past the radio station on the right hand side of the road the major spoke up, "The Brigadier is over there now, he's about to make an announcement I think you'll like. You'll hear it on the seven o'clock news."

I knew it was fast approaching seven and it now suddenly seemed that it was by design that I had been kept in custody for the day. Now I was being taken back to my hotel so that I could hear the Brigadier make an announcement on the seven o'clock news.

To my complete surprise the major said, "You might be pleased to know that the Brigadier is adopting your idea for an amnesty, a 30-day amnesty for the arms, to let the situation cool down and your 21 men are included, they will be released tomorrow."

"Bullshit," I said.

"No, that is true. You had some worthwhile suggestions. You'll hear it back at the hotel. The Brigadier, this morning he got up and he went and saw the President and he spoke to the Chief Justice, and then he went and saw the cabinet, and then he had a meeting at the army barracks and it was decided that the 21 were in the amnesty."

"Hey if you're not fooling me, from my point of view the case is over," I said. "I go home. I've got no reason to criticise. I came to do a case. If the accused are out of jail, who am I to get involved in your internal politics?"

I was ecstatic. I was absolutely over the moon. I knew this man was being sincere. Criminal law teaches you to reasonably assess a person's character. It does not take much of a logical discussion with a person to perceive peculiarities of nature, and I intended to believe the Major when he said what he did. I asked if we could get Fa over. It was celebration time. I was excited. They were quite excited that I was excited and I was keen to hear the news at seven o'clock.

At seven o'clock, sure enough, the Brigadier announced the 30-day arms amnesty in his solemn voice, calling upon the people to surrender their arms and keep the peace.

CHAPTER TEN

A DRINK WITH THE BOYS

"Can you get Fa, I mean he's entitled to come in on this. He was involved, there's no reason why we can't come together eh? Order up some drinks, get some beer for the boys. It's on me." I could see they would love a beer but none were on wages or expense accounts that freely allowed such luxuries. So I told those who were left to call up room service and send up what they wanted. The others had gone to get Fa.

I was eager to see my lawyer friend. I had been deeply concerned for his well-being when I first saw he was no longer in the cell on the Wednesday night. A knock at the door and in came Fa.

"Jesus brother, how are you?"

"Aawwh, Christopher it's good to see you."

I was thrilled to see him. We met in the middle of the room, patting each other on the back. Everybody was smiling until the radio came on at seven o'clock and the Brigadier commenced his announcement.

As soon as the news of the amnesty was over, a reporter came on with the announcement that lawyer Tevita Fa had criticised New Zealand lawyer Christopher Harder, who was released from detention today and taken back to his hotel, for being insensitive to the cultural needs of the Fijians.

As I heard the words blare from the radio my blood pressure leapt to the point of explosion. I rose to my feet and stepped towards Fa with an anger that I had not felt before, not a person flinched, not one made a sound. As I took that second-to-last step, I halted and slowly forced my hand out to Fa.

"We have come too far and through too much to end it like this. We have made a major accomplishment here, you and I and the others. This is not on. This is not called for and I will not accept it — why would you say . . .?" I stopped my tongue and grabbed his hand, "We are still friends." I squeezed and squeezed and we stared into each other's eyes for the longest time.

"You phone and make the retraction." In seconds the major had the radio station newsroom on the phone and was passing the receiver to Fa, who was obviously thinking of what he would say.

He simply told them that the interview was taken out of context, that it was not accurate and that it should not be repeated, that it was wrong. Fa's phone call set the major in motion. He barked out an order that sent two of his men dashing from the room.

"They are going to the radio station," he said. And miracles of miracles, within a few minutes there was a complete and absolute retraction — an apology by the radio station such as you would never hear in New Zealand.

That minor matter out of the way, Fa and I and the military people began to talk in an upbeat fashion. Everybody was thrilled that the sting of the situation had been drawn and that I wasn't harbouring harsh feelings about my treatment. They wanted to make my stay as pleasant as possible. Somebody joked, "Get him a girl." And one of them said "Which does he want? Fijian, European, Indian, or Melanesian?" They laughed.

"Well, I presume if I said Indian that Rabuka would think I was racially prejudiced," I answered and the conversation about girls ended.

After three trays of beer Fa stumbled off with the rest of the security people. I was left with my two guards, Liga and Peli. They said they were assigned to sleep in the room, so I offered one the couch. The other wanted to sit up.

"Fair enough," I said and went into the bathroom with my waterproof Walkman and climbed under the shower. Headphones on I leaned back in the cubicle and semi-dozed under the tepid water spraying out of the antiquated shower. Ahhh, wonderful. Three days in the tropics without a swim or shower is more than enough. I must have been asleep for a while. There was a bang, bang, bang

142

on the bathroom door. It was my guard wanting to know if I was all right.

Clean and dry and in my dressing gown but still hyped up I headed for bed only to be disappointed that my Walkman batteries had finally given up and I couldn't listen to my music.

Like a junkie without a fix I reacted. "Can't we get some batteries somewhere?" but I knew Fiji was not like New Zealand or British Columbia where you can get things around the clock. One of the guards offered to send someone to get batteries at the market instead we decided to try the front desk before sending this other man off into the night.

Liga and I went down to the lobby but as we stood there a senior officer came in and flew into a rage because I was out of my room. In rapid-fire Fijian he ordered me back to my room, immediately. Soon he was pounding on the door, fuming.

"I have a good mind to put you back in the cells until you leave Fiji. I told you to stay in the room!"

"We were just going to get batteries for my music," I said.

"I could send you back to the cells!!" he warned again.

"Hey major, for you I'll do without my music."

With that he began a lecture. The message was crystal clear although I didn't understand a word of Fijian. They were not, under any circumstances, to take me out of the room until he returned in the morning. It was about 3.30 by the time I finally got to sleep. I had trouble trying to doze off, my stomach churning, my chest on fire, I was excited I was going home.

Major Mataitene had promised they would bring the prosecutor over in the morning. I had asked if I could see the prosecutor just to confirm the details and they said it was not a problem. They would bring John Semisi, the New Zealand trained acting Director of Public Prosecutions and Babu Singh, one of the prosecutors. Dawn came and the Friday morning paper announced the amnesty. The *Fiji Times* front page article speculated that the 21 were included in the amnesty but said this had not been confirmed.

Afterwards I was to learn that the *New Zealand Herald* had once again had a more telling account of what was going on in Fiji than the local newspaper did.

143

In a bizarre twist the Fiji Government last night announced a 30-day amnesty for illegal arms — a move advocated by a New Zealand barrister on Tuesday, hours before he was detained.

The announcement follows the imposition by decree last week of draconian powers of search and indefinite detention without charge.

. . . Within hours of his letter reaching the cabinet, security officers took him into custody.

Last night Mrs Harder said the whole affair had been very worrying but she now expected her husband home on Saturday morning.

"Where he is you just do not know what is happening.

"How many days are there until Saturday?"

It was a long day. It dragged on and on and on. No prosecutors came. No majors came. No phones rang. No nothing. But they did get me some batteries, so I sat on the balcony listening to my tape over and over. Cold bottles of tonic and menthol cigarettes kept me going. I looked at the horizon out over the harbour and took some pleasure from watching big boats slowly manoeuvre while little boats sped among them.

Elderly Fijian ladies were fishing on the shore, throwing their tiny, baited hooks into the water with a practised flick of the wrist. It was alive and shimmering with one to two inch fish whose names I could never remember. They glistened silver in the sunlight as one by one they plopped into the fisherwomen's bags. This scene was repeated along the waterfront.

Their fishing reminded me of my own passion for fresh water angling and an incident with a sequel in court. As a student at the University of Calgary I was poor by North American standards, my one proud possession was a convertible Volkswagen Carmen Ghia car. It had stereo speakers, sheepskin seat covers from New Zealand and a good motor. It was nothing special, but it was a bit different and did enable me to indulge in the great pleasure of going fishing. Not far from the city I could get down to the Bow river just below a big hydro-electric dam.

Then one day I found the gate locked. Further up the road I found a spot where the only thing between me and the road to the fish was a railway track and a three foot embankment.

Over the summer I developed a technique of jumping the tracks with my car so I could drive to the other end of the dam. I would lay two thick planks leading up to the side of the track and another pair across the two rails. On one very successful venture I had been fishing for several hours. Just as I was about to leave the water my Royal Coachman fly disappeared from the surface of the water, then my line began to run down the rapids as I struggled to keep balance.

I stood in my hip waders on a bed of rounded stones, the current whipping through my legs pulling me off balance. I struggled to keep the rod at an 11 o'clock position and the line taut in my right hand. Fifteen yards downstream my rainbow trout broke the surface of the rapids in a dazzling display of aquabatics. I tried to slow his dash down the rapids; carefully thumbing the reel trying hard to keep my knuckle out of the way of the hand piece zinging around like a flea in a fit.

The reel began to slow. I changed the rod to my left hand, stopped trying to wind the line up and began to slowly gain it back hand over hand. I knew this one was a beauty.

Twenty minutes later the trout was beginning to tire as the sun sank down behind the hills. The fir trees on distant mountain ridges were now backlit. I stretched out over a last little eddy with my net where this monster was now lying, exhausted, on the end of my line.

By the time the fish and I got back to the railway track it was getting dark. The full moon was out as I got my jumping track ready for action. With a Beach Boys tape playing "surfing on the crest of a wave" I floored the accelerator and drove like a wild man up the launch pad. Bang! I was thrown onto the steering wheel by the force of the sudden stop.

The car had slid off the boards and now hung half over one of the tracks. No amount of revving or pushing would budge it. My prized Carmen Ghia was firmly stranded on a well used railway track and it was not insured.

I heard the sound first, then came the long beam of its light searching around the corner. Eyes fixed on the light, it was not until I heard the whistle that the extreme danger registered. Yet I just sat there, frozen, like the time hitchhiking in the back of the Chevy with the Charlie Manson look-alike gunrunners.

It seemed minutes before I snapped to and leapt out of the car; headlights on, music bellowing out to the foothills of the Rockies. My heart and chest heaved, the likely consequences of a train derailment caused by me jumping the tracks to get to a rainbow trout were considerable.

Faster and faster I ran towards the diesel engine lumbering down the track. I yelled, screamed, waved my shirt and arms, all to no avail. It did not slow a bit. Finally, out of breath and shaking from shock and fear, I turned towards the hill but kept running. One last glance over my left shoulder saw the unstoppable force of the Canadian Pacific train bearing down on my car. Like a feather in a storm the Carmen Ghia flew into the air, somersaulting over and over.

The train took several hundred more yards to stop. The remains came back to earth about 40 feet from tracks, headlights still shining brightly into the night sky, stereo blaring. Fish lay scattered, glistening in the moonlight.

Self Defence

My first-ever appearance as an advocate was the result. I was my own client in the Calgary Magistrate's Court, charged with driving without an existing driver's licence and crossing a railway track at an unauthorised railway crossing. It was important to win — and not just because I didn't like losing.

As a student at the University of Calgary I also worked part-time for the Canadian Pacific Railways, steam cleaning train engines. If convicted I would lose my job and be liable to pay the $6000 worth of damage my car did to the train's cowcatcher.

I will remember that day when I walked into court. The police prosecutor stood: "The prosecution is ready to proceed with the case of police versus Harder." The first witness was a policeman for Canadian Pacific. He had examined the initial contact points on the car and train and believed the train hit and demolished my car travelling at about 30 miles an hour, a full train pulling 46 cars and a caboose.

146

The policeman said that when asked for my Alberta driver's licence I had replied I did not have one. Despite having been at University in Calgary for nearly three years it was one of those things I had just never got around to doing. The engine driver told the court he saw a person, presumably me, running towards the train about 300 yards from the point of impact.

I cross examined all three witnesses about the evidence. Photographs I had taken of the scene the day after the accident showed the "road" worn in the grass where I had been driving the car up to the track. I showed the photo to the Canadian Pacific policeman and asked if he saw what looked like a road leading to where the accident was alleged to have occurred? Begrudgingly, he said yes.

Did he see any official train post or fence blocking the path at the end of the grass road to the tracks? "No." I showed him another photo of a wooden crossing on the inside of the track. This picture showed an area used by linesmen for turning around their little push carts called jiggers, when they check the tracks for fallen rock.

The Judge asked to see the photos again. He looked at them for a moment, then he raised his head and spoke. "Mr Harder, you have successfully raised a doubt in my mind in relation to your state of mind at the time."

To this day I don't know if he meant I was crazy or that the Crown had not proved the *mens rea*, the mental element of the offence, whether or not there was the required intent. I was acquitted on the accident charge.

On the charge of not having an Alberta driver's licence, with the permission of the Judge, I recalled the arresting officer and asked the court crier to show the witness a British Columbia driver's licence in the name of Christopher Lloyd Harder, born 27/9/48 in Vancouver, and asked him if it recorded my details. He replied, "Correct".

I then asked if the licence had expired. "No," he said.

I then put it to him that I did have a driver's licence, just that I did not have an Albertan driver's licence.

"That is right, that is exactly what you are being charged with."

I had the clerk hand the charge sheet to the officer in the witness

147

box. "Yes," he had seen the wording of the charge. I then asked if the charge used the word 'existing licence' rather than 'Albertan driver's licence.'

"Yes."

"Do you accept that the British Columbia licence is presently existing?"

"Yes."

Surprisingly the prosecutor declined to re-examine the witness, when asked by the judge if he wanted to do so.

"The defence rests, Your Honour," I said in my most impressive legal tone and sat down with a smug look on my face knowing I had done well. The decision of not guilty on both accounts brought an ear-to-ear smile.

Please Sir, Can I Go Swimming

Down at the water's edge of Suva harbour where I could see the women fishing there was lots of garbage; coconut fronds trimmed from the trees, part bags of concrete, odd bits of plastic, decaying vegetable matter, wood and other debris.

One o'clock came; I was hot and sticky and requested permission to go for a swim. So far they had brought my food to the room. I was not allowed to discuss anything of consequence with the maids but they still greeted me "Goodday Mr Harder", very courteously. My guards were obeying their orders to keep me confined to the room. Liga and then Peli began making phone calls seeking permission for me to go for a swim. Finally they got through to the major on duty at Queen Elizabeth Barracks.

One of the guards gave me the phone and the major said that Philippa had got through to him on the phone the previous night. ". . . and she made me take a royal oath that I would come and see you and tell you that I had spoken to your wife and that she was okay. She just wanted you to know that. She hoped to see you home soon. And I told her that I didn't think that it would be very much longer. I told her I didn't think you were in very much trouble and that I thought everything would be okay."

I enjoyed the swim, a 20-minute respite in an otherwise monotonous day until I got the nod that it was time to get back to the room. Just as I went out to the balcony to lie in the sun there was a knock at the door. My security men turned to look at each other. Liga went off to the door.

The gentleman who announced himself said he was from the New Zealand Embassy and would like to see Mr Harder. He had spoken to the major, the same one that Philippa had extracted a promise from, and got permission for the New Zealand Consul to speak to Mr Harder.

"You'll have to wait outside. We have no such instructions you will just have to wait. We will make contact," Liga said shutting the door, leaving the diplomat out in the hall.

I don't know if he saw me. I could hear him but had not seen him in that first instant.

They called the barracks again. The situation soon changed and he was invited into the room to sit down and talk to the men, but he was not to converse with me.

I wasn't foolish enough to try talking to him. I looked at him as he sat down and gave him the thumbs up.

"Would you like a beer or a cold drink? Just help yourself in the fridge," I said. He asked for a cigarette and I gave him one of my menthols, winked and went back outside and sat down.

Instead of trying to listen I put on the Walkman headphones. It was obvious things were slowly getting better. I had been told I was going home. The consul was here and I had just heard him say: "I'm here at the request of the Canadian Embassy." That made me feel better because I had heard tales from a Canadian Jewish businessman who didn't have too much faith in the British High Commission whom he believed would look after the rights of Canadians in this part of the world. I was pleased that despite my long absence they were still concerned for my well-being.

But my lack of New Zealand citizenship, when I was eligible to hold dual citizenship, was to cause me some embarrassment. I had not applied for New Zealand Citizenship because I thought there was a possibility some labour supporter of days gone past might try to throw a spanner in the works over my association with Strike Free. I had not stopped to think it through. There was a chance it

149

would rekindle old political battles and I had found it easier to just let the status quo run.

For many years I had faced animosity. There had been verbal threats, nasty telephone calls and derisive comments from the union movement. I didn't think everybody had forgotten about Christopher Harder just because he was now practising criminal, not industrial law. Industrial law was left to John Haigh, barrister and top industrial advocate.

The consul's mere presence in my room gave me a feeling of confidence that this ordeal was about to come to an end. Finally the phone rang and there was instant Fiji chatter. Now I was allowed to speak to my consul friend from the New Zealand Embassy. It was indicated that we should talk in the living room where the three security people were.

"Hey major, you've got no problems with me, let me talk to him alone," I said. "How can I complain? The 21 — they'll go free today."

"It may take until tomorrow," he warned.

"Well, as long as that's the case. How come tomorrow?"

"Well, they're scattered all over and the orders will have to go out to the different locations where the prisoners are; they're not all at Natabua. Some are here, some are at Lautoka Police Station. I just say it could take until tomorrow."

On the sundeck I offered the consul a cold bottle of tonic or a beer. He had a tonic. Then we both lit a cigarette. I had a Bic-flic that blew out in the warm wind. He cupped his hands and looked at me, "You must be reasonably proud of yourself. Tell me about this letter that hasn't been published."

I gave him a copy of the letter which he read.

"Well, the amnesty, that was an accomplishment."

"Quite an accomplishment," I said.

"And the 21, are the 21 in the amnesty?" asked the diplomat.

"That is my information. I was told by the major on the way down. I was told by both of them after the seven o'clock speech and they said that they would bring the prosecutor over.

"But you haven't seen him yet?" he continued.

"No, no I haven't seen him yet."

"Well in diplomatic circles you sometimes take what you can get," he said. "But you don't necessarily get what you want," he said. "But you take anything that's a step in the right direction.

"We have been informed you will leave on the Saturday flight which leaves about four in the morning. Your wife has been notified. She's been in contact with the consul and your young son, is it Justin, he called the New Zealand Ambassador in Fiji wanting to know how you were."

My case was getting worldwide coverage. The media had not stopped calling. The Prime Minister had made an announcement that I would be coming home on the five o'clock flight from Nadi.

"So you can expect to have a little bit of a media presence when you arrive. If you need any assistance don't hesitate to ask," the consul said.

"Thanks. I've talked to my wife about that on the phone. She's not terribly keen about what's happening, she's been harrassed morning, noon and night by reporters from around the globe and she's finally had to put the phone on answer service."

She couldn't keep looking after the children, and get enough sleep, with the media forever trying to get comments. Philippa is basically a quiet person and she was getting dragged into something much further than she would like to be.

I assured the consul that I would be all right. They would probably let me have a swim after supper and I had enough to keep me occupied if I had to until midnight. The guards told me I was to go up and see Konrote, the number two in the army, before I flew out. They would take me up to the barracks at seven o'clock.

"I think it'll just be a bit of a pep talk. I'm not terribly concerned. I don't think the embassy need to be concerned. Thank you for all your help and I hope to see you again one of these days, real soon. Thank you." The consul turned and left.

Now I felt confident enough to become a bit more assertive with my guards. "I thought you called the major, you know, about the prosecutor. He was supposed to come and visit this morning and I haven't seen anybody, and I'd like you to get hold of the major. Get him now please."

Liga went to the telephone and dialled the operator. It was a curt message. He seemed to ask for the major to come up.

"Hey is Major Matt down at the front? Is he sitting out in the car at the front of the hotel?" I asked.

"Yes."

"Is that the radio car?"

"Yes. Major Matt."

No News Is Bad News

The afternoon dragged on. I tried to phone Philippa just to pass the time. My phone calls had been limited to and from my wife. But when I tried to call her the guard said he didn't know anything about it and he couldn't help me, he would have to wait until he got orders.

I tried to explain to him that the major had given specific instructions to the hotel staff that those were the two calls that were allowed and that I would want to call my wife. But he did not budge from his official stance. A short time later the phone rang, Liga answered it again. He was obviously talking to the front desk and trying to understand what was going on.

"New Zealand Law Society?" he asked as if to say, who's that?

I took great warmth and comfort from that. For the first time in my career the New Zealand Law Society was speaking out on my behalf.

In the cell I had wondered who would come to my rescue. Would somebody do something or was this an occasion where everybody would clap and say, "leave the bastard in jail". I didn't know for sure. Even though he did not get through it was great to know that the society's president, Graham Cowley, had tried to call.

"Would you please get the major up to see me. Tell him I'm concerned that the people he promised to bring to me this morning have not arrived," I asked once more.

I asked the other guard to tune the hotel radio to the best news station. He turned on Suva FM96.

I was beginning to feel uneasy. None of the promises of the morning had been kept. My front door was silent to visitors. There were no phone calls at all. The major, who had been drinking my beer the night before, was nowhere to be seen. I turned on the two o'clock news to hear Dan Thompson from FM Fiji Radio say that

152

the 21 arms-accused were not included in the amnesty. His exact words: "They were not included in that amnesty." The comment attributed to the Brigadier was broadcast on the two, three and four o'clock news bulletins, all of which I listened to in my room.

By five o'clock I was perturbed. There was a degree of back-sliding, that in retrospect I guess was only appropriate in a dictatorship. I sat back on the balcony and sunned myself. How should I respond, or should I respond at all? I was primarily interested in going home now that my status in Fiji had been changed by the Brigadier.

Major Matt, dressed in smart civies — pressed shirt, pressed pants, shoes and multi-coloured casual shirt — came into the room and confirmed that I would be taken up to see Colonel Konrote at the barracks at seven o'clock.

I didn't have much time to ask Major Matt about what I had heard on the radio news. Just as quickly as he arrived, he disappeared. He was gone and I stood there facing three new body-guards. They were tattooed young men, similar to the last group. They appeared uneducated and unsophisticated but well able to enforce the order that I was not to leave the hotel without express permission of the major.

At six o'clock I was again reminded that I would be taken up at seven and it dawned on me that seven o'clock was the time of the news and I didn't wish to miss the news. I asked if the meeting could be delayed. My request was ignored, no response and no reply. At 10 to seven I was taken from the room and escorted down the hall, down the stairs and through the conference room so that I didn't have to be taken out through the main lobby.

As we drove up the hill, my Tontons left and right, the radio news came on. Christopher Harder, lawyer, was to be sent back to New Zealand by Sunday at the latest because he had written a letter critical of the Government in relation to the arms case.

The news went on to say that Mr Harder had been released from Queen Elizabeth Barracks and was back in his hotel under room arrest. The same bulletin had an article about the application for bail by the lawyers who attended the Lautoka Court earlier in the week. They were referring to the Thursday hearing the day before

153

where bail was refused for all but Haroon Shah whose High Court bail was not interfered with by the District Court. The bail hearing had prompted prominent Fiji lawyer and politician Sidiq Koya to say lawyers would no longer appear in the Fiji Court if the orders of the High Court were not obeyed.

It was obvious that the police and security forces were not interested in the sanctity of the individual. They were obviously relying on the new security decree to detain people without charge or bail. Under their loathesome decree suspects could be held two years without appeal to a court of law.

When the bulletin indicated Koya was fighting hard in the Lautoka Court on the question of bail, one of my guards offered an opinion, "We'll fix that bastard, we'll get him, we'll fix him." It was the same type of rough shod cowboy tactic that seemed to permeate most of the security force.

Confronting The Colonel

This time as the car approached the Queen Elizabeth Barracks' obstacle course, a pre-arranged light signal flashed on and off in the growing dark and the entrance bar was raised and we scooted into the inner compound. The major climbed out and went into the Military Police barracks, spoke briefly with somebody inside, then returned to the vehicle and drove up into the army compound proper, where the car was again stopped. The men quickly altered their pace, smartly getting out of the car and standing to attention. I slid out the backdoor.

Standing on the pavement in my court suit feeling the cooling wind of the early night I was thankful not to be back in the cell. Then "one-two, one-two", I was marched forward into the office of Colonel Konrote.

It was a sparse room. The curtains had been drawn across the windows as we approached up the sidewalk. Major Matt was seated to my right and a few feet to the left of him was an empty chair.

With his back to the opposite wall and window was a man I had never met before. I looked at Major Matt who didn't say boo. Clearly, by implication, I was to sit in the empty chair. It was a very basic chair with metal legs and a wooden seat. Not something I

154

would want to use for extended periods. Last time I had sat on chairs like this for very long was to do detentions at high school in British Columbia.

I turned and took three steps. It's funny how sometimes in life I come to a point where I'm about to take a step and I consciously think whether I should step there and say this or sit there and say that. Here, as I turned and began to sit, I stopped before the momentum carried me to the seat. Instead, I continued to walk toward Konrote.

He was in his khaki dress uniform with a number of ribbons that meant little to me. A man with an intense face, balding. He looked very uptight, with splotchy red patches on his brown face hinting at high blood pressure. You could see he was not a relaxed man.

"Major Konrote I presume," I said, offering him my hand. "Christopher Harder — how do you do?" The wind was temporarily taken out of his sails. He didn't know what to say or what to do. He paused then spluttered into a poison on Gagaj Sau Lagfatmaro.

"That Henry Gibson, you know if he ever comes back to Fiji, I will personally shoot him. When you go back to New Zealand you tell him, I will execute him," he said with some emphasis.

"Well, that doesn't really seem to be an appropriate way to resolve the problem," I replied, backing away from both Konrote and his threats. I sat on the chair and crossed my legs.

Then the major began to rave about the damage Gibson had done to the people on the island, trying to divide and conquer.

Konrote interrupted, "You know my people, they wanted to hurt you when you were there last time, and I wanted you arrested. It was only Magistrate Seru who stopped you from being arrested."

I stood and paced around the room. "You know Colonel, an amnesty for the men, it won't cause any further problems to Rotuma," I said. "They're old men, they're not sophisticated, they have no money, there's nobody outside New Zealand who has money for them. I do not see them as a threat to you. I think you should be merciful to them." Little did I know when I said there was no money for the Rotumans outside Fiji, that earlier that afternoon Fiji security forces had detained and sent packing a senior official of the World Muslim League, his briefcase and contents, some $US250,000 still intact.

At this he exploded, saying that it was a serious, serious matter, the sedition case involving Henry Gibson's Molmahao clan. They would be dealt with by the full force of the law.

He seemed to find it difficult, me standing up and taking the lead in the conversation, and it was apparent that the question asked of me in the car by one of the security men would not arise: "Will you drink kava with Konrote until the car leaves for the airport?"

"If they want to drink kava all night, I'll drink kava."

It was clear from the way the Konrote looked, his veins puffed up, his face growing redder by the moment and the sweat oozing from his brow, that he was not going to sit and drink kava with me tonight.

"I have an important meeting that I must now attend," he announced at 7.30.

We had spoken for less than 20 minutes. I had made it clear that I did not consider what the Rotumans had done was a major problem, and that I thought he should be merciful. I asked the Colonel to apologise to the Brigadier if the picture in the *Fiji Times* had caused him any embarrassment. I understood he had been embarrassed, losing face for not accepting the traditional Fijian savusavu of kava roots and tabua that I sought to offer him.

Then I told Konrote there had been no choice but to go public because nobody would make an appointment, nobody would return my calls, nobody would give me the courtesy of the time of day, and when people acted like that you sometimes had to take unusual steps to get their attention.

The Colonel was clearly concerned with the regime being criticised by me on my return to New Zealand.

"If the 21 men are in the amnesty, then I have no problem. But I am concerned because the radio has said three times this afternoon in words attributed to the Brigadier that the 21 are not in that amnesty. Now that does cause me concern colonel."

"Major Matt," said the colonel, "You were there, and I was there, when the Brigadier turned to the Commissioner of Police and said the 21 were in the amnesty. Is that not correct?"

"Yes colonel."

"If anybody is putting false news on the radio station, they will be arrested within the hour for disseminating information that is not correct. Do you understand Mr Harder?" the colonel asked.

"Yes I heard what you were saying."

"I must be off, I have a meeting that I cannot delay. If you require written proof from the Brigadier that the men are in the amnesty, then I will get that for you before midnight if that is what you require."

"Thank you."

CHAPTER ELEVEN

HOMEWARD BOUND

Konrote's promise to obtain written confirmation with the Brigadier's signature was too good to refuse. We shook hands and I climbed into the back of the car for the ride back to the hotel.

Again they took me through the conference room so that nobody in the lobby could see me. Back in my room where time dragged I tried to occupy myself listening to my music and reading the paper for the tenth time that day. Liga wanted to give me a universal reason for the significance of all the tattoos he had. But my experience in life and law suggested most of them had been engraved in jail at some time in the past.

One of the guards wore a teeshirt with the military crest of the Fiji Military Police. Under the crest a slogan read, 'Who dares to challenge'. Inside the letters the graphic face of a bulldog glared straight ahead.

Who dares to challenge, was a phrase that summed up most of my life. Here I was matched against a stubborn dictator, a giant of a man, who didn't want to know about criminal defence lawyers at this time in Fiji's history.

At midnight exactly, I was told to pick up my suitcase, come down to the front desk and pay my account. It was quite clear that I should pay for the privilege of being under hotel arrest. The security forces told me I was required to pay my bills.

Thank God for Visa. As I checked out I got the staff to pose together for a photograph and took some pictures of the surrounds.

Major Matt just said it wasn't possible for him or his boys to be photographed. Anyway they would come to see us in New Zealand.

I walked out of the hotel for the last time with a heavy feeling in my heart. I was unlikely to come back for a long time; genuine sadness that my future in Fiji, for work or pleasure, was indefinitely interrupted. Neither I nor Philippa were likely to holiday here again in the foreseeable future.

Again I was seated in the car with one man on either side of me. By this point we were developing a relationship and beginning to discuss matters. They had read the letters I had written Rabuka, and the one about the decree.

Most of the security people assigned to look after me had begun to warm a little and discuss everyday affairs. Major Matt was an interesting but relatively normal chap with wife and children. Because of the second coup and the decree, and now my own incident, he was seldom getting home to his family, even on weekends.

The saga of the guns was on-going. There were always people to locate and interview, apprehend and detain. They just wanted to get to the root of their problem and hang the person who introduced guns to Fiji.

Whatever other criticisms had been levelled against the 17-year-old Government of Ratu Sir Kamisese Mara, the man who had been Prime Minister since independence, until now they had done a good job keeping firearms out of Fiji.

Apart from a few village chiefs with a Second World War vintage Lee Enfield .303 well hidden and a handful of privileged people with hunting licences, they had virtually kept guns out of public hands.

In particular they were tough on visiting yachties. Many American sailors, especially those with Vietnam experience or who had been thrown out of the Carribean during the upheavals of the early 1970s, had firearms on their boats when they arrived in Fiji. They were given no option — hand the weapons over for storage in bond until they left or head back out to sea immediately.

The authorities had always feared what might happen in such a volatile society if people were able to arm themselves with anything more than sticks, stones and cane knives.

For my brief involvement in the guns affair I was being shepherded out of the country. It was a two car convoy. In the front with the two majors all I could see were dark shapes in the glow from the dashboard, but I could relax and feel well supported on either side. Big, football player shoulders held me like the filling in a sandwich.

We drove out of Suva at great speed. About 60 miles from town as we began winding around the coast again the driver swerved suddenly, startled by the flash of a black beast of some sort lurching into the middle of the road then off again into the darkness. We skidded to a halt in time to catch a glimpse in the headlights of a horse disappearing into the bush. We could have hit it at 60 miles an hour.

I could see little or nothing from the car except the road ahead as the miles rattled by. There were no street lights. There was no moonlight. It was dark except for the high beams reflecting off the tarseal and the oxide-red dirt on the road's shoulders.

As we rounded a bend just outside Korolevu our driver again screeched to a halt. In front of us was a group of 200-300 villagers walking along the main highway miles and miles from nowhere at almost two in the morning. We were 20 miles from the last villages. But for a good set of tyres our journey to Nadi could have ended fatally for the poor souls wandering along the road. Nobody offered a word to explain why they were there.

Major Matt said nothing to me during the first half of the trip. Somewhere near the town of Sigatoka, I ventured, "What is the situation with the men? Are they in the amnesty or are they not?"

Without turning his head he said, "They're not."

I was stunned, shattered. I felt impotent, but I was hardly in a position to protest. There was nothing to say and nothing to do. They had made a promise and broken it, and I was being escorted out of their country.

What I did when I got out of the country would be up to me except for the message given to me by the security people that my friends and acquaintances in Fiji would suffer if I was critical of the Fiji Government or the decree or any other matters that I had observed during my brief stay in Suva.

160

We were driving along one stretch with the radio car behind us when suddenly out of nowhere came a blur of fur, but as the car yet again braked violently there was an awful crunch, the sort of crunch where you know bones have been broken and death is likely. If we had not had to stop to fix the bent fender we would not have known it was a calf we had killed. The driver just wanted to keep going.

He swore loudly in Fijian while the radio car man came forward with a small sledgehammer. They bashed our relatively new vehicle on the fender, splaying it so that the wheel could turn again.

At Sigatoka the vehicles stopped. We all got out and they asked if I wanted a coffee.

"No, I'll just have an orange." I ordered an orange and paid for it myself. They paid for theirs. We stood around stretching our legs. Riding for two and a half hours on the axle hump in the back seat, tends to jar the tailbone, so I asked the major if it was possible to dispense with one of the guards and allow me some room in the backseat.

I wasn't about to go anywhere. When we started from Suva, the glovebox was purposely opened and a clip of ammunition was slammed into the officer's .38 pistol. They all obviously carried pistols in their line of security work.

Over the drinks I puffed on a cigarette. I was back smoking like I had in the yesteryears of alcohol haze and was frightened that tobacco would be too hard to give up a second time after getting out of this jam. But I kept telling myself I would quit.

As we wandered around stretching it was easier to talk to the major. "You said the 21 aren't in it. Why?"

"Because the public prosecutor told us we had to take them out of the amnesty," he said. "It would affect our chances of extraditing those actually involved with importing the guns. The man who introduced guns to Fiji, he's the one we must have and, I told you before, we will hang him. He will not be forgiven for what he has done to Fiji. He has set a fire in the bush and the grass is still burning. That is why they have been taken out of the amnesty but they will get amnesty. If the guns come in they will get amnesty."

"If that's what you really want, to have the guns in, then you

161

should leave me here. You should let me go talk to the men and see what the situation is with the guns."

He laughed and looked at me with that "nice try Harder" look. "No, you're on your way home." He called out to one of the boys. "Hey you ride in the radio car. Give Christopher some room to stretch out."

"Thank you, I appreciate that," I said.

As we neared the airport I thought about Fa. It was obvious we would not see each other for a while. He was probably still at home celebrating the birth of his baby daughter; his fourth child. His wife was a lovely Fijian schoolteacher who was concerned that the decree could be used against teachers to arbitrarily disqualify them from teaching. It was said they would have to be certified as fit and proper by the Minister of Home Affairs in charge of the security decree and the Minister of Education. The arrest of Fa on Wednesday morning had caused great anguish in his family.

His wife's parents blamed me for the fact that their daughter's baby was being born 30 days premature. Fa stayed quietly out of sight and I never got to say goodbye to him, nor to discuss the change in the amnesty circumstances for the 21. I was going to miss Tevita Fa.

The Rotuma case had a constitutional appeal, but more importantly it was a winner. I didn't believe the Director of Public Prosecutions could prove seditious intent simply by the fact that our clients had declared loyalty to the Queen.

The Government appointed Rotuma island manager had gone to the extreme of shooting the Union Jack with his pistol when it was raised on the Molmahao flagpole. He had to be taken off the island for his own safety after that incident.

The Price of Freedom

We approached Nadi Airport about three in the morning. The army roadblock to the entrance was manned by eight soldiers in green uniforms and wearing caps, polished boots, shiny buckles on their belts and carrying M16 rifles.

They were very casual, one had a clipboard and was leaning against the wall. As our Falcon pulled up one of the young lance corporals came around and muttered a question about identification. When the major looked up and said "You don't remember us, security forces," the men all snapped to attention. The lance corporal saluted and the others followed suit, realising that somebody of importance was in the vehicle. We were ushered through.

In the airport lounge Major Matt tried to find a line out so that I could phone my wife and tell her that I was on my way. But the lines were all toll-barred. I had to wait until I was on the Air New Zealand flight out before a message could be sent to Philippa confirming that I had indeed left Fiji.

The airport was moderately full at this early hour. Fijians and Indians sat around, security staff down by the international lounge were sitting on pew-like benches, drinking from a bucket of kava.

I sat down, still with my company, and began to drink the kava. And when I asked Major Matt to have my friend, Big Dan the doorman from the Gateway Hotel, asked over for a bowl of grog he dispatched a guard to find him. Big Dan was another person I wanted to explain things to, and to farewell. But Dan wasn't working and the guard could not find him.

The Air New Zealand security man approached and introduced himself. "Hello Mr Harder, I just want you to know that you will be coming back on the plane as an ordinary passenger. You will not be treated as a deportee and we'll see you at the plane at the appointed time. Thank you very much. We'll look forward to you flying with us."

Upstairs my friends and I wandered the halls of the duty free shops looking to see what I could buy my wife on my now seriously overcommitted credit card; some perfume, some music, some toys for the kids. I enjoyed the freedom of walking among other people, looking at what I wanted to look at, doing what I wanted to do. I bought a bottle of whiskey for a friend in New Zealand; the friend who had gotten the message through to the Prime Minister that I had written the letter about the decree. He had earned his bottle of whiskey.

As I sat in the lounge outside the bar with Major Matt, he said

"You know Fa, he got out 7.30 on Wednesday. He may have said some things to New Zealand, I just thought I should tell you that."

"You mean that was his price for getting out on the Wednesday night?" I asked.

"Well he went straight from the jail to the radio station, I say no more. But there may be some comment he has made in New Zealand. Just be prepared."

"Yeah I'll be prepared but if you made him do that, if I find you made him do that I will be disappointed to say the least. You can muck around with whoever you want but I came up here in good faith. I wrote to your Brigadier and I put it all in the letter. I tried to see him and you guys made a promise, now I find you changing your word and undoing your promise."

Finally the boarding call came for TE 04 flight to Auckland. The first call was for all transit passengers who had flown from Vancouver and Hawaii and were continuing to New Zealand. The office manager stood by the gate counting the individual transit cards. If one passenger was missing the security forces would not let the flight leave, these were difficult times in Fiji.

Finally I was led to the very front of the 747 at the Air New Zealand ramp. I didn't have to go through the baggage check procedure, or customs. I was given V.I.P. treatment.

Major Matt turned and shook my hand. "We'll see you again. We'll see you again, when I come to New Zealand I'll look you up."

"All right my friend. Just remember to tell your men that although they've got a job to do they must be polite and fair to the Indians. If they do that it will go a long way to making things better." I turned and boarded the plane. A seat was designated for me.

The Fijians had been very considerate from the time they decided I was going home. They had seen me smoking cigarettes and so, as a courtesy had booked me into the smoking section. I had a window seat and the husband and wife next to me smoked like chimneys. I had declared not to smoke again once I was on the airplane.

I put my seat back, fastened my seatbelt, put a pillow on the window as we climbed out of Fiji and closed my eyes. When I woke

164

up, the plane was flying at 2,000 feet approaching Auckland's Mangere Airport. It was the quickest flight I have ever had.

CHAPTER TWELVE

BACK TO EARTH

I walked off my bird of rescue, thanking the purser who had given me a copy of the *New Zealand Herald* with the front page story of my arrest by Rabuka's boys.

Down the corridor and onto the escalator, between the walls covered with colourful rural scenes, it was great to be back in New Zealand. One of the stewardesses walked off with me explaining that Prime Minister David Lange had taken Fiji to task for interfering with a New Zealand citizen. I cringed.

I was not yet a New Zealand citizen. I knew my Canadian passport had caused difficulty for the New Zealand Embassy in Fiji. What I hadn't known until this moment was that I had caused the PM embarrassment over my lack of New Zealand citizenship.

Now I was embarrassed. Maybe I should apologize to the Prime Minister for the blunder. After 12 years of residency I should do the proper thing.

It was not until I had nearly finished putting this book together that I learned of another reason why Rabuka may have been ill disposed toward Canadians.

A Canadian piggery farmer named Carl Petersen, who lived at Tailevu, had caused some concern for him and his bully boys just after the first coup.

A number of Fijians rioted burning some houses in Baulevu near Petersen's farm. The Canadian, himself a physical fitness freak, organised his Indian neighbours into a neighbourhood defence force.

When the Fiji military raided his pig farm they found all manner of notes in his garage indicating where people should stand guard at different outposts around the area.

Petersen and his neighbours had feared that the Fijian rioters would come back for a second go at the Indians. Petersen took the lead and arranged for the women and children to be moved out of the way.

He showed them how to make weapons for self defence out of broom sticks and assembled cane knives and various farm implements suitable for use as a weapon.

Finding this evidence the military over-reacted and arrested Petersen. The fact that Indian youths of the area had taken up Petersen's suggestion and organised themselve and that Petersen had generated a measure of solidarity and organisation for the locals was taken personally by the bully boys.

Petersen was badly beaten by the military and detained in the Queen Elizabeth Barracks. Two local Indian lawyers worried about him, put a call through to the spokesman for the army: "There are 700 young Indians about to storm the barracks to release Petersen. We are having trouble holding them back."

The army spokesman asked the Indian on the phone to call back in five minutes. When the call came again the spokesman responded that: "We will release him within the half hour."

Petersen was found later that day in a disoriented state walking around Nabua just down from the army barracks. He was taken home by some Indians and nursed back to health. Little did the authorities know that they had been conned. The 700 Indians ready to storm the gates were no more than a bluff by a couple of resourceful Indians.

At the baggage machine I loaded a trolley with a Visa card flag and headed for the Immigration and Customs barriers. For a fleeting second I wondered if I could now be excluded from New Zealand. My experiences of the last week now seemed so unreal that anything might be possible. After all I had been formally declared a threat to the peace and good order in general of a neighbouring country.

Luckily New Zealand and most other civilised law doesn't work like that.

I handed my documents to the immigration officer. He looked at my passport, punched a number on the screen and looked up at me, then quickly stamped it, authorising my entry into New Zealand. "Welcome home Mr Harder. Good to see you back." The words were a warm greeting. The airport staff were efficient and friendly.

Leaving Immigration I sighed with relief, as I had when I stepped off onto the ground at Rotuma after our plane had nearly fallen from the sky way out over the Pacific.

The press would be waiting outside to interview me. Many times before I had been involved with the press on a variety of issues. I had not objected to talking to them in the past, today it would be different.

My chest was fit to burst when I came through the exit doors looking for my family. I saw a sea of faces, such a loud noise was buzzing through the place, as if everybody was speaking all at once. All manner of persons; friends and families recognising each other, waving in excitement. I was in an absolute state of shock. My stomach felt like it was in my throat. My eyes searched around the lobby looking for a familiar face.

To my left I saw lawyer friend Christopher Reid. My focus on him was fleeting. The kids and Philippa were number one on my list today. All I wanted to do was give them all a great big hug.

The homecoming was almost as traumatic as my detention was at times in Fiji. Other times Fiji had been enjoyable and thrilling. It was an emotional and frightening experience, but one I would go through again tomorrow, given half a chance.

Kate was the first one to come into sight. I saw her recognise me as I came into her view. Her angelic little face lit up like a 200 watt bulb. I scooped her up in my arms as she dashed towards me. Then six-year-old Joshua jostled his way in. Philippa was nowhere to be seen. She would be back behind the madding crowd. The children and I were surrounded by reporters, cameramen, soundmen and clusters of microphones.

Lights flashed and everybody started asking questions. My brain was in a completely other phase and could not comprehend what was being said. All I wanted to do was get out of the airport and take off with my family. I was simply very glad to be home.

I gave Kate a great big hug and a kiss . . . squeezing her so tight I thought I'd never let her go. Joshua was pulling at my sleeve so I bent down and picked him up in my other arm. Josh blushed and put his face on my chest. Then I put both of them on the luggage cart and started to push.

Almost every segment of the media was present; television, radio, a pack of newspaper people, even some wire service reporters.

"Mr Harder, did you meet Rabuka?"

"Mr Harder, did they hurt you?"

"Why were you arrested?"

"What was your involvement with the guns?"

"Mr Harder, Mr Harder."

I shook my head. My mouth was dry and I found it hard to speak. I tried swallowing to get rid of the lump in my throat. I said, "I am sorry folks, I can't talk right now."

Part of my inability to talk to the press was the emotion of the moment. The other was that Subash Parshotam, secretary of the Fiji Law Society, was still in detention at the Queen Elizabeth Barracks. Silence on my return to New Zealand seemed appropriate if he was to be released.

I turned the buggy with my luggage and children and headed for the door. There was Philippa standing back by the wall wearing the purple tracksuit I had bought her in Canada the year before. Our eyes met for a second. A smile grew across her face and I knew she was glad I was back. "Pip" would be there once we were outside. She preferred to stay well away from the cameras, notepads and tape recorders. A shy person, she did not like being invaded by the media. We would say our hellos in the privacy of our home.

Straight ahead, not looking left or right, I went. As if I could shake off the press, the longer I walked the more reporters seemed to join me. Questions, cameras, tape recorders. Finally I had to stop because I had nowhere else to go. I had come to the end of the sidewalk on the far side of the car park. "Please," I said, " I can't talk to you at the moment. Some of my friends are still in jail."

"Chris, can we call you later at home?"

Not wanting to be obstructive or ungrateful for past assistance I

169

told them all "Yes, but give me an hour or two to settle down please." This seemed to calm the raging storm of questions. So I turned the cart around, gave my kids another big hug at the request of the cameras and walked off to find the car.

Joshua pointed me in the right direction and I ran pushing the cart as fast as it would go. Then I saw the TV camera. Obviously I was not going to get away that easily. As I approached the car the camera began to roll. I quickly put the baggage and the children in the stationwagon. Philippa was already in the front passenger seat.

"What was your first thought when you were thrown into the cell, Mr Harder?" said the reporter. I stopped by the back of the car. I thought for a second as I began to move my lips, but no words came to my mouth. My lips were dry. My throat was frozen and tears began to run down my cheeks. I could not utter a word.

The thought at the moment I was thrown into cell five at Queen Elizabeth Barracks had been a question: how was Philippa going to settle on our new house we had just bought next to Mt Hobson in Remuera. There would be no work or fees coming in. How would she get a mortgage without me. But I couldn't tell the television reporter that. I was too choked up to explain it. All I wanted was to get into the car and go home.

CHAPTER THIRTEEN

SUPPORT IN FAR AWAY PLACES

We met on the Stanley Park sea wall in Vancouver. He was about 55-years-old, medium build, dark Indian skin with a black handle bar moustache hiding most of his upper lip, but not his pearly white teeth that shone in the sun. The major had recently retired after more than 20 years' military service in the Indian Army. Vancouver in early August was still warm and Stanley Park seemed the prettiest park in the world; 1,000 acres of forest, park and seashore walks almost in the middle of the city. A perfect place, out of harm's way, for a meeting with my old military friend from bygone years.

We had first met 18 years before while I was a university student at Calgary. A young economics student I shall call Hari for obvious reasons, befriended me one day at our local watering hole, the Highlander Hotel.

Hari was a little person, possibly five foot two. I don't know what it was that brought us together, maybe I was just nice to him and he needed a friend.

The major, Hari's father, was introduced to me in the early 70s at his son's graduation as an economist. He had flown halfway around the world to beam his joy and pride as his fourth-born son was capped.

Ring, ring . . . the phone, I hurried to put down the *New Zealand Herald* of July 6th, 1988. "Long distance calling for Mr Chris Harder." People in Canada called me Chris, New Zealanders tend to call me Christopher.

"Hello, is that Chris Harder, the lawyer who was arrested in Fiji last month?" asked an Indian voice.

"Yes," I replied.

"Do you still remember Hari from the University of Calgary and his father from India?" the caller asked.

"Major, is that really you, how the hell are you? Where are you calling from?"

"I'm fine. I am calling from Bombay. How was your trip to Fiji? I heard of your arrest on the BBC World News. Are you all right?"

"I'm okay, they treated me all right, but I wouldn't want to be an Indian in Fiji at the moment," I yelled down the phone.

Despite depending on telephones for many years in my daily business I still talked on the phone like I was yelling down a long pipe.

"That's what I would like to talk to you about, the Indians in Fiji. Have you time for a short holiday in another world?" he asked.

I could sense a determination in his voice. Many years ago, when I still drank alcohol, I had spent a good number of evenings and the odd morning or two sharing a 26 ounce bottle of Canadian Club Whiskey with him as we talked about India, Ghandi, and the world situation in relation to the Indian race. I had learned from his son's example that the basic Indian was a good, clean, hard-working person. After much discussion and soul searching I had concluded that the Indians from India, were on the whole, an unfairly maligned race.

Vancouver, British Columbia, was the logical choice of meeting place. Most every year I went home to Vancouver; with its large Indian community I was sure the major would not be lonely.

I leaned against a fir tree that was at least 200 years old and looked out over the harbour to Vancouver's North Shore. Small white caps lapped the sea wall as the gulls glided by. I was fascinated by seagulls. My twin brother Greg, who owns Conti Computers in Vancouver, has a young son Jake who tamed a seagull for us one summer. Jake's seagull?

The popcorn cart down by the children's jungle gym at 4.15 on Wednesday afternoon was our agreed rendezvous. If either was more than 15 minutes late we were to try and meet again the next day at the same time. I had an emergency unlisted number to call if

172

all else failed. The six digits for the back-up call were firmly in my memory, the major had requested that I not write them down.

The last salty dregs of my pop-corn carton were in hand when a man strode into view. He wore a light grey cotton suit, a silver tipped cane twirling in his hand. There was a glimmer, then a sparkle as he saw me standing waiting. The Major stopped and stood ramrod straight. He was waiting for the horse carriage to pass before he crossed the road.

"Hey my friend, I rushed towards my long-lost confidante. We embraced on the sidewalk. It must have looked awfully funny. Here I was, six foot two, winter-white arms bared for some summer sun, wearing a purple and pink Hawaii singlet. My friend with his deep, dark complexion was in a formal suit and spit polished shoes and hardly came up to my shoulders. His firm hands clasped mine and shook me like a long lost son.

"How are you and where is Hari these days?" I asked.

Slowly he lifted his head. He paused then as he looked up a tear rolled down his cheek. At that moment I knew I would never see Hari again.

The major quivered as he tried to speak. "Dead," he said. "Two years ago in Delhi. He was killed when a bomb went off. Three people died in the explosion. Nobody ever took credit for the bombing. They couldn't tell if Hari was an innocent bystander or whether he was carrying the bomb," his explanation tailed off. "They identified him by a finger print, only by the digit finger from his left hand." The major's voice began to crack as the pain of death surged back for an anguished moment. The subject was still too fresh in his heart and mind to take it any further for now.

The mouthful of salt and pop corn I had swallowed moments ago was calling out for relief. I saw a water fountain down by a duck pond. "Wait a minute my friend until I get a drink of water," I said, both to quench my thirst and give him a chance to regain his composure.

I stood up from the fountain, straightened my shirt and looked around for the major. He was down on one knee by some trees trying to feed a squirrel a peanut from his right hand. He had once shown me a scar on his right arm that extended from his shoulder to his wrist. But for the luck of God and a very good British surgeon he would probably have been a cripple.

"Shall we go for a walk and talk Christopher?" he asked.

"How about a ride in the horse and carriage?" From a security point of view any potential follower or eavesdropper would soon be unmasked plodding around behind us.

I looked long and hard at this spry, middle-aged Indian I had not seen in many years, yet it seemed I had seen him only just the other day.

He had been a major when he retired in 1984 and among the people in his home village in India he still retained his rank. His exploits as a paratrooper over many years and in many countries ensured he kept it.

As we talked his eyes lit up when I said something that reminded him of Hari, as if for the moment his boy was still alive. For his pain he carried a silver flask of whiskey, my old favourite, C.C.

"For you," he offered me a drink. I could smell the nose tingling alcohol vapours.

"Eh, I don't drink any more, I quit over six years ago never to drink again. Hell, if I had continued drinking I would have been struck off, dead or in jail by now," I said.

"Major, when you and I used to drink, I was just a student. Nothing bothered me then. You always saw the pleasant merry fellow, but there was another side of me. When I used to get really drunk I used to get violent to all manner of people."

"Well have a bottle of your favourite coke then," he said. It was time to stop reminiscing and tackle the real issue.

"I believe help is available to the Indians in Fiji. It is only a matter of time before help comes. The foreign policy of non-intervention outside the Indian continent is slowly changing. The Prime Minister's think tank has discussed broadening the policy to other areas where significant numbers of Indians are suffering under oppressive regimes."

The major sat back in the carriage as the driver began our journey through the enchanted underforest of maples, vines, berry bush and ferns. Above towered Douglas fir and cedar trees. They gave off a natural bouquet of growth, and of decaying leaves.

"When you go home I want to help," the major said. "The Fiji Indian is close to my heart."

Our carriage swaying in the summer breeze, the horse pulled us past the aquarium from where the shrill sounds of trained killer whales, splashing and whistling, came.

"I want you to meet a friend of mine who's come all the way from India too. He understands the problem and is in a position to help."

His friend understood the problem all right. He understood that Indians had been given a hard time, and not just in Fiji. But he also knew how strong, and from how many millions of people, was the support available.

While there was one gun unaccounted for in Fiji, and there were free men outside, there would always be one to lift a finger. For that matter guns would be available to the right people, he said.

CHAPTER FOURTEEN

THE KAHAN CONNECTION

I was sitting at my desk preparing for a murder trial, Fiji far from my mind, I hadn't talked to anybody about Fiji for a couple of weeks. In fact I had hardly talked about it since I'd come back from Canada. Being fairly keyed up after several long periods of concentration on the murder case, the ringing of my fax phone was a welcome relief.

I strode over to the corner of my study to see the fax paper start reeling up from the machine . . . "VICTOR LISSACK & ROSCOE SOLICITORS, 8 Bow Street, Covent Garden, London."

The lawyers of Mohammed Kahan. He had been arrested in Britain and the Republic of Fiji wanted his extradition for gun running. My interest in the message coming off the fax machine quickened.

13th September 1988
Harder Esq.
Dear Mr Harder,
Mohammed Rafig Kahan

As you know we represent Mr Kahan who is currently in custody awaiting the Home Secretary's decision on whether or not to give the Authority to Proceed on his extradition to Fiji. The next Court appearance in this matter is 10.30a.m. September 30th 1988 at Bow Street Magistrates Court by which time the Home Secretary will have made his decision.

We intend to make representation to the Home Secretary before asking him not to make this order on the grounds (among others) that Mr Kahan is wanted by the Fijian Authorities for purely political reasons and that if extradited to Fiji he will not receive a fair trial, if he receives a trial at all.

We would be grateful if you would write a letter on an affidavit setting out whether, in your opinion, you would expect Mr Kahan to receive a fair trial in Fiji, which we could then send to the Home Secretary. Please send it by fax.

We also understand that Dr.Cameron, who used to be a Magistrate in Fiji, is now living in New Zealand. We would like to contact him and would be grateful if you are able to tell us his telephone or address.

Yours sincerely, Robert Rosco.

I finished reading the letter, put it down and looked across the room at my wall covered in law books, wondering if I should tell the whole story for the sake of Kahan. He sounded like a thorough rogue with a list of criminal convictions across Canada, Australia and England. An Australian police spokesman had described the Fiji Indian suspect as a man with an international criminal record.

The federal police in Sydney said he was a member or associate of the Coalition for Democracy in Fiji. Kahan was handsome, black haired, swarthy; he was a man of proven ability, able to pass himself off successfully under a variety of aliases.

I knew long before I received the letter from Kahan's lawyer Robert Roscoe that I would probably go to bat for the gun runner if I got the opportunity. I remembered the letter I had sent to Fiji's senior prosecutor back in early August. The intent of it was plain. I had warned the Fiji military regime that I would not withhold my criticism of Fiji if they didn't honour their promise in a letter to the Public Prosecutor, Major Iskeli Mataitoga.

The Department of Public Prosecutions
Government Buildings, Suva
REPUBLIC OF FIJI

Dear Sir
As you are no doubt aware I was excluded from Fiji pursuant to an order signed

by Brigadier General Sitiveni Ligamamada Rabuka on the 22nd day of June, 1988.

When I was released from the custody of the Queen Elizabeth Barracks on the Thursday night just before the Amnesty speech, I was taken to my Hotel where I was kept under room arrest. At the Hotel I was told by Major Mataitene that the 21 people accused in the guns affair were included in the Amnesty. This significant point was confirmed by Colonel Konrote, Chief of Staff. He assured me the twenty one accused were included in the Arms Amnesty. Colonel Konrote and Major Mataitene discussed this matter with me in very plain English. There was no misunderstanding. The Brigadier turned to the Commissioner of Police and confirmed that the 21 were in the Amnesty. I was promised the men would be set free. Clearly this has not happened.

On the way to Nadi Airport my security people advised me that the men were taken out of the Amnesty at your Department's request. The reason I was given was that you or your designate while you were away, said that any subsequent extradition would be rendered a nullity. I disagree. The arms possession charges and the rest are all relatively minor charges compared to the alleged offences facing Mr Kahan, currently being held in British custody awaiting a formal documented extradition request by the Republic of Fiji.

Unless the promise to release the 21 arms accused is honoured within 14 days of the date on this letter I intend to make myself available to Mr Kahan's defence counsel in London Magistrates Court to give viva voce evidence of senior Fiji Security Forces personnel who advised me that the man who had imported guns into Fiji would be hung by his men on his return to Fiji. "We will hang him".

Furthermore I have first hand experience of serious manipulation of the existing Judicial system in the Republic of Fiji. Finally I would inform the Court I have read the original of the Security Decree 1988 and will give evidence that under the Decree the onus of proof is shifted to the accused.

I believe my testimony would be of some significant assistance to Mr Kahan in the defence of his extradition.

I require a photograph, showing the men after they have been released from custody, to be published overseas confirming the release and amnesty, consistent with the Christian principle of forgiveness. Forgiveness was and still is a valid concept.

Should Anand Singh request his passport for travel to New Zealand, I trust you will facilitate his departure and return.

I trust that the book I am writing on Fiji will have a good ending.

I look forward to your reply. My Auckland fax number is 504-694.
Best of luck

Yours faithfully
CHRISTOPHER HARDER, BARRISTER

The one thing that Rabuka and his henchmen hated more than the Indians was world press publicity critical of their actions.

Running a campaign against Rabuka and his band of cowboys was a time consuming and expensive task. It was like preparing for a great big trial step-by-step, building a case against these constitutional criminals. All the time I had local work around me that required attention. This meant taking on extra staff so my practice didn't suffer.

I decided to go to London to try and see the Home Secretary face to face before he made his decision on the first step of Kahan's extradition treaty. Perhaps I could stop Kahan being extradited before the court procedure began and claim an early round from Rabuka.

If at the same time the Queen would strip Rabuka of his OBE it would be like a standing eight count against this giant of a man. If he was stripped of his title Rabuka would probably falter. Then it would just remain to help expose where the guns had come from, and who was involved. Accounts I was still receiving from both Fijians and Indians in and out of Fiji all suggested Rabuka was fast losing support on ground which he could not hope to regain. The sooner he went the better.

It seemed the cabinet that sat in the grand old Government building in Suva was still more or less just a puppet front for him and his army mates. The civilian cabinet could discuss matters but the military ministers remained silent, never speaking more than a few words and never offering any positive substance to the debate.

I could imagine the difficulty administrators had in dealing with these shallowly educated, thoroughly indoctrinated gunslingers who had been given a taste of power. After every cabinet meeting they were still going off to their barracks to discuss the events

179

among themselves, often returning to the next meeting to simply veto what the ministers wanted.

I thought of Fiji and the palm trees, the white sands and crystal blue waters lapping at the shore. I wished I was back there lying on the sand listening to the Fijian music on my Walkman. Instead I was sitting at the desk in my office in front of a wood fire, hoping the affidavit I was about to write would hot things up for the Brigadier. I started to type . . .

IN THE LONDON MAGISTRATES COURT

IN THE MATTER OF The Fugitive Offenders Act and an application for extradition by the Republic of Fiji

BETWEEN *MOHAMMED RAFIQ KAHAN*

DEFENDANT

AND THE REPUBLIC OF FIJI

Applicant

I, Christopher Lloyd Harder, Barrister and Solicitor of the High Court of New Zealand, make oath and say:

1) I was admitted as a barrister to the High Court of New Zealand at Auckland on May 20, 1983 and have practiced as a barrister sole since May 31, 1983.

2) I was admitted as a barrister on a temporary admission to the Fiji High Court on the June 21, 1988 by the Chief Justice.

3) Attached to this affidavit and marked with letter 'A' is a copy of my affidavit sworn and filed by me on the 17th day of June 1988 in the Fiji High Court in relation to the Lautoka (Arms Case) and the Rotuma (swearing allegiance to the Queen) sedition case.

4) My admission to the Fiji High Court was supported by the Fiji Law Society as is evidenced by the letter marked with the letter 'B' and attached hereto.

5) Following my admission to the Fiji High Court in the Chief Justice's chambers on Tuesday the 21st day of June, 1988, I signed a letter addressed to the Solicitor General and cabinet of the Government of the 'Republic' of Fiji criticising the

draconian measures of detention without charge or bail for up to two years at a time, retrospective life imprisonment penalty, and the shifting of the onus of proof to the accused, all of which are contained in the Fiji 1988 Security Decree.

6) A copy of the letter containing my criticism of the 1988 Security Decree and a recommendation for a 30 day Arms Amnesty referred to in paragraph five of this affidavit is attached hereto and marked with the letter 'C'.

7) I prepared the letter with the full knowledge and approval of my instructing solicitor Anand Singh of Singh and Fatiaki, Solicitors, of Lautoka, a copy of the letter having been sent to him for approval.

8) The letter referred to above was signed by myself and SubashParshotum, Secretary of the Fiji Law Society in his private capacity, the four remaining Law Society members abstaining from voting on the letter or not being available to discuss the material, the more vocal members of the council having left Fiji for other parts of the world.

9) I personally delivered the letter to the office of the Solicitor General at Government Buildings with sufficient copies for the rest of the cabinet. The papers were supplied to the personal assistant of the Solicitor General on the understanding that the papers would be handed to the cabinet forthwith.

10) The following morning I was approached at the pool of the Travelodge in Suva, across the road from the Government Buildings and the High Court, by a male Fijian about 24 years of age, covered in tattoos telling me, "Security Forces, come with me." After a verbal altercation with this "Tonton Macoute" looking lad, I went up to my room and dressed. I was then taken to a four-wheel-drive vehicle with three other casually dressed men also covered in tattoos. Subsequent inquiry of my captors revealed that the tattoos were in part from previous periods of imprisonment either in the Army or in civilian life.

11) My Fijian instructing solicitor for the Rotuma sedition case, Tevita Fa, was also taken into custody with me. Subash Parshotam, Secretary of the Fiji Law Society, was arrested at his home on the night of Wednesday the 22nd of June. All three of us were jailed at Queen Elizabeth Barracks, Suva, in small four foot by six foot cells. The bare concrete floor, with drain hole exiting the wall, was used to drain water used for washing the floors. The hole also doubled as a perfect rat door.

12) While I was detained in cell five I observed or heard grossly improper interrogation practices taking place. Half naked Indians, dressed in pants or pyjama bottoms with a blanket draped over the door to hide who was inside the cell, were subjected to real mental torture. The grey army blankets also stopped other prisoners

181

from actually seeing what went on in the cells, but did not stop us all from listening to the frightening interrogations taking place.

13) On one particular occasion the Indian male in the cell across the hall and down one to my left was questioned, threatened and then promised execution by shooting under the Decree for denying talking about the Brigadier over lunch to another person in a little restaurant not far from the barracks.

14) A second Indian was verbally threatened on a number of occasions when he failed to give the 'right' answer to a series of questions put to him by a security man swinging an M16 rifle at his side. The interrogator then grabbed the jail door by the bars and shook and rattled the padlock and chain screaming out for the uniformed soldier to bring the key for the lock so that this tattoo-covered security forces person could gain entry into the cell of this distraught Indian, now being terrorised by one of Brigadier Rabuka's security men.

15) The soldier obeying the Brigadier's security man's order unlocked the chain and let the interrogating security forces person into the cell. He replaced the blanket on the bars so that I could not see inside the cell. The sounds of fear and pain I heard coming from the cell sounded like the Indian was on his knees pleading not to be hit again after several slap sounds were heard from behind the blanket.

16) On several occasions the man at the far end of the cell corridor was taken down the hall to the bathroom. I now identify this person as Som Prakash, university lecturer, arrested by the security forces from the University and questioned, within my hearing, as to why he wrote the critique on Rabuka's book, NO OTHER WAY, about the two military coups.

17) On one occasion a security forces man strode down the concrete floor in the jail corridor with a three foot iron rod, approximately a third of a inch thick. I heard the standard question asked again, "Why you write about Rabuka's book?" Then shouting, "Open this door." The soldier complying with the order opened the cell door. Then Som Prakash was hit several times with a swack, swack sound as the rod connected with some part of his body, followed by yelps of pain from his cell.

18) During my 32 hours in the cells I recalled guards walking up and down the corridor with their M16 rifles yelling out, "Make my day" click, click, click as they pulled the trigger on their rifles, imitating Clint Eastwood with his standard line in the film Dirty Harry. On these occasions the ammunition cartridge was either in the other hand, stuffed in a pocket or inside a belt.

19) When I was finally released from the Queen Elizabeth Barracks about 6.45 p.m. Thursday night, I was taken back to my room at the Travelodge Hotel and placed under room arrest. There I became quite friendly with my guards and a

Major Mataitene, Head of Security. Following the announcement by Brigadier Rabuka on Fiji Radio on the 30 days arms amnesty, I was informed by the Major that the 21 arms accused were in the Arms Amnesty. For the rest of the evening we discussed personal philosophy, the arms case and the military attitude to Indians in general.

20) Major Mataitene in discussing the case said the gun runner who brought the guns into Fiji would be brought back to Fiji and "He will pay" were the words uttered to me, "We will hang him."

21) During discussions on the Thursday night, June 23, in my hotel room, Major Mataitene spoke of how the Brigadier had taken the Amnesty suggestion to the President of the Republic of Fiji, the cabinet, the Chief Justice and finally a meeting with army and police officials, including the Commissioner of Police at Queen Elizabeth Barracks. I was told by the Major that the 21 persons would be freed under the Amnesty 'tomorrow'(Friday 24 June 1988).

22) I was promised a meeting the next morning with the acting prosecutor, John Semesi, and a deputy prosecutor Babu Singh who had appeared in the gun case. The meeting never took place. Three times that afternoon I heard a retraction on the radio attributing words to the Brigadier that 'the 21 gun accused were not part of the amnesty.'

23) At 6.45 p.m. on the evening of Friday 24 June I was taken back to the Queen Elizabeth Barracks by the security forces in a Falcon motorcar with its radio on. The seven o'clock news spoke of Suva criminal lawyer S.Koya campaigning for bail for the accused, telling the magistrate at Lautoka that "the lawyers will no longer appear in the courts if orders made by the High Court were continued to be ignored by security forces people."

24) This comment was made in relation to Haroon Shah, lawyer of Lautoka, who was one of the 21 men arrested who had been re-arrested by security forces personnel despite his grant of High Court bail. Shah was one of six clients I then represented along with Lautoka lawyer Anand Singh.

25) The two security forces person in the front seat of the car got very angry and said they would "fix Koya by giving him a taste of life in a cell soon enough."

Shah, the lawyer whom Koya was talking about, had been charged for standing by while allowing a felony to be committed. The Magistrates Court denied Shah bail on this charge. An appeal to the High Court was successful but Shah's release was shortlived. Shah was arrested for a second time, this time without any charge or reason being given.

26) On his return to court the magistrate ordered that Shah was free to leave the court in line with his grant of High Court bail. For a second time Shah was apprehended, in full view of court staff and Lautoka lawyers, and taken away by security forces personnel. Shah has been under house arrest without visitors since June.

27) The seven o'clock news finished as the car drove back in through the gates of the Army barracks. I was taken to see Colonel Konrote, second in charge under Brigadier General Sitiveni Ligamamada Rabuka OBE, Minister for Home Affairs, Commander of the Security Forces and Minister charged with the responsibility of Internal Security.

28) Colonel Konrote confirmed the 21 gun people were in the Amnesty despite what I had heard on the radio. The Colonel looked to Major Mataitene who was also in the room, and said, "You were there with me when the Brigadier turned to the Commissioner of Police and said the 21 are in the Amnesty."

29) During the course of my brief interview before I returned to New Zealand it was made clear to me that my friends in Fiji would be better off if I did not criticise Fiji on my return to New Zealand. The colonel also asked me to pass on a message to Henry Gibson, de facto King of Rotuma residing in Auckland, New Zealand, that he (Konrote) would personally execute Gibson should he return to Fiji.

30) As I left Konrote's office he said he would obtain written confirmation from the Brigadier that the 21 accused were in the Amnesty before I left Suva that evening for Nadi and New Zealand. In return I said I would not criticise Fiji if my clients were set free. He told me the people broadcasting false news on the radio would be under arrest within the hour.

31) During the course of my car ride to Nadi and deportation from the Republic of Fiji, I was told by Major Mataitene that the 21 were not in the Amnesty. When we stopped for a coffee at a roadside stop I again asked, "Why, that wasn't the deal?"It was then that Major Mataitene said, "The D.P.P (an army officer appointed as Director of Public Prosecutions) said that we wouldn't be able to extradite the gun guy when he was arrested if we let these guys go now. We will let them go when all the guns come in," he said.

32) Consistently throughout my May trip to Fiji about my admission and the Rotuma case I found that I could not rely on the word of court officials or the D.P.P involved in the Rotuma case, Mr Iskeli Mataitoga. Neither could I rely on the Court Registrar or his staff.

33) Documents that I personally served on Rusiate Lauwedrau, chief clerk of the High Court and taken into the office of the Chief Justice as I stood at the foot of the spiral stairs to his office, were later denied as ever having been served. An assurance that the Department of Public Prosecutions' copy of the 'application for urgent fixture' in relation to the Rotuma sedition case in the High Court of Fiji would be served on them by the Court staff, was never carried out.

34) A tactical mistake by the D.P.P to allow the Rotuma jurisdiction case to be referred to the Fiji High Court brought about a severe reprimand by the Brigadier to Mr Mataitoga. The D.P.P. had tried to return to the Magistrate's jurisdiction at a time when the matter was properly before the High Court, the magistrate being functus officio.

35) The first call of the Rotuma jurisdiction case in the Fiji High Court on June 9th, 1988 was turned into a full hearing without notice to instructing counsel Tevita Fa by the Chief Justice of the High Court. Tevita Fa was forced to go on with a full hearing despite the fact that I had been told the case was still some three weeks away. The court clerk had confirmed a date after 18 June at the earliest when I could return with legal submissions prepared for the complex jurisdiction question.

36) Prior to my arrest by the security forces in Suva I was told of an incident as witnessed by a lawyer in the Suva Magistrates Court where Magistrate Rabuka, half-brother to Brigadier Rabuka, in sentencing a woman on a serious matter where prison was likely, told her, "Woman, I am going to send you home but if you ever come back before my Court again, I am going to [expletive deleted] your arse." The prosecutor involved in the matter ensured that the issue was taken up with the Chief Justice within hours. The Chief Justice required that the magistrate resign. A two-hour reprieve at the request of the magistrate brought about a situation where Brigadier Rabuka walked into the office of the Chief Justice and threatened him if his half-brother was not reinstated immediately. Rabuka was quoted as yelling, "You remember, I could have put an Indian in your chair." Magistrate Rabuka was reinstated within 20 minutes. This is the second such "[expletive deleted] your arse . . ." comment from this magistrate. This incident was described to me by one of the lawyers present in the court at the time. The second person relayed the story to me as told to him by the Chief Justice himself.

37) Since my return to New Zealand following my expulsion from the 'Republic' of Fiji I have been visited by a high ranking judicial officer from Fiji who has related to me the gist of a discussion held between the Department of Public Prosecutions, Army Major Iskeli Mataitoga, Magistrate Seru, Chief Acting Magistrate of Fiji and Magistrate hearing the Rotuma Sedition case, and the Chief Justice of the Fiji High Court days before the Rotuma jurisdiction hearing of first call. The crux of the conversation was that Major Mataitoga was 'not to worry, the C.J. would look after the Rotuma affair following his 'mistake' to let the matter develop as it did.'

185

These remarks were said by Magistrate Seru in the presence of the Chief Justice who nodded his head in agreement.

38) The judicial system seems to be manipulated by a variety of different persons both in and outside the judiciary in relation to both the sedition and the arms cases to the extent that I would have no faith in a person charged with gun importation or similar offence receiving a fair trial in the Republic of Fiji.

39) The volatility of the security forces is best described as criminal, dangerous, untrained, undisciplined, threatening, uncaring. They are bully boys owning blind allegiance to the man who gave them food and a job or freedom from jail — Brigadier Rabuka, OBE.

SWORN at AUCKLAND   *this 19th day of*
SEPTEMBER   *1988*

BEFORE ME ———————— *L.A. LAWSON* ————————

It was 8.15 in the morning London time when I began to the send the signed affidavit to London by facsimile. Robert Rosco was waiting for whatever information I might be able to supply him in the defence of his client, Mohammed Kahan. Barrister David Jones would be running the battle in the old Bow Street Magistrates court. I decided to watch my back. The possibility of a Fijian-backed hit man had crossed my mind. Hell, if someone could walk down my driveway at sunrise in mid-summer and blow up my Mercedes, then I thought anything was possible. My insurance was paid up, I thought to myself as I got ready to fly off to London.

I was feeling a bit like an athlete psyching up for the Olympics. Criminal lawyers have to prepare and above all they must be competitive. They must know how to absorb punishment and to hit back when the time is right. When my fax beeped, signalling the affidavit to London had been sent, there was no turning back. The gauntlet had been thrown down, the next question was who would pick it up for Rabuka and his new Republic.

Bow Street Bound

In casual clothes I boarded the Air New Zealand flight to London. It was midnight on Saturday and the rain was pouringdown. I

186

wondered what Fiji's chief prosecutor Isikeli Mataitoga was doing at this moment. The newspapers said that Fiji had hired a Queen's Counsel to help Rabuka's man extradite Kahan. I wondered what my reaction would be if we met on the street in London walking down Piccadilly. I certainly did not expect to pull any punches when it came to speaking out against Rabuka and his hired guns.

I pushed my seat back and tried to get comfortable on this 22 hour flight to London. There was plenty of time to reread the file and the documents of record to refresh my memory on small matters that might suddenly become important. I read the press clippings from the first mention of smuggled arms into Fiji. The gun case had taken so many ducks and dives it was difficult at times to tell which end was up.

Nearly three months had passed since I had been shoved out of Fiji. Rabuka would have been well advised to check my determination level before he had me arrested. Immediately on returning to Auckland after my arrest I began my campaign by speaking to the Foreign Affairs departments in Australia, New Zealand and Canada. Everybody wanted to help but didn't know what to do. They were all lacking reliable grassroots information, which made policy decisions difficult.

My decision to see Rabuka and the guns case through to the end was a matter of habit, it was hardly necessary to remind myself to see the battles through. But this was a case with no end yet in sight unless the Home Secretary accepted my affidavit describing Rabuka's follies. I hoped the contents of this sworn document would make unpleasant reading, leaving no room for any reasonable person to doubt that it would be impossible for Mohammed Kahan to get a fair trial in Fiji.

CHAPTER FIFTEEN

TRADITION AND SAFETY PINS

The escalator going up to Charing Cross Station was broken so I walked from my underground introduction to the tube. People were milling every which way. A busker sitting on his Diamond amplifier played piano organ with a sound that ebbed and flowed through the enclosed walkways. I nearly always tip a busker on the street. It takes talent and a special courage to entertain their way. The sound of church bells in this grand old lady of a city rang cheerily over Sunday morning.

In London the population of 10 million makes sure the business part of the city sings. All manner of folk walk the streets. Punk rockers in the most extreme and garish outfits dot the side walks. McDonald's clientele were adorned with purple spiked hairstyles, or painted blue mohawk hair cuts, rings and diamonds in their noses and safety pins in their ears; real anti-authoritarian attitudes. Probably not much different from my independent stance of younger years, just differently presented.

We wore skin tight jeans, black pointed bankers on our feet, and shirts hanging out. Hair styles were Elvis, long-back-and-sides with a swished up duck's arse at the back. In the mid 60s that style was replaced with Beatle cuts as British music hit North America. But we didn't quite run to safety pin jewellery.

Sometimes my fine hair falls back like a Beatle cut and I wonder if maybe I am still trying too hard to hang on to the adventurous times of youth. But then who said only the young could have adventure? While I was in London my mate Peter Williams, at 54 years of age was on sabbatical for a year, about to chase adventure up the Amazon River.

Here I was ducking the pan handlers who urged the passing throngs to give up their loose change. Down the lane from the Charing Cross Hotel I stumbled on numerous drunks, both young and old, male and female, mostly white. Many were sprawled out vomiting, drunken, revolting enough to boggle the mind at how man or woman could put themselves in that condition. Things were getting worse. As I walked up the Strand towards Fleet Street I saw a number of old folk making their beds under pieces of cardboard in office doors and alleys. The lucky ones had a woollen blanket wrapped around their shoulders trying to ward off the chill.

But around every corner in London stood historical buildings, so appealing to the eye, so refreshing to behold. Even in London though, the battle for preservation and restoration went on. I saw the local soldiers of the preservation societies hanging out their painted cloth signs protesting at the proposed demolition of a magnificent old building in the heart of London.

Sunday afternoon in London is an experience all its own. The rushing masses have disappeared. I took a traditional black taxi from the front of the hotel.

"Where to governor?", came the inquiry from a fish and chip monger filling in for his mate. He rented a cab from the company for 97 quid a week. This covered his hire, repairs and insurance. On top of this he had his diesel totalling about 75 quid. On a gross income ranging from £350 to £650 a week, a London cabby could have a fairly reasonable standard of living.

"Take me for a ride to Henley-on-Thames please," I called out loud enough to be heard through the sliding glass partition and over the throaty noise of the muffler. Henley-on-Thames, famous for its annual rowing regatta, was a most peaceful place where willow trees hung out over the grass covered banks of the River Thames.

I got out of the cab and gave the driver a 10 note. It was the smallest that I had.

"Here you are Gov," he dumped eight heavy one coins into my hand.

189

I contemplated a quick stroll around some shops. The week to come promised to be busy, with little time for sight-seeing. Jet lag was crawling up on me, dragging my head and neck down like a ball on a chain. It was time to check into my hotel for a some rest.

Charing Cross Hotel is an establishment of yesteryear hanging on to its share of the market with reasonably priced rooms, £55 for a room in London was very cheap. That price covered a single bed and shower, colour TV and a hot water jug. When I asked if I could get a double bed I was told "Yes, Mr Harder, that will cost an extra £30."

"I'll sleep on it," I told the Scottish lass at the desk. Hotel prices in London are astronomical, usually anywhere between 150 and 400 quid a night. I reckoned I would have to do some very special sleeping to justify that kind of five night stand.

I was handed a key card by the front desk to show to the porter. Security was tight in London. On the wall behind the porter's desk was a 'BOMB WARNING' notice, a reminder to be forever on your toes about strange packages. Two Arabs waited at the desk for their keys and messages.

I took my Walkman headphones off for a moment and joined the real world. "Yes sir, can I help you?" spoke the young man behind the desk.

"Could I have a key for my room please and are there any messages for Harder?" I enquired.

"No sir, nothing as yet."

"No fax messages?" I asked.

"No sir."

I knew something was wrong. My reliable wife would never let me down unless it was beyond her control. I was expecting papers from her and some from a young, up-and-coming Maori barrister called Charl, without an 'e' Hirshfield. Charl was preparing a murder case for me which was awaiting my return. He too was reliable. He was one of those rare breed who would always go to extreme lengths to ensure the job got done. Charl was sending over my bedtime reading so that I would be ready to fire straight into court on my return to New Zealand.

"Is your fax machine working?" I enquired.

"I am sorry, sir. We no longer have a fax machine. The hotel was taken over by new owners recently and the fax was taken out."

I wanted to scream. I had picked the Charing Cross because of its British sounding name and because the travel representative had assured me the hotel had a fax. All manner of people had been given the hotel's old fax number so that I could keep in touch with New Zealand. Accurate and up-to-date information was crucial to sound decision-making. Now I faced the fundamental problem everybody was having when dealing with Fiji and the guns case.

What A Good Idea

Room 458 had a view of Nelson's Column and Trafalgar Square. I put on the jug for a cup of coffee and took off my suit, pulling the curtain before changing. I don't know why. The only things that could see into my room were pigeons or someone with a telescope. I had heard about the British spy service and its various agencies. I guessed what was happening in Fiji made me fair game. Anyway, by now almost everybody knew I was writing a book. I was determined to finish the story despite all manner of interference, threats and blatant blackmail by some of the Fijian players.

I had never thought to do a book about my arrest in Fiji until one of my more senior security forces guards first raised his fear of me writing about my experiences while in Fiji.

It was one of Rabuka's boys who had said it was obvious my real purpose in Fiji was to write a book. Nothing could have been further from the truth at that point. I had taken no notes, made no tapes, kept no postcards. All I had was ordinary tourist pictures of local beauty spots, not jails, dock yards and bridges. Until that moment the thought of really doing a book on Fiji had not crossed my mind.

I shall not name this security officer for fear he might cop the blame for this book or at least the name of one of the book's chapters. One of my Tonton Macoute-looking security guards had been wearing a blue teeshirt with a crest on it. My eyes seized on the motto below the Fiji Military Police Crest: *WHO DARES TO CHALLENGE*. There it was, the riddle of my life used as a military slogan. At that moment I knew I would reply to the challenge with the word, "Me."

I sat down and called Robert Roscoe on the phone. "20 pence a minute," said the price card on the phone. This could be an expensive week by the time I finished making my calls. I was not yet sure how far I would have to cast my net.

Mohammed Kahan was an enigma to me. I had certain ideas about this Mr Kahan whom I hoped to see.

My enquires had led me to believe this fiery little Muslim Indian, rogue that he might be, had a certain courage that rivalled some of life's braver souls. Once in a while you meet a person who because of their past has nothing left to lose by risking their future, someone who wanted to change before it was too late, who wanted to be accepted back into the mainstream. Kahan knew his chances of rehabilitation were next to nil unless the traitors of Fiji were banished, possibly at the point of a gun. Kahan would not be alone dreaming that his wish to help end Rabuka's rule could come true.

My subsequent time with Kahan in the little interview room allocated for Category "A" designated inmates at Brixton Prison was to confirm that he was such a character. Justifiably he was hounded by his list of previous convictions for dishonesty, now he was looking for one redeeming moment in life so that he might seal off the past. A gamble to help himself and Fiji's Indians.

Kahan was dealing in what he thought was a pragmatic manner with the lesser of the two evils now existing in Fiji. He hoped that despite his past record and his history for unreliability people would accept him. He prayed, like so many, that Dr Bavadra might one day reclaim his proper place as Prime Minister of the Government of Fiji.

A bit of money at the end of the day also featured in Kahan's decision to involve himself in the guns affair. But not to the exclusion of his higher principled goal of attempting a $40 million fraud to give Fiji sugarcane farmers sufficient funds to live on while they supported a campaign of civil disobedience by refusing to harvest their crop. It was a plan to cripple the economy without going to war. A policy dream designed to bring Rabuka down because sugar is Fiji's main export.

Now Kahan was residing, courtesy of Her Majesty, in Brixton Prison, about the only place a Fiji Indian could be sure of feeling like he still belonged to the Commonwealth. Somehow I didn't think it was exactly what Mohammed Kahan had in mind when he became involved in the guns affair.

I had first heard of Roscoe when I read his name in the *New Zealand Herald*, along with London barrister, Alun Jones. Each of these gentlemen, I later learned, had practised in the true tradition of the English bar, Roscoe and Jones prosecuting and defending alike, a standard procedure in London.

"Hee..low," went the strange sounding voice on the other end of the telephone. A woman, probably Asian, was obviously struggling to make herself understood.

"Is Mr Roscoe, the solicitor, home please?" I asked.

"Paardon," came the reply. French maybe, I thought. She had me confused and my accent had her confused as the two of us struggled to make each other understood.

"Mr Roscoe, he is out, sorry. Your number please." I could imagine a dainty little person answering to Mr Roscoe's needs in some stone and moss covered mansion out in South Croydon. From the little I had seen of London I knew I would be back and next time with my wife. Keeping her away from this lovely town was a crime for which, unlike Rabuka, I was not likely to be pardoned.

I had nothing else to do on a Sunday night, so I turned on the TV and watched the Seoul Olympics flash onto the screen. The announcer was outlining high points in the career of Canadian sprinter Ben Johnson in the lead up to what promised to be the track highlight for the games, the clash between rivals American Carl Lewis and Canadian world record holder Johnson in the 100 metres.

The jostle of the champions I thought. This would be a race to remember. Johnson, a Canadian transplant from Jamaica, had beaten Lewis in Rome at the World Champs and held the world record. Lewis was determined to repeat his four gold medal effort at the 1984 Olympics and take the record back. It was a race I could follow with a sense of pride. Even though I had just applied for New

Zealand citizenship, I would always have one big toe in Vancouver, British Columbia.

Sitting on the single hotel bed my stomach began churning and my mind racing as I struggled to analyse my position. The Republic of Fiji was trying to extradite Kahan for arms smuggling. Rabuka had taken over the Queen's parliament with a group of Fijian army soldiers and one other, fairly new to the parliamentary hit squad. This one other person was said to have worn a blackened face on the day of the first coup. The situation did not seem fair. One thing I felt reasonably able to assess was fairness. Somehow, this whole Fiji thing had a bad smell about it that just would not go away.

A Stitch In Time

Before I left New Zealand for London I had sent Robert Roscoe's legal clerk, Miss Carolyn Wood, a facsimile asking her to arrange a meeting with the British Home Office. I knew that the Home Secretary, Douglas Herd, had to first sign a certificate authorising the Fijian government to proceed with Kahan's extradition, if the court case was to go past September 30.

I am a firm believer in nipping things in the bud. Throughout my career as a lawyer I have had many criminal charges against my clients dismissed simply by dealing to the police case at the very first available moment. Strike before the concrete sets had been the practice: who dares to challenge, my successful motto.

My first criminal case as a barrister was for a young lady charged with importing heroin. Customs officials at Auckland International Airport found a straw of heroin and a match box of opium in her suitcase. Customs asked if the drugs were hers and she replied "Yes" to both.

The next day her parents approached me in the District Court building. "Excuse me sir, my daughter has been arrested on a drug charge and we wish to get her out of jail. Can you help us?"

I agreed to try.

Successful on the bail, the parents asked me "How much would you require to look after our daughter?" I thought for a moment then said, "Five thousand dollars, all up." I waited for the response.

194

"That will be fine," said the father, "I'll arrange for that in the morning."

The next day I interviewed the young woman and quickly established that although she had been involved with drugs in Singapore, she did not knowingly import them into New Zealand.

After a fight with her boyfriend, who worked on the oil rigs off Singapore, she had decided to go straight home, making a plane reservation for later the same morning. She dumped her clothes drawer into her suitcase, at the same time unwittingly dumping her boyfriends drugs into her suitcase.

Before anybody can be convicted of an offence, it must be established that they had a guilty mind. This mental element is called the *mens rea*, the physical act is the *actus rea*. For example, if you rolled over in bed at night and knocked your wife on the nose, you would have physically assaulted her but you would not be guilty of the offence of assault because you did not have the required state of mind. You did not have the necessary intent. This was my clients defence.

I hired a private detective in Singapore and obtained statements from the boyfriend, the taxi driver and the airline reservation people. All the evidence pointed to the fact that my client had left in a hurry and may well not have known she had the drugs.

The case book was typed up. All the affidavits were enclosed. Why wait for trial? My case was strong, I had nothing to hide. I marched up to the Drug Squad at Auckland Central Police station and laid my cards on the table.

The next morning I appeared in the District Court. The second in charge of the drug squad, Detective Sergeant Wally Hayes, sat in the first row. "I commend you on your admissions, Mr Harder," he said. A warmth began to grow in my chest, I felt I had found my calling.

My client stood in the box as the police prosecutor Roger (pink carnations) Stevens told the judge that the police wished to offer no evidence against my client. She was free to go. My client and her parents were ecstatic and I was $5000 better off for two minutes spent in court and some hard work gathering evidence.

However, if the evidence was running against a client, I found that time was a great healer and often the deciding factor in whether a person ultimately had to go to jail or not. This latter proposition normally excludes violence, sexual assault and hard drugs cases.

It was Sunday night in London and my jet lag had won round one. As soon as my head hit the pillow I was asleep. Some time later I awoke half dreaming of Fiji and wondering what was happening with some of the other players in the guns affair case.

No matter how many times I had tried, I could not get a hold of Anand Singh, my ex-instructing solicitor for the guns case in Lautoka. Both his phones had been disconnected. Neither was Subash Parshotam, secretary of the Fiji Law Society, contactable. I did not know if these brave souls were still working in Fiji, in jail or worse. The Fiji security forces had pulled a tight shroud around Fiji protecting it from prying journalists and worse, from New Zealand lawyers.

Bow Street, London: Monday September 26

Number 8 Bow Street is directly across the road from the Magistrates court where Kahan was to appear later in the week. The court is an old sandstone building. Attached to it is a police station, handy for processing people through the system.

I walked up the rickety stairs to the office of Victor Lissack & Roscoe, solicitors."Hello," said a female voice, as I walked into the waiting room. I could see an attractive English lass getting up from her typewriter.

"Christopher Harder to see Mr. Roscoe," I said and she welcomed me explaining that Mr Roscoe would only be a moment.

Robert Roscoe is about six feet tall, 35-ish with fair, thin hair, a reasonably handsome chap who, as a solicitor, appears in the magistrates court with regularity.

I introduced myself to Roscoe with a firm and cheerful, "How do you do." His office looked over Bow Street and the tree lined lane by the court. In the streets I could see a large contingent of press gathered outside the main entrance. The mob were waiting for the accused in the Guiness insider trading case, currently appearing in the Number One court. Typical Fleet Street journalism, I thought.

Roscoe's law clerk Carolyn Wood walked into the room. We had previously spoken on the phone. Carolyn was a pretty looking young woman with a special sparkle in her eyes, wearing white stockings, black loafers and green dress with a page boy style hair cut. She appeared to be an eager student keen to specialise in criminal law. I would be able to rely on her I thought to myself.

"This is the young lady who is doing most of the work with Kahan at the moment," said Roscoe. "Carolyn will arrange a meeting with the Home Office if that is what you want. Then the two of you can take the tube out to Brixton Prison."

It was Carolyn who was talking to Kahan. It was from her that I received my most important piece of evidence pointing towards one of the persons who had an interest in the guns that had been imported into Fiji, and a motive for wanting to keep Kahan quiet. A time bomb was slowly ticking away in Fiji, the fuse being lit in London, I thought. It was only a question of time.

Roscoe suggested we all go out for a coffee and sandwich. The three of us walked up the lane to the Golden Arms pub on the corner. This little hideaway buried in the basement, perhaps once a dungeon, was a quaint place to sit and chat.

Carolyn told me that she had spoken to the Home Office and the indication had been that permission would be given to the 'Republic of Fiji' to commence extradition proceedings against Kahan.

"I would like to see the Home Office people before that decision is put to pen and paper," I said. I was trying to be careful in what requests I made. I did not want to be seen as pushing into someone else's territory but I had to see the Home Office staff and that was that. Again I was following my established practice. If a decision had to be changed or influenced, then it was critical that I go straight to the top and talk with the decision maker. Douglas Herd was that man. I would try, I thought to myself, I would try.

Also I am a firm believer of never giving up without a struggle and sometimes refusing to accept the pessimistic word "no". I remember doing a big drug case in New Zealand for Peter Fulcher, a close associate of Terry Clark of Mr Asia drugs fame. Fulcher had been charged with all manner of heroin importing charges in New Zealand. It had been alleged that Fulcher was Clark's right hand

197

man. Clark had previously been convicted of conspiracy to import drugs into Great Britain and of murder involving the handless body of New Zealander Christopher Johnson, whose body was found weighted down in a water-filled disused quarry by divers. Clark was tried, convicted and jailed till he died a sudden death in 1984.

Fulcher needed to score every possible point in his trial or he was likely to die in prison like his mate Clark. In that case I was assisted by my good barrister friend Aaron Perkins, now the assistant Crown Prosecutor. Nine times during the trial Perkins and I retired to Mr Justice Tompkins' chambers to argue points of law with New Zealand's top Crown Prosecutor, David Morris.

On no less than eight occasions I had sought a particular ruling on the evidence only to be turned back by the eloquent submissions of the prosecutor. Perkins and I, aided by submissions from my researcher, persisted to argue the point.

Each time we went into chambers I knew it would be a battle. And each time when we walked out of the judge's room the two of us were grinning because every time the judge had reversed his decision after persistent argument. It prompted the court registrar, Phillip Milwood to ask me for a copy of my Canadian dictionary. Having turned eight NO'S by the judge into eight YES'S, he now wanted to see where in the dictionary 'NO' was defined as 'YES'. Whether I could get the Home Secretary to turn yes into no was now the question.

After coffee I thanked Roscoe and Woods for their time and company, deciding to return to the hotel to shake off some of my jet lag. Bow Street runs off the Strand down beside Covent Gardens, which is a conglomerate of old English buildings housing barristers, surveyors and the like. It is a quiet, serene atmosphere to work from in the middle of a big city. Three taxis came down the road. I waved in the hope of flagging one down. None stopped.

Another taxi came round the corner. Up shot my arm as I yelled out "Are you for hire?" The driver motioned affirmatively as I took a puff on my cigarette.

I had been smoking on and off since my release from Rabuka's jail cell last June. But I am sensitive to others' feelings about smoking. I remembered back to before that time when smokers would force their vile, filthy habit thoughtlessly upon me. As I approached the cab door I saw a big sign saying 'No Smoking.' Not wanting to offend the drive, I changed my mind and said no thank you, without explaining.

The cabbie slammed the door, pushed the shift lever forward and engaged his clutch. A loud crunch and a clank indicated he was having trouble changing gear, no doubt brought about by my frustrating actions of declining a ride in the first place.

Still not wanting to walk to the hotel I looked around for another cab in which I could have a cigarette. In a couple of minutes a black car came around the same corner. I stepped out into the middle of the road and waved him down.

To my horror it was the same driver. He must have thought I was crazy. He began to yell and swear, warming up the air around us with all manner of obscenities.

I turned away, my tail between my legs, lost for words when for the second time this Pommie taxi driver crunched his gears and tore off up the road.

A New Tradition: Bomb Alters

Now too scared to flag another cab for fear of causing someone to have a heart attack, I walked back along the Strand towards the hotel. As I came closer I could see fire trucks parked in front of the building. People were walking up to the fire officer and asking, "Is it a bomb?"

In London the chances of having a bomb go off in your hotel are probably about the same as having one explode in a barrister's Mercedes car or on the Rainbow Warrior in Auckland harbour. Different countries, different places but still the same old thing; violence is everywhere.

"No bomb," said the fire warden, " Someone reported smoke in the underground."

The recent deadly fire at the King's Cross Station with the loss of many lives has made people sensitive to tube fires. Nobody, but nobody was supposed to smoke on the subway. I recalled a story I had read in London's *Daily Mail* the day before. A cocky youth under the influence of something had dared to light up a cigarette

199

in one of the tube cars. A middle-aged lady had asked this lager lout to put out his cigarette without any success. Instead the yob lit up another cigarette and stuck it in his mouth. Two at once, now that was cheeky. When he lit a third and began to puff, a little old woman, with one quick action picked up a fire extinguisher and begun spraying the delinquent from head to toe. Everybody cheered. Some broke out in laughter as the youth had to be restrained. Point made, this perky little lady quickly stepped out of her car at Notting Hill Gate and disappeared into the crowd.

Back in my hotel room I phoned Philippa. It was noon in London, but midnight the day before in Auckland.

"Hello, just checking in. How are you?" I said, missing her like hell and wishing she was here.

"You were talked about on TV last night," she said, "on that mastermind show, *Krypton Factor*. The question was 'who was the lawyer who was arrested in Fiji?'"

"Oh ya," I said, my Canadian accent popping out. "Did they get it right?" Her reply, yes, brought a smile to my face.

I wanted to come back to London. It really is a lovely place, particularly if you have lots of money. I guess that's why Philippa was not here. This whole Fiji Affair of mine was getting to be awfully expensive.

"I'll bring you to London next time." I promised. "Sleep tight."

I hung up the phone and climbed into bed but before putting the light out wrote a note to remind myself in the morning: "CALL BUCKINGHAM PALACE." I wanted to talk to the Queen's secretary, Robert Fellowes about Rabuka's OBE.

I had first written to the Queen about a month after I got out of jail in Fiji last June asking her to deal to Rabuka, suggesting she be fair and consistent in line with other cases where prominent persons had brought disgrace to the Royal Honours List. Sir Albert Henry had been stripped of his Knighthood when he was convicted of vote-buying in the Cook Islands some years ago. Lestor Piggot, loved and respected by British racing fans was similarly stripped of his OBE when convicted of income tax evasion involving several million dollars.

Would Her Majesty consider stripping Rabuka of his award on

the grounds that he was no longer a fit and proper person to hold such an honour? Rabuka had twice committed treason against the Queen. I bet that if a letter was written to the Fleet Street press, some of the recipients of other awards might express their discomfort at being on the Royal rolls with a traitor. If the Queen did not act on Rabuka she could be seen to be siding with the indigenous Fijians. I was sure she did not want to be seen siding with a traitor.

On August 16, 1988, a letter had arrived at my new office from Balmoral Castle. I was sitting at my desk with the fire blazing away when my Fiji Indian secretary Ameta handed it to me.

Dear Mr Harder

The Queen has commanded me to thank you for your letter of 22 July

Her majesty would not normally consider the forfeiture of one of her honours, unless she first received the advice, in this sense, from her Representative or Ministers in the State concerned. Fiji has, as you know, been declared a Republic. It follows that any initiative in matters concerning British honours in Fiji would be made by the Queen on the advice of her British Ministers.

Yours sincerely
ROBERT FELLOWES

I had thought that if the Queen wanted to take away Rabuka's OBE all she had to do was pick up the phone. I wrote a letter back to Buckingham Palace, addressed to the Queen, seizing on the words her secretary included in his letter of 16th August, "would not normally consider forfeiture." I thought the words plainly acknowledged that the Queen had a residual power to act on her own bat, so I pointed out that Rabuka's actions were anything but normal.

As a fallback on September 14 I also wrote to British Prime Minister Margaret Thatcher at Number 10, Downing Street. I told her that Sitiveni Ligamamada Rabuka OBE, should be struck from the rolls. How could a Prime Minister of a western country ignore a royal traitor who had also publicly declared his intention to convert 300,000 Indians to Christianity? One thing was for certain, telling a Muslim Indian you were going to make him a Christian against his will was a sure fire recipe for dissent. Such threats were guaranteed to provoke some Muslim to take up arms against such a religious zealot.

Rabuka's views on "God talks to me", were given much publicity in New Zealand. He had announced his religious edict to the world on Radio New Zealand back in July. The New Zealand churches, to their own disgrace, remained silent. They let this religious freak get away with talking religious genocide.

When I had decided to go to London to help Kahan fight extradition I had not yet received a reply from Balmoral Castle. I remember coming home from the new marble and glass Auckland District Courts building, which could double as a set for the *LA Law* television show, two days before I was to fly out to London. "No mail from London," said my secretary as I walked into my office.

"Ameta, send the Queen and Thatcher a copy of my affidavit about what I saw in Fiji when I was arrested. Maybe that will prick their consciences into some kind of action."

I had always thought of the Queen as fearless, like the imagery of the Royal Lion. "Courier it. I want the papers in London before I get there, please."

Birthday Blues At 40

Tuesday morning I woke early to the sound of jackhammers in London and a birthday telegram from my son Joshua and daughter Kate. What a bitch, I had to celebrate my fortieth birthday on my own. They say life begins at 40. I was hoping a Fijian did not end mine before I was 41.

Eager to get going but having three hours to kill before the 9.30 opening hour of most London business, I decided to go for a run in St James Park off the Mall leading up to Buckingham Palace. This might be the closest I got to Palace.

Robert Fellowes had not left a message as I had asked in my couriered letter. Not very good public relations I thought. Give him one more day. If he doesn't call I'll release the letter I sent to the Queen to the press. There was more than one way of skinning a cat. Rabuka's turn would come. Like most novelty items he had a limited shelf life. He would go with or without the help of the Queen.

I put on my blue Fiji military forces teeshirt, hooked up my trusty Walkman and my new Richard Clayderman tape, *Romantic America*. Down the Strand through Trafalgar Square I ran slowing for the traffic. As I passed under Admiralty Arch, heading for the Birdcage walkway along the south side of the lake in St.James Park, and as I ran towards the south wall of Buckingham Palace, I wondered if Robert Fellowes had made any inquiries in New Zealand about this chap Christopher Harder who kept sending him letters for the Queen about Rabuka and Fiji.

I ran along the side of the water listening to the music and watching the ducks and swans float along beside me. It was a most enjoyable jog. I savoured the excitement of the moment, wondering what was around the corner in this real world drama. What would the future hold, I wondered. I knew that I had to make my break sometime. Now seemed to be the moment. I had always wanted to write a book but I'd never quite had the justification. Now, with Fiji and detention, it was my chance.

The park walkway behind me was bare of followers as I looked back over my shoulders. While in London I did not intend to run down any dark streets by myself. I was alert to my surroundings. The last thing my wife said before I left was watch out for the Israelis. We had discussed some new information I had received from Fiji just the day before I left, confirming Israeli involvement with Rabuka. Some sort of trade off for good will in Lebanon where Fiji has more than 1000 troops standing guard as United Nations observers. Some people have asked me lately if I thought the CIA might also have been involved; in answer to that obvious question, I just smile.

When I first secured my room on Sunday I had stepped out for a brief stroll ending up at Nelson's Column in Trafalgar Square. I was walking around behind the stone lions when from out of nowhere jumped two young women. I got quite a fright from the suddenness of the incident.

"Will you take our picture against the lion?" asked one of these pretty tourists. "Just push this button, okay?"

I stood back trying to get both the girls in the frame. "Where are you girls from?" I asked, trying to guess the accent.

"Israel," said the blond-haired one.

"And you, where are you from?" she quickly followed up.

"Canadian," I said. " From Canada."

For some reason I felt like hiding from the two. Not normally one to shy away from talking to pretty ladies, commonsense told me to get back to the hotel.

"Are you a tourist on holiday?" asked the brown-haired beauty with big brown eyes and olive skin. "Which hotel are you staying at in London?" went the questioning. Paranoid or cautious, I am not sure which, I mumbled something about the Savoy and turned and walked away making sure I had no followers.

The clock on the television news said 9.35. It was an early morning breakfast show such as we don't see in New Zealand. Britain has a lot more world news than New Zealand. The American coverage was absolutely mind boggling, full American news on all manner of topics was shown on TV. The rest was taken up with IRA bombings, killings, trials, and security measures.

There was no doubt in my mind that the IRA situation weighed against Kahan. The Home Office would not want to be accused of being soft on terrorism by refusing the preliminary certificate allowing the Fijian authorities to at least proceed to step one of the extradition procedure. Guns and extraditions were always a problem for Maggie Thatcher and her government.

They were continuously seeking to extradite alleged terrorists from around the world back to Britain for trial. She would not want to be seen as being soft on a suspected gun runner found hiding in her patch.

At 9.30 a.m. I picked up the phone and dialled nine, three, zero, four, eight, three, two and waited.

"Buckingham Palace, can I help you?" said the pleasant voice on the other end of the line. No waiting here I thought.

"Could I speak to Mr Fellowes, please?"

"Just a moment, what is your name?"

"Christopher Harder," I said. I always hated giving my name on the phone. Nobody could ever understand my pronunciation.

When I was a young boy I had a decidedly noticeable lisp. It took many elocution lessons learning to recite "the big brown cow jumped over the moon," and many other enriching phrases before I mastered my speech impediment.

"I am sorry Mr Harder, Mr Fellowes is very busy at the moment. Can he call you back please?"

"Most certainly," I said. "Ask him to call me at the Charing Cross Hotel before ten o'clock or after five thirty please."

I knew I would be late coming back from Brixton Prison after interviewing Kahan. The prison visit was set to last from one thirty to four in the afternoon. By the time I walked to the bus, transfered to the tube, with changes at Victoria and Stockwell stations, it would be well after five before I got back to the hotel.

Inside Brixton

Miss Woods and I arrived at Brixton Prison just before one thirty. I thought of rough and tumble New Zealand Queen's Counsel Michael Bungay who had lived in Brixton as a young boy.

We opened the door marked 'Solicitors Entrance' and climbed up 22 steps to another locked door. 'Push the buzzer once' said the sign by the bell. In quick response to the bell the door opened and a female prison guard invited us into the security room. Like going through airport security at Gatwick International Airport, we emptied all metal objects from our pockets and one by one walked through an upright metal detector. Both of us having cleared security, we were asked to open our briefcases so that staff might examine the contents: papers, two tape recorders and some Consulate cigarettes for the interviewee.

"Please sign the register here," the guard pointed towards the guest register. "Each sign twice," he said.

"Why twice?" I asked.

"One for getting in, and one for going out," the guard explained.

"You mean I could disappear in here and the records would show that I had left?"

"Yes, it saves you from having to come back upstairs."

We followed the friendly well dressed officer through several stark rooms and out into the internal court yard of the prison; old brick everywhere. A tall brick chimney stretching to the sky was obviously the incinerator. A bull pen for holding prisoners while staff sorted them out was next to us as we walked towards the category 'A' visitors block. All of the prisoners in the pen were black, except for one blond youth who looked very out of place.

"Heh, maan," called out a Jamaican with braided dreadlocks, "Caan I bludge a smoke?" I was tempted to help this man, trapped inside this hideous place but I knew better.

"This way, sir," said the guard opening a door which lead the two of us into a corridor 300 feet long if it was an inch.

The excitement of getting this far was nerve-racking. "Have you got a toilet I could use before I see Kahan?" I asked.

"Just a moment, sir. Yes, come this way." When I came back into the interview room a handsome Indian, standing about five foot nine inches and dressed in blue prison denim, stood to shake my hand. A smile broke on his face as I introduced myself. He sat down at the little table. The room was smaller than my Fiji jail cell by a hand each way. The table was about two foot wide by three foot long. Layers of paint covered the stone walls.

"Have a jube or a cigarette."

"I don't smoke," he said.

"Neither did I for six years until Rabuka arrested me," I replied lighting up a menthol.

"Good of you to come," said Kahan. "You have come halfway around the world just to see me."

I told him I also hoped to see the Home Secretary to reinforce the contents of my affidavit in person. "I am writing a book on my recent experience in jail in Fiji. I would like to do your story at the same time." I showed Kahan a promotional copy of THE GUNS OF LAUTOKA. He was impressed by the cover. The back sleeve mentioned 'Mohammed Kahan, suspected of master-minding the arms shipment to Fiji, now in custody in London opposing extradition by Rabuka's military forces.'

"Do you mind if I record what we say?" I asked Kahan." That way neither of us makes a mistake." The conversation roamed all over the world and back to Brixton as we tried to get the measure of each

206

other. Carolyn sat silently beside me as I slowly probed this mysterious man.

Fiji-born Kahan was 46. His father died and his mother remarried a carpenter who took over as a step-father to Mohammed at a young age. One side of his family was in commerce, the other was in the transport business, both in Fiji.

A Muslim, Kahan practised his religion when time allowed. His ties to the Mosque were firm. He would always have a friend in the Holyman. "It's not really easy, if you're not born with a silver spoon in your mouth," he explained. "You just have to go and battle it out and during my battling with the system, sometimes I thought I knew too much. I suffered for it."

Kahan acknowledged there had been some good opportunities to make something of his life, but he hadn't taken them when they arose.

Violence did not feature in Kahan's background; it was not his way of life. "We were brought up not to fight. We were brought up to be passive, chained to the ground growing and harvesting the cane."

"What about the guns?" I asked. "Where were you when you were first going to try and get some guns?" I finally raised the topic I had come to talk about.

"It was not that I decided we would get guns. The committee was set up very, very early," he said, "a group of individuals, international individuals. They were in Canada, America, Hawaii, Fiji, Australia and the UK and the group gradually got bigger. The initial group was only about five."

At first the group talked of civil disobedience but it was difficult to get the Indians to participate. Fear of the native Fijians and a need to make some money just to keep a subsistence level of living were the two big problems. The money factor had been the main difficulty; nobody could afford not to harvest.

"We were dealing with two Indians in the beginning, Mahendra Patel of Motibhai and Company and Hari Punja of Punja and Sons. Motibhai is a money-hungry man. He and Lady Mara are both partners in a Nadi duty free store. Motibhai has managed to get

207

concessions out of the government to form deals which were maybe not quite *kosher.*"

Kahan went on to describe how Motibhai, often known as MacPatel, was a great mate of Fiji Prime Minister Ratu Sir Kamasese Mara, and how he had leaked the tip about the coup two days before it happened.

Knock, knock at the door. "Five minutes, okay!" said the guard.

"I hope to see someone from the Home Office on Thursday morning about my experience in a Fiji jail. Maybe it will influence the decision on the preliminary extradition warrant," I said "But it looks like the Minister has already made up his mind on this one. By my calculations the full appeal process up to the House of Lords could take 18 months, so you won't be going anywhere for a while my friend." We shook hands.

He gave a firm shake but I could see Kahan was putting on a brave face. His hand lingered in mine. Mohammed Kahan was genuinely scared for his life if he went back to Fiji. He didn't need to be told what would happen if the security forces got their hands on him back in Suva. Unless Rabuka retired from the army and returned to his village and the security forces disbanded, Kahan would never be safe in Fiji.

"Tonight write out your story in your own hand so that I can read it at my leisure, please," I said as we walked out of the interview room and down the hall to the prison exit. Throughout the time we were with Kahan three guards stood outside the security glass looking in.

The trip back to the Charing Cross hotel took 50 minutes. Sitting on my bed with my shoes off I put on the Olympics special programme to hear the announcer say, "Ben Johnson, fastest man alive and champion of Canada, is to be stripped of his gold medal."

They said tests had shown he used banned steriods. I was shattered. I had always been proud to be a Canadian. For the first time in my life that had changed. I hoped the test was wrong. Maybe it was all a great big mistake. On Tuesday night I did not sleep well.

Charing Cross: Wednesday Morning

Why does the phone always go when you are in the bathroom? The Regent in Auckland caters for such laws of nature with telephones in the bathroom. The Charing Cross hotel was not so sophisticated.

"Hello, Mr Harder, my name is Julie Fitzgerald from NZPA London. Can I speak to you a moment about the Kahan extradition case?"

NZPA London is the New Zealand Press Association. For a moment I was suspicious. Earlier in the year I had played a practical joke on my good friend Auckland deputy crown prosecutor, Aaron Perkins, who had gone for a two week holiday in London. A small article was concocted and made to appear it had been published under the heading "KIWI HERO" in the London *Daily Mail*, attributed to the NZPA.

This phone call from the real NZPA news-hound in London had me a little concerned at first. But Julie only wanted to know if there was anything to report on the Kahan front.

"There is not too much I can tell you at the moment. I am here in London at the request of Kahan's lawyer to see if I can add my weight to my affidavit about his chances of receiving a fair trial in Fiji if he gets sent back by Great Britain."

I told her I'd be seeing Kahan later that day at Brixton. I gave her the number of Alun Jones, the barrister and told her where to contact Robert Roscoe the solicitor; number 8 Bow Street, just across the road from the court.

I told her Miss Woods from the solicitor's office and I would be seeing the Home Office tomorrow about Kahan. Off the record I thought he would give the O.K for Fiji to at least start proceedings. The Home Office would not want to be seen to be soft on gun smuggling in light of all Thatcher's condemnation of terrorism. Only the week before the Prime Minister was quoted saying 'We shall never surrender to terrorism, it would be the death of democracy.' A pretty good catch-phrase but she had not applied the same principle to the terrorism of Rabuka and his gun toters who destroyed an 18 year run of democracy in the former Commonwealth country of Fiji.

"That is about the extent of things at the moment. See you for a coffee on Friday and I might have something to add."

"That would be nice," Julie replied, and hung up. I sat on my bed for a moment, smoking a cigarette, rehooked on nicotine. It must have been all the nervous energy and the excitement of the whole scene. A fight was going on. It would turn into a battle, but not with guns. From other battles in my life I knew the campaign would be based on that old cliche: the pen is mightier than the sword. I would reply to my arrest and Rabuka's rampage with a book.

Exposure was what Ratu Mara and Rabuka needed. Take away their Knighthoods and OBEs. Shame them. Both could have rehabilitated the political situation in Fiji and both refused. One was a thug, the other a commercial bandit. If the rumours are true, Mara has amassed significant wealth in different parts of the world on the moderate salary of a Fijian Prime Minister. The military is now inquiring into the use of the Hurricane Rehabilitation Relief Fund an agency set up under the Mara government. In another question-raising incident Kamisese Mara met and received a lieutenant of Adnan Kushoggi, Guru Chandra Swami, not long before the 1987 election in which his government was defeated. Chandra Swami arrived with 14 people on arms dealer Kashoggi's private jet. Kushoggi is now wanted by a New York grand jury for allegedly helping Ferdinand Marcos carry out transactions involving millions of dollars stolen from the Manila treasury.

A blue piece of paper lay on my bedside table. I picked it up and examined the dates. Carolyn Woods had copied them from the Brixton Prison visitors' books herself. Three times since Kahan's arrest, the Republic of Fiji's Ambassador Brigadier Ratu Epeli Nailatikau, Ratu Mara's son-in-law, had gone all the way out to Brixton to visit a one time con man, now a remand prisoner. Why? Why, indeed, I mused. It was one question I would not forget to ask Kahan.

Brigadier Nailatikau was head of the Royal Fiji Military Forces during the first coup, but was conveniently out of the country at the time. Ratu Epeli is not only Ratu Mara's son-in-law but also has chiefly connections with most high ranking officials in the Fiji government. In between diplomatic stints with the Fiji High

Commission in London and the United Nations in New York he has spent the last 10 years in Fiji's armed forces.

Just how close Ratu Epeli is now to the seat of power in Fiji is hard to evaluate. Since the first coup, when he was apparently out-ranked by a junior officer — the then Colonel Sitiveni Rabuka — he has kept a low profile while maintaining his standing in the Fijian nobility. Besides, the diplomatic privileges and the social connections that accompany an Ambassadorship in London could make life very interesting.

Representing a former Commonwealth member in London soon after that country had been made a Republic as the consequence of an armed overthrow of a democratically government was surely a confusing prospect.

However, looking at the situation from the viewpoint of the military commander whose very own troops had been used to stage the coups, was an odd perspective; even the most imaginative minds would find this difficult to reconcile.

Had he been given a job to get him out of the way, or because it was a payoff, a perk, to have all the privileges in London? How much absolute power did his father-in-law Ratu Mara still wield and therefore, how close was he to the big chief? There is definitely some feeling that Mara and Nailatikau don't agree on all subjects. How closely was he working among the old boy network of military contacts?

Fijian soldiers had long since found their way into the ranks and beyond of the military world, particularly the British forces.

When in 1963 Britain did away with conscription, 200 fit young Fijian men, prime troops if ever there was such a species, were signed up to help fill the gap in recruiting. Many of them stayed on for more than 20 years and nearly as many served in specialist units such as bomb disposal, Special Air Services and other anti-terrorist roles. Many of them served in Northern Ireland.

During this period Nailatikau had risen to lead Fiji's military forces. Under his command Fiji had been a faithful member of the Commonwealth clan. Certainly he would have strong contacts in the upper end of the military spectrum in this and other parts of the world and maybe this was why he had the top job in London. Then again, he had expressed some support for Dr Bavadra's Coalition Party. Yes, I'd definitely be asking Kahan about his visitor.

"Carolyn! I'll meet you at the front of the hotel in 15 minutes." London telephones are efficient but getting a number from a phone book was difficult; to cover the Greater London area there are four hefty phone books. My budget hotel did not run to copies in the rooms.

Automatic wakeup for me is between five thirty and six in the morning. I had already drunk three cups of coffee; cranked up for the day with a heavy fix of caffeine while I watched the replay of Ben Johnson and his world record run. The British commentators never stopped running Johnson into the ground, calling him a cheat of the first order. I thought Johnson should be banned for two years, then be given an opportunity to rehabilitate, under Olympic rules there was plenty of precedent.

The president of Fiji had pardoned Rabuka; an act Christian in spirit but not valid in Fiji law. For a pardon to be effective in law a person must first be charged and convicted. Major-General Sitiveni Rabuka, OBE had not, to my knowledge, been either charged or convicted. Seventeen months ago he had been a lowly lieutenant-colonel.

I wondered if a new government would try Rabuka or just send him back to his village with his great big pension, justified by his meteoric rise through the ranks; it was said he had failed three attempts at the basic New Zealand School Certificate examination.

The hotel maid had left me with only three foil containers of milk for my morning coffee. Where could I get some more? Recently I had been part of a practical joke, an account of which appeared in the *Auckland Star*.

"Counsel Would Not Be Cowed"

The cream of the criminal bar have sprung a surprise on Crown lawyers at the High Court in Auckland — of a dairy variety.

No fewer than 100 bottles of milk were delivered to those gentlemen the other morning, complete with labels reading: "Roy the Boy Big (Udder) Dairy (Sharemilkers) Company — Official supplier to the New Zealand Criminal Bar."

Word had got around the court that a defense lawyer's request for a bottle of milk from the Crown Prosecutor's fridge had been turned down. There wasn't enough to go around, the counsel had been told, so he arranged the early morning delivery which left the crown room fairly flooded with milk.

A press release anonymously claimed the donation was the first production run of Prosecutor Roy Ladd's new milk company.

"Colleagues said Mr Ladd was as surprised (and dismayed) as they were. They are advising defense lawyers to pull the udder one."

Back In Brixton

"Good morning Mr Kahan," I said as the guard showed him into the room. I turned on the outside fan so that I did not smoke the place out. Unlike my cell in Fiji this room had no window. Nor did it have any drain holes big enough for rats.

On August 17 Mesake Koroi, the *Fiji Times* chief reporter, who had gone to Rotuma with Tevita Fa and I, had been taken in by the security forces. Throughout the difficult times since the first coup Mesake had done his utmost to present as much information as he could without stepping over the fine line which would trigger the regime to march in and shut down his newspaper.

But even this affable Fijian had eventually fallen foul of the military system, despite his impeccable contacts within it.

Mesake replied to his 46 hour detention in a tiny Suva police station cell by publishing a story about how he had befriended a huge rate that had climbed in through the drainhole.

He ended his story saying that the difference between himself and the rat was that the rat was free and he was not, it could come and go through the drainhole.

His very last words perhaps had a double meaning.

I would appeal to future occupants of the cell at Suva Central Police Station to keep a look out for my friend . . . Mr King Rat.

At least in this part of Brixton prison Kahan did not seem to be worried by any rats.

"Here is my story Mr Harder. It is the story behind my being in this place today."

I took the three pieces of paper and turned them over. Five sides, single spaced. It would take me a little time to read. I turned off the tape, sat back in the chair stretching my feet out and absentmindedly lit another cigarette.

Had I consciously thought about my smoking I would have been ashamed. But I was engrossed in Kahan's statement. It was the statement of his defense.

"Mara's initial deal with Colonel Rabuka was that Rabuka hand back power within 30 days from the bloodless coup to [a] Mara controlled interim civilian Government, and that Rabuka return to the barrack(sic). Governor General in place take executive power and bless as Mara's interim Government in the interest of peace in Fiji.

But when Rabuka played the "Rambo" and carried out the coup with the blessing from Mara and assurance and help from overseas connection (US and Israel), he started to enjoy the fame and feel of real power, and started to back track on his original deal to return to barrack with 30 days. Instead he demanded active participation in any new Government and to reserve the right to veto any of Mara's policy or decision. Monetary assistance to Rabuka soften him a little but he was not going to give up power that easily.

Rabuka's association with "Radical Taukei" and "Terror Squad" increased. He stated to some inner circle that he could not believe how easy it was to take control of Fiji Government and have real power. Rabuka's nagging fear was that since he was used for others gain, and if his usefulness might fade away when the job was done, he could be dispensed of if he gave up real power. With this fear he could solidate (sic) his power base and influence. Rabuka's trump card was "Ratu Penaia" and his faithful chief. He knew Ratu Mara could not do too much to hurt him. After all, it was his chief Ratu Penaia who in his capacity as G.G (Governor General) pardoned Rabuka for "treasons."

Mara started suspecting Ratu Penaia when Ratu Penaia started siding with Colonel Rabuka during their many inner circle meetings. This caused Mara pain and distrust. But Mara also knew that both Rabuka and Penaia need him for his experience in any new interim Government and his overseas connection. But the question that worried Mara was that the longer Colonel Rabuka stays in effective control of power and learns from Mara, Ratu Mara will become dispensable. And it would be harder for Mara to get rid of Rabuka or even control him with his crazy ideas.

All these fears and frustrations were revealed to a few selected Indo-Fijian friends and business people, who in turn started to worry. Their fears and loose talk filtered down to our "listening posts" and our intelligence gathering unit. We heard that

Mara was a very worried man. He did not want to ask his overseas connection to set up any contingency plan to deal with these fears "if" and "when" the need arises.

Our executive group decided to capitalize on this fact and put out feelers and floated an insurance policy plan for Mara — 'If Rabuka try to ditch you, Indians and certain Fijians will take up arms for you, and we have access if need arises.' To this Mara was very touched and emotional. He admitted to selected source that things went wrong and he was losing control, and could lose total control.

Mara wanted the "Deuba Accord" as a compromise but Rabuka and Penaia put too much pressure on Mara with difficult and impossible demands which they knew that Dr Bavadra could not possibly agree to or sell out his supporters.

Here we see Mara did not want to die with a label of traitor, dictator or cheater. He wanted to stay in power and keep the Indians in Fiji to help Fiji because he knew that without Indian business know-how and Indian farmers, Fiji will become like Uganda — bankrupt. Also, he knew that it would take 15 — 20 years for Fijians to learn to effectively run a country.

To our feelers, Mara really surprised us. He signalled that he can help divide the Army to weaken Rabuka but he needed Indian assistance to obtain arms for this divided Army. We signalled back — "divide the Army and we will help". When we are satisfied we will show you the arms to prove our faithfulness to him.

Ratu Mara's man was Colonel Budromo, ex-commissioner of prison service, permanent secretary of Home Office under Mara, and Colonel of R.F.M.F. It was this man who helped us to really infiltrate Rabuka's army and establish a solid cell group. Before this, we had limited infiltration.

Before Colonel Budromo's connection we managed to infiltrate the army through our connection with "FURPOP" — Fiji's United Revolution for Poor and Oppressed People, an underground movement but very secretive with network on both larger islands [Viti and Vanua Levu.] This organisation was set up in 1979 after the mini-coup of 1977 when N.E.P. won the election. The aims of this organisation were to help the poor and oppressed people of all races in Fiji if the military coup of Alliance Government was floated in 1977 and formulated as contingency plan in the event of the alliance lose another election.

Our mole in Alliance party inner circle was Mahendra Patel of Motibhais. This man knew of the coup but he did not tell Dr Bavadra because he did not like some of the people in the NFP — Labour Coalition Government.

Anyway, since Mara showed his good faith to help divide the Army, we had to show that we can get arms for the divided Army. That is why some of the Arms were stored at Saha Deo's place to show Mara. Saha Deo is a strong and faithful

215

supporter of Alliance Party and Ratu Mara. So, (the) Mara faithful or . . . was shown the arms to prove that we can help Ratu Mara. Very few people know about this fact. My job was to co-ordinate with all connections either directly or with the help of other faithful.

Mara is not aware that "Fiji Defence Force" and "Fiji Malitia"(sic) exist. There are mixed group of both Indians and Fijians, including Solomons, Rotumans and a few Tongans in a highly secretive and disciplined underground force. The aim of the Malitia was to support the divided Army during counter-coup. The Militia and Defence Forces were "Insurance" for the poor Indians and Fijians, and an invisible force to correct things if the divided Army ever tried to double cross Dr Bavadra.

If the counter-coup took place, Dr Bavadra would have returned to power as Prime Minister. But compromise was that in the event a Government of National Unity would be formed to incorporate Ratu Mara to defuse any urge for foreign intervention, to appease the greatest majority of Fiji people and the majority of the Fijian Chiefs. This Government of National Unity would return Fiji to democracy; Commonwealth and Queen. It would have defused radical demands and bring the country to the near pre-coup confidence and future for propriety.

And the deal was that Government of National Unity could stay in power for its full term of the Parliament (five years) or call new elections when the situation is satisfactory. If there was any new election, Mara would not run but allow his son to take his safe seat, and Dr Bavadra would not prosecute Mara or carry out witch hunts.

If the counter-coup went ahead, Ratu Mo, brother of Ratu Mara's wife, Adi Lala Mara, would have become Governor General and Penaia pensioned, Rabuka and his gang in prison and the military controlled would go to either the British Army Office or New Zealand. All major and key positions would have gone to overseas expatriates, i.e. Police, prison, chief justice, etc, to bring back confidence and stop any bickering.

Further, the deal was that no Ratus will be patronised or given favourable or privileged treatment in any national affairs. All citizens will be treated equally but special programme to encourage the natives to go into joint venture with Indians or other qualified people who could assist to bridge the gap. Also, special treatment for poor of the country to narrow their gap between rich and poor.

Before I forget, Rabuka suspected Mara and he strengthened his secret alliances with pressure and harrassment of Mara. Both Taukei and Rabuka wanted Mara out. Therefore, with Rabuka's blessing, Taukei started to openly criticise Mara and

216

demanded him removed on the grounds of corruption, etc. The stage was being set for Rabuka's third coup which was planned for April 1988. We had to show Mara's emmissary those arms at Saha Deo's to calm him down. He was under intense pressure. When we heard about the planned third coup or sacking of Mara from our internal military source, we quickly signalled to Mara. He quickly moved to consolidate his power base with Council of Chiefs, and for them to pressure Ratu Penaia to control his boy, Rabuka, and not to be stupid. Rabuka was shocked that this was leaked out and now he was sure that his inner circle had holes, and someone has infiltrated his closed circle.

When Rabuka back-tracked on the deal with Taukei, Taukei's executives got very desperate and our intelligence was that we should make contact with Taukei to feel them out.

As a result I posed as overseas businessman representing people who are very interested in affairs of Fiji, that we are pro-West based in London, and we could help Taukei if they moderate their demands and work with Dr Bavadra.

It was at that meeting (April 1988) Ratu Mo, myself and Ratu Meli met for lunch in a hotel room for four hours that I learned that Taukei also had their men in the army and they had a contingency plan to take control by force, meaning eliminating Ratu Mara and Rabuka with his close friends to grab power.

Of course we did not want to be part of that blood-bath because we knew that Dr Bavadra would not go for it. We advised them not to, for international opinion would be against them and the people might not support them which will lead to civil war among Fijians and dragging others into the vortex to ruin the country. But if they consider working under Bavadra in an Unity Government, we could help."

Written by Mohammed Kahan, Wednesday 28 September, 1988.

"Interesting story Mr Kahan. Who would believe it?"

"Kamisese Mara would believe it because it is true, Mr Harder. They know you were coming. Everyone know that you are coming to see me. Mara's son-in-law, Ratu Epeli has come to see me three times, first to see what I would say, then to dissuade me from talking."

Kahan had answered the question without me having to ask. The son-in-law looking after father-in-law in hopes of getting Mara's seat in parliament I wondered?

"You want to question Saha Deo. Ask his neighbours if when the security forces arrested him did his wife yell out, why don't you arrest Mara," he continued.

"Ask Deo what he said in Lautoka police? It's common knowledge."

"Question Mara about his Indian mates. You question Mahendra Patel and Motibhai, ask them if they agreed to help. Get them to produce their bank records, look for transactions from Singapore and Australia to India."

I interrupted Kahan's planning of his defense. "I don't honestly think we will get the chance to question these guys in the very near future. They are unlikely to let the ones we want come to London and I don't think they will let me back into Fiji. It would be tantamount to putting Fiji on trial."

Later in the week Kahan's suggestion was to take on some prospect that I and my London colleagues might be able to go to Fiji after all.

A Call From The Palace

Back at my hotel, a consistent 50 minutes from Brixton, I put my feet up on the bed. No messages from the Palace.

"If Mr Fellowes doesn't have the courtesy to return my call, I'll give it out to the press. That will cause some heat to be thrown on the subject of Rabuka's OBE." I muttered out loud. The matter had been reported in New Zealand. It was as if the British Government had put out a wartime style D-notice censoring or suppressing the subject.

It was five past five when the phone rang. "Mr Harder, this is Robert Fellowes from Buckingham Palace."

What a fast response to my threat to go public in London, it was as if he had been listening to my muttering!

"Mr Harder, I am sorry I did not return your call earlier. What can I do for you?"

"You have received my correspondence to the Queen about Rabuka and his OBE?"

"Yes, I have, but the Queen must await any advice from Her Ministers on this matter."

"I would have thought from the simple reading of your letter to me dated 16th August 1988 from Balmoral Castle, 'Her Majesty would not normally consider the forfeiture of one of her honours . . .'"

Our conversation continued with words to the effect that I thought the Queen could act in abnormal situations on her own initiative.

"I am sorry Mr Harder, I can't help you any further. I understand you have communicated with the Prime Minister's office."

"Yes, that is correct." I thanked him for returning my call.

The response was not unexpected. I hoped the letters would raise the British Government's level of awareness of Rabuka and Fiji.

The security checks and escort systems at the Home Office are designed to prevent terrorist attacks. We had to sign in, then have our names and appointments confirmed. Although ostensibly a modern government office, I was surprised to see the receptionist looking through all manner of books to find the person we wanted to see and his correct extension number. The poster on the wall encouraged people to stop and open their briefcases if approached by security people in the building.

The middle-aged lady at the front desk behind the bullet-proof glass was very helpful. "Mr Tom Cobbley will see you now Mr Harder and Miss Woods. Follow me please." We were taken through different colour coded parts of the building. Obviously different security clearances were needed for different areas.

As we walked in a well dressed government officer arose from his chair to greet the pair of us. "Mr Cobbley, I presume," the words slipped out without thinking.

"Cup of tea," said one of the other two gentlemen standing to one side. After brief introductions the conversation came around to the question of whether the Home Secretary was still amenable to submissions.

"Is there anything new that you can add to your case Mr Harder?"

"Yes there are certain matters I have not committed to writing in the interests of protecting some individuals still in Fiji. But I require your assurance to keep this information within the Home Office." I had some concern over security of information.

News had travelled fast when I faxed my affidavit to Robert

Roscoe in London five nights before I left New Zealand. By noon the next day I was aware that people in Fiji knew I had sent an affidavit to London to try and help Kahan.

That I had sent a fax from my office to London should only have been known to me, Roscoe and the Home Office. How the information got to Fiji so fast is still a puzzle.

A short burst of cross-examining the Home Office officials in a polite way established that the Minister for Home Affairs had in fact signed the certificate authorising the extradition proceedings to commence three days ago, on the Monday. Nothing I was to say would change that point.

The officials explained how the Minister was impressed with the fact that all but two of the 21 accused in the guns affair in Fiji had received bail only days before the certificate was to be signed.

It was a working office despite the glass table for my brief case and my cup of coffee. The Fiji file sitting on the desk before Mr Cobbley was nearly 12 inches thick and bulging. The officers had an indication that the Security Decree might be dropped, but nothing of definite nature. Furthermore, the matter still had to come back before the Minister for Home Affairs even if Kahan was ordered by the court to be extradited back to Fiji for trial.

"We will assist the lawyers to obtain visas if that is necessary. You should approach your own consultate."

At least they were offering some practical signs of assistance. "Gentlemen, you have the whip hand in relation to Fiji. I would appreciate your assistance in obtaining a visa in light of my exclusion order under the Security Decree from Fiji," I said, immediately indicating an interest in their offer.

" We will see what we can do Mr Harder, but I am not sure if we will have a response before you leave on Friday."

"Here is my card. I would be obliged if you would write to me once you have made inquiries of the appropriate authorities. Roscoe the solicitor, Alun Jones, the barrister and I each require a visa. I know Fiji. I've been there three times and have been admitted to the Fiji High court for the gun case."

"We will see what we can do, Mr Harder."

"Thank you gentlemen, for your time." We were escorted to the door by one of the men in the office.

As we walked to the elevator, he said, "Remember, the case still has to go to the Home Secretary for final approval. A lot of water may have flowed under the bridge by then."

"Thank you again," I said as the elevator door closed behind us.

Last Chance With Kahan

Thursday was to be the last visit with Kahan for some time. I had two hours to get a number of matters sorted out; a release to publish the information was one of them. Kahan quickly agreed, he saw the guns as a political affair.

"I, M.R Kahan, authorise Christopher Harder, Barrister, to use the tape recorded interviews given by me this 28th day of September, 1988 and the documents supplied to him by Miss C. Wood of Victor Lissack and Roscoe in the preparation of his book in relation to my extradition case, including the documents to be supplied by the Fijian authorities in support of my extradition.

Signed M.R. Kahan

I plonked the four bundles of papers down on the small table.

"Mohammed, we have not got much time so I want to go straight to some of the documents." I tried the tape recorder to make sure it was working, pushed play, and nothing happened. It was not even turning, not at all, let alone recording. As I prodded at it a little piece fell out and I was certain the recorder was buggered.

Thank goodness I had a spare machine. Philippa had arranged to have it fixed before I left Auckland. "Testing, five, ten, fifteen, twenty . . ." I pushed rewind and then play. A garbled ffiivvvveeeee, teeeooooooon ground its way out in an inaudible and useless mess. I was in an absolute flap. My writing was far too slow to be of any use. "Guard." I called out, "Do you have a tape recorder I can use for the afternoon?"

Very obligingly the warder went off and returned with a Sony that could play a tape but not record. It would be of no help. In desperation I tried the black recorder again. The red light was on, it was recording. Somebody was looking after me. The piece I had broken off was the erase head. It would not be needed today.

"Mohammed, I do not want to waste the afternoon, so I will get straight to the point. The documents found in your briefcase have been included in the depositions. It means the papers have been given to the Fijian authorities. I believe the move was unlawful."

It seemed that the documents had been surrendered to Fiji, a foreign Republic no longer part of the Commonwealth, without first gaining the proper court authorisation.

"I will talk to Alun Jones about it tonight when I see him at his chambers," I explained to Kahan.

I could see from the first few pages of this pile of depositions before me that they would reveal a complex trail by the time I got to the bottom. The detailed record of conversations.

The cover sheet to the depositions was headed up with a statement of witness from Detective Sergeant Barry Waterman of New Scotland Yard's Serious Crimes branch. Waterman, who had been involved in the arrest of Kahan on July 22 had examined a brown briefcase seized at the time. The list of exhibits outlined a grand scheme by Kahan to ferment a counter-revolution against military strongman Sitiveni Rabuka in Fiji.

The photocopied bundle of exhibits the Fijian authorities intended to introduce as evidence in support of Kahan's extradition told an amazing tale. It was an intriguing and extensive trail of international jet travel, guns, the PLO, the plotting of a counter-revolution, and much more. What was not revealed might have made even more incredible reading.

Mohammed Kahan's plan to save Fiji and make himself rich at the same time started back in December 1987. The Marriage Registrar at the Elstree and Potters Bar in the country of Hertfordshire was a Mr S. Kelly. It was a cold winter's day that Mohammed Rafiq Kahan married Homewatti Dharamdas, a 32-year-old nurse and daughter of a farmer called Dhawamdas Ramadhin.

Mohammed needed a base to operate from. It was back to London that he would go if things got too hot in the South Pacific. London to him was the best of all places. With its significant Indian population Mohammed could blend easily with the masses. If London got too hot he would find some quiet job in the country and lie low for a while.

In London anything was possible. You could make political contacts, you could raise a mortgage on your wife's home for working capital. You could meet gun dealers and revolutionary minds who often passed through on their way to the Middle East. There was also a 'Friends of Fiji' movement in London.

Undoubtedly to the Fijians the diary entry of January 29, 1988 was of extra significance. It was a list of weapons Mohammed had taken down from a phone call.

4 Boxes
1. Inside: 300 Mortor Ammo. 60mm
                300 Mortor Ammo. 82mm
On top of No. 1, Box Mortor Barrell
2. 5000 Heavy Duty Rounds and
      100,000 AK 47 Ammo
      200 more (underground)
  3. 9 x 2
        1) Bag 6 complete AK 47
        2)   7 " "
        3)   7 " "
        4)   4 RGJ-7
        5)   10 Ammun/RGJ
        6)   10 "
        7)   6 Electric charge 10 timers
        8)   180 grenades
        9)   (illegible)
        10)   2 AK 47 700
        11)   A
4. 102 AK 47 complete
      4 RBJ 120 Ammo

On the February 11, Kahan took mortgage papers to a Mr Bender of Herbal Life looking for a loan.

The diary recorded a message reminding Mohammed to phone

Mike Sepay about shipping. Somehow the guns had to be delivered and the sooner the better.

On Wednesday, March 2 Kahan opened a new Barclay's account ready for a direct debit. The next day he bought a Skoda car. Over the next two weeks he contacted a number of banks trying to raise a mortgage without success. Among those he tried were J.P. Morgan Trust, Lloyds Merchant Bank and a company called Walberg's Investments.

A 3 p.m. appointment, again about a mortgage, was followed by the notation: "Channel 4 (20-20 production) Israeli lobby 8-9 p.m."

Delhi India: March 28

A two hour stopover in the transit lounge before continuing on to London on Air India flight 141 was noted.

Air India flight AI 116 departing London 9.35 a.m., destination Delhi was another leg of an ever increasing adventure for Mohammed. It was to be a mysterious journey. Nobody knew he was going except the people he was to meet. The wheels of the 747 touched down on the runway at exactly 11.10 p.m.

The airport was crowded as he worked his way through customs and immigration. He had no trouble. The baggage belt was delayed when he came down the escalator. He had hoped his bags would be offloaded by now. Hundreds and hundreds of passengers all off flight 116 from London were waiting in the sweltering heat. Baggage claimed, Kahan went to the Kailash Inn, a quality hotel. It had a centrally air-conditioned guest house with closed circuit TV.

This international traveller carefully recorded his costs as he went about his task of finding arms for his friends and money for himself while supporting a Fiji uprising. He spent 100 rupees on a taxi, 260 on a meal and another 130 for a taxi to take him to a meeting. It was too far to walk in Delhi. His hotel cost 675 and he consumed another 80 on lunch.

Bombay was a two day jaunt which hardly got a mention in the diary. Kahan wrote two letters and gave them to a hotel clerk for urgent mailing and flew out of Bombay at 1.45 p.m. that afternoon on Air India, flight IA 404, headed for Singapore and Sydney. He arrived in Sydney at eight in the morning on April Fool's day, no doubt planning to give Fiji its own Fool's Day soon enough.

Kahan thought on a grandiose scale. He wanted to make a fool of the world for allowing Rabuka to hijack Fiji at the point of a gun, never having fired a shot.

Nadi: Saturday, April 2

Kahan spent some time making long distance calls from his Fiji hotel room. He arranged a rental car in the morning to begin moving around. But he almost felt too sick to make the effort. His chest was tight and his body tired. He had been fliting around the world and had still to adjust to the confusing number of time zones this travel had taken him through.

He made an appointment to go to Carpenters Shipping at noon on Tuesday 5, to pick up some import paperwork and check out the warehouse procedures. His diary reminded him to call a man named Shiva on Sunday.

On Tuesday he went to Carpenter's Shipping — a division of the long established Carpenter's Fiji Limited. They are shipping agents for a number of lines, including Pacific Express Lines, a service between Australia and Fiji, which calls at ports in Vanuatu and Noumea if required. The line is operated by Sofrana Unilines (Aust) Pty Ltd using the vessel Capitaine Cook III on a monthly schedule.

Wednesday, April 6, was a day of annoying events. The telephone between his room and Sydney ran hot for a time early in the morning. To be sure he got his contact before he left for work he had to call early.

For all of Monday and part of Tuesday, Mohammed travelled about by Legion Cab. If he needed a cab he just called 382-024; one would soon be at the hotel. He finally picked up a rental car on the Thursday but it was a nuisance. First it had a flat tire. Then he found a parking ticket under the windscreen after a meeting in a Lautoka curry house. Who would believe it, a country controlled at the point of a gun and he got a parking ticket. The fine was paid promptly. He did not want officialdom inquiring into his car rental because of an unpaid $2.50 parking ticket.

Thursday was spent driving around Lautoka and the

surrounding countryside searching and surveying; meeting his friends and talking to some reliable strangers.

On Friday morning Kahan dialled 64590. He asked for "Anil" and enquired about a bill of lading, number 400050137046, wanting to know whether it had been unloaded.

At a "please call back while I try to find the paper," Kahan hung up. His heart began to race. Was something the matter or was the person on the other end of the phone just disorganised? Under the lading number in the diary Kahan wrote a note, "Nitya Piasif Agr/ Lautoka."

Ravin Dutt was the managing director of the firm R.J. Dutt. He was responsible for clearing from customs any goods for the company Vinod Patel and Co. Ltd. Every Wednesday the *Fiji Times* newspaper listed a schedule showing the arrival times for various container ships. Dutt's clerk had been to the Shipping Department earlier that day and had taken details from the manifest list for clients of R.J. Dutt.

Ravin Dutt had looked at the list the previous Wednesday morning when he saw the reference to six packages of used machinery. He had phoned Arvin Patel at his office in Ba.

Dutt told Patel that there was a consignment on the Capitaine Cook for him of some used machines. Patel replied that he would check the documents with the bank and ring back.

About an hour later Vinod Patel called Dutt at his Customs clearing agency. He had checked with the bank and there was no consignment to show a container of used machinery for him.

Dutt then took a pen and put a rule through the entry on the manifest book and took no further action on the matter.

It had been a busy day for the Carpenter Shipping clerk. He did not pay much attention to the person who presented the original bill of lading for stamping by the Lautoka office. He just plonked the Carpenter stamp on the papers without asking the man his name.

The bill of lading the clerk stamped corresponded to the number recorded in Kahan's diary. It was for one container of six packages of used equipment. The shipper was given as S.A.F.E. Freight Services, A/A Qunitex Trican Ltd, with no consignee, but there was an instruction to notify Vinod Patel and Co, Kings Road, Ba,

Fiji. Freight and other charges had been paid in Australia. Quintex Trican is a shelter company used by Adnan Kashoggi.

Not Quite Speedy Clearance

Taimud Dean's garage was not far from the office of Speedy Clearance. He often called in to see his relative, Mohammed Shariff, at the transport office.

It was about ten in the morning when Dean came into the office and the two of them began to speak. Part way through the conversation Dean said in Hindi *"Hum ek bhari client tumar lage bhejega"* (I will send a big client to you). After a couple of cups of kava with the other workers Taimud left.

At about five that evening a white Mitsubishi Lancer rental sedan pulled up in front of the Speedy Clearance sign. The driver walked up to Shariff just as he was about to close the door. "Excuse me, he said, my name is Mohammed Kahan. I have been sent by Taimud."

As a customs agent Shariff was used to people calling at odd hours. "Come into my office."

Mohammed began to talk. "I've got one container with a lathe machine coming. I would like your services. What is the clearance charges?"

They negotiated a fee for wharfage, full container cartage to Ba and empty container return to Lautoka.

The sun was shining bright as Kahan walked to the Speedy office around ten next Monday morning.

Kahan handed over an original supplier's invoice from Quintex (UK) Ltd for two used lathes.

Shariff pointed out that the consignment was for Vinod Patel and he was not the agent for Patel. He advised Kahan to try R J Dutt, whom he thought handled Patel's imports. But Kahan was not easily put off. He said the bill of lading was "consign to order" and he was the owner of the goods.

Shariff looked at the bill of lading, saw the word 'order' written in the section marked 'consignee or order', and agreed to handle the container.

On Thursday Kahan called Shariff to see if clearance had been arranged and was told that Customs wanted more information about the consignment.

"I'll come to your office," said Kahan as he hung up the phone. He was sweating. He had worried from the very start that something like this might go wrong.

The Customs entry documents had come back to Speedy earlier in the morning. The comparing officer's signature had been struck through. The entry on the back addressed to Speedy requested more information about the documentation.

It was eleven in the morning and Shariff had just returned from out the back of his building drinking some kava when three men walked in. Shariff recognised Mohammed Kahan, who was accompanied by an Army officer and another person he did not know. Kahan introduced the third person, a Fijian as Ratu Mosese Tuisavou. In typical Fiji style the four made small talk and drank kava for awhile before getting down to business.

"Customs want more information about the value of the lathe machines and the age of them," said Shariff.

Kahan asked him to ring 61823 and get Taimud over to the office.

Shariff spoke to Taimud's mother, leaving a message for him. Then he phoned the Customs and Excise Department in Lautoka and spoke to a person called Mahendra Rao. "Can I make an appointment to see you with Mr Kahan and his customs problem, please." Shariff turned the form over in his hand. On the back he had marked the words, "according to the client documents not in hand".

A few minutes later Taimud Dean arrived. Kahan, Ratu Mosese Tuisavou and Shariff then left the office through the side door. Shariff had the customs documents in his right hand. The three of them climbed in Kahan's car. The windows had been left up and the vinyl seats felt like they would burn up in the sun. Shariff sat on a copy of the previous day's *Fiji Times* so as not to burn his legs on the seat. Kahan had on long pants. Ratu Mosese had a green Fijian sulu protecting his thighs from the searingly hot plastic.

In Lautoka the Customs officer Mahendra Rao asked Kahan about the value and age of the lathes.

"They are fairly old. What's on the invoice is their value. Mosese is going to buy these machines," Kahan said.

Rao asked Mosese if this was true and he replied that he was going to set up a factory in Ba in partnership with some other people.

The men then walked back to the Customs building to have some more kava. A number of people were standing around talking. Kahan had a conversation with the Senior Collector of Customs, Mr Rokodovu, and the Collector of Customs, Mr Saukoro. After a brief period all five walked towards Kahan's Mitsubishi. The rental car was proving most unreliable. For the second time in a week a tyre was flat.

Shariff offered to help change the tyre for Mohammed, who was still dressed in his suit. Once the tyre was fixed Shariff left the site with a staff member to be dropped off at a nearby Mosque.

About two in the afternoon Dean and the Army officer were standing back outside the Speedy office waiting for Kahan.

"Where is Mohammed?" Dean asked. Shariff replied that he had gone for lunch and would be back shortly.

A few minutes later Shariff phoned Rao at the Customs office. Shortly after the call Shariff left his office in the company Bedford, picking up Taimud from his garage as he went. The two of them drove to Carpenter's Shipping. Shariff turned the motor off and told Taimud to go into the office and "get me a copy of the freight sheet." A couple of minutes later Dean climbed up into the truck, paper in hand, grinning.

Rao stood in the Customs Office looking at the freight sheet handed to him by Shariff, who looked a bit nervous. He wondered why there was so much fuss over a couple of lathes.

"There is $1500 difference between the amount of freight shown on the original supplier's invoice from the UK and the bill of lading," said Rao. Shariff decided the best way out of this was to amend the documents to take account of the larger figure. This meant there was more duty to pay but it removed the likelihood of further Customs enquiry. He passed the paper back to Rao. But the customs officer had one more challenge for their nerves. "I will pass the entry but I want the container examined for valuation."

Shariff, no doubt feeling pleased with getting this far, went to the cashier's office and joined the queue. Seven Indians stood in front of him in the hot, dusty office waiting to pay. Nothing ever happened fast here. Finally his turn came. He pulled a long folded BNZ cheque book from his pants pocket and wrote a cheque for $973.75 to cover the duty.

The Fijian cashier took the cheque and rang up the till. Methodically she picked up the Customs entry documents and stamped each with a warrant number. The bottom copy was handed to Shariff.

By 3.30p.m. the three of them were standing outside Shariff's office awaiting his return. Kahan was leaning against his car door, Dean drawing little pictures in the sand then scratching them out and starting again. Mosese Tuisavou stood against the chainlink fence stretching his arms to get rid of some tension. At 3.30 exactly Shariff walked into the yard. Mohammed Kahan walked up to him and spoke in Hindi and it was all over for the day. There was absolutely no chance of liberating the container at such a late hour on a hot tropical afternoon.

Clearance Day: Friday, April 15:

Kahan and his colleagues appeared at the Speedy office at nine on Friday morning. Shariff knew they would be back today. He had tried to get the container ready for these persistent men by sending his boy Sarjit Singh down to Customs to help the process along. But the morning dragged. Eleven o'clock came and went and the container had still not arrived. It was hot and humid in the office, outside was worse and it was not even noon.

Shariff was panicking now. He picked up the phone and spoke to a Customs officer called Ali.

"There are no examining officers available at the moment, why don't you get an officer from the main office?" Ali said.

Speedy Clearance was not proving to be a terribly efficient office. It sometimes took months to clear a container at Lautoka unless you knew the right person. Even then it was quicker with some gesture of goodwill. A week to clear a container was definitely the fast track in this port. After all, Fiji is in the tropics.

The phone rang in senior Collector of Customs Rokodovu's office. It rang and rang and rang. Finally Rokodovu picked it up and gruffly identified himself.

By this time Shariff was very frustrated. He was trying to keep his patience. There was no point in getting cross at the boss. "Can you please help me to get this container cleared? We are having so much trouble," he begged.

"Ok, ok I'll get you a man this afternoon, is that OK," snapped Rokodovu. He pushed his chair back screeching on the concrete floor.

Shariff told Kahan about the promised clearance. But he also had to tell him that Carpenter's could not provide a truck to pick it up until after two o'clock. It was time to have some lunch. The four men returned just after two, and waited. Nothing happened for several more hours, but that did not cause any panic, doing nothing much during the afternoon heat was normal. Finally the container arrived on the back of a brown truck. It stopped on Sadurugu Lane, in front of the Speedy office.

Now five of them stood around in a group. There was Kahan in his suit, Taimud wearing shorts, teeshirt and thongs, and Tuisavou in his wrap, cotton shirt and dark brown leather sandals. For all the casualness of Fiji, most Fijian men have their sandals polished by street vendors; 10 cents gets a shine.

With them were two army officers who either polish their own boots or had some poor soldier on fatigues do it for them.

Shariff approached and spoke to the truck driver. "Could you unload the container here?"

"No, it is too narrow this place, the drains are on both sides and the ground is too soft."

"What do you want to do? We cannot unload the container here?" Kahan turned to the men and asked. "Why don't we take it to Ba to the Steel Rolling Mill and do the examination there?"

Rao, the Collector of Customs, said he would have to ask his boss and went in to use the phone. He returned in a few minutes. "Okay, go ahead with it." It was 3.30 in the afternoon when Shariff climbed into the cab of his truck and headed for Ba.

Beside him, cool and calm, sat Kahan with Rao, his arm out the

231

window directing the breeze with his hand. Dean drove Kahan's rental car carrying Tuisavou and the army officers. Another truck with an army officer and an unidentified Indian came last. It was an odd convoy of destiny. They passed through canefields, many of them standing more than six feet high and nearing maturity. After about half an hour Nagan's Steel Rolling Mill came into view. A watchman stood off to one side checking their arrival. As the truck rolled to a stop Kahan opened the door and directed one of the men to hook up the truck's crane onto the container. The chains tightened and the box was slowly hoisted off the truck.

Shariff gave Kahan his opportunity when he asked "Where's the forklift and the other gear?"

"It's almost five o'clock now and the forklift people have gone home," Kahan replied.

Shariff lifted the leather flap on the container door to reveal the heavy metal seal.

"Since the forklift is not here and because the seal is on the container, why don't you do the examination on Monday?"

Rao got down and looked at the seal. Then he went and talked to the watchman. After a few minutes he returned to the container and put an extra padlock on the doors.

Nagan's Mill: Monday April 18

The Customs officials arrived at the steel mill on Monday morning with Shariff. As they approached they saw Kahan, Ahmed Ali and a few other Indian men standing around a petrol bowser about 50 metres from the container. A green car parked nearby started up and pulled across the truck's path. Kahan got out of the passenger side and spoke to Shariff. "Naushad, instead of two lathe machines, I have only one," he called out.

"How do you know there's only one?" a slightly alarmed Shariff inquired.

"I have opened the container."

Shariff was flabbergasted. He could not believe it. Nobody opened a container without permission.

"Look Ali," said Shariff, "He's opened the container. You take the matter up from here." Annoyed, Ali sharply asked Kahan why he'd touched the container, let alone opened it.

"I got a forklift on Saturday," was Kahan's simple reply, so simple that it took the wind out of their sails.

Shariff and Ali walked forward and looked into the container. It was empty.

"Why was it not kept here?" demanded Shariff.

"Ratu Mosese refused to buy it."

"Well your customs duty won't be refunded," chipped in Ali.

As the Customs men drove away from the steel mill with Shariff, Kahan and his friends were heading for Rafiq's not far away. The crates would be there soon. Kahan smiled to himself as the car whistled along. With a little help from his friends his plan to get the container through unchecked had worked. Their friend in the Army was still loyal.

I stopped reading the papers. Most of the two-hour prison visit had flown by as I had skimmed the documents and Kahan had filled in the details of this amazing story.

"Mohammed", I said, "Two letters stand out because of their signatories." I showed him the two documents signed by Dr T Bavadra, Prime Minister. The first letter was addressed to the Tamil Tigers in Madras seeking support for any help "Mohammed Kahan, special envoy," might seek on behalf of Dr. Bavadra.

June 4, 1988
The Chairman,
LTTE Central Committee,
MADRAS, India.

Dear Sir,

The National Federation — Labour Central Committee, I as the Democratically elected Prime Minister of Fiji, and my fellow Cabinet members, hereby give authority to MOHAMMED 191366, our special envoy and the Commander-in-Chief of the Fiji Militia Forces to discuss and seek positive assistance, guidance and implementation of the strategies to overcome our oppression; to de-stabilise

Rabuka regime and to return the rightful and democratic government of Dr. Bavadra.

There are many areas we can help each other which will be discussed by Mohammed so that whatever we do, there will be mutual benefit for both of us, and create a bond between our people. Your help will be appreciated.

Sincerely yours,
Dr.T Bavadra Prime Minsiter of Fiji.
cc:file

The second letter was addressed to the PLO asking for assistance to fund an uprising in Fiji.

OFFICE OF THE PRIME MINISTER
CONFIDENTIAL

JUNE 30, 1988

Chairman Arafat,
Palestine Liberation Organisation TUNIS, Tunisia. Dear Mr Chairman: Re: Fund raising for uprising — letter dated 15.6.88/ F.O.F Barclays Bank guarantee for 40 million Atg./ London.

Further Friends of Fiji's letter dated June 15, 1988 in reference to the planned uprising in Fiji similar to the ones in the occupied territories of Palestine, we the N.F.P Coalition Government of Fiji and the Central Committee of the said Party, seek your assistance to raise the required 40 million pounds sterling against the irrevokable bank guarantee from Barclays Bank, London for the repayment of the loaned sum.

Mr Chairman, please don't abandon us but assist us vigorously in the memory of our late brother Abu Jihad to counter Israeli and Zionist presence in Fiji.

Our set-back in Sydney, Australia has given us greater strength and determination to overcome the military government of Col. Rabuka and the Israelis.

Your assistance and guidance would be greatly appreciated by the people of Fiji.
"LONG LIVE PALESTINE & P.L.O."

Sincerely yours,
Dr.T Bavadra,
Prime Minister elected by the people of Fiji.
cc:file/ TB-OLP-05
Seal of N.F.P. LABOUR GOVT OF FIJI

" I put it to you that these two letters are forgeries, Mohammed." I showed him the two documents. I also showed him copies of blank letterhead for the office of the Prime Minister and some from the Friends of Fiji. The small 'm', typed on the letter had a fault on it that stood out a mile. Another letter signed by Kahan contained what looked like the same noticeable fault on its 'm' characters.

"Yes, the letters signed Dr.T Bavadra are forgeries. They were written to give weight to my position."

Then I went into a little cross examination routine to make sure Kahan had signed the letters and was not trying to cover up a more sinister plot.

"The letter addressed to Arafat signed by Bavadra on 30 June, that's a forgery too?"

"It's a forgery, anything with Bavadra's name on it."

"Where did the blank paper from the Prime Minister come from?"

"The committee. We have a committee."

"Somebody gave it to you?"

"Yeah."

"And the stamp?"

"They also had the stamp provided."

Another letter showed the grandiose scale this conman-turned-revolutionary was thinking on. Written on Friends of Fiji letterhead it asked Arafat for help in raising £40,000,000 for an uprising in Fiji. Kahan was not wasting his time on any small-fry objectives. If he pulled this off, he would be rich and have a position of influence after the change of government. It was a wild plan.

FRIENDS OF FIJI
40 Clarendon Road, London, E11-1DA. U.K.

June 15, 1988

The Chairman,
Palestine Liberation Organisation
Tunis.

Dear Sir,

Re fundraising for Fiji uprising — 3 to six months

To stage uprising similar to the uprising in the occupied territories of Palestine, namely the West Bank and Gaza, we would need to raise substantial funds to sustain it.

Initially, we anticipate that we will have to commit what-ever resources we have left which of course is not much. But we did manage to get the support of Barclays Bank in London to guarantee the repayment of principle amount loaned to us and not exceeding 40 million pounds sterling and for period not exceeding 12 months.

This guarantee can be made through bank to bank to secure the lender who is willing to assist us. Barclays Bank will give unconditional and irrevokable guarantee for the actual amount lent to the Trustees of the Friends of Fiji.

Therefore, we officially seek the help and guidance from the PLO to identify and introduce to us the possible lender or lenders who can assist us in this cause.

Sincerely yours,

Mohammed 191366
Special Envoy & Committee member.

cc. Dr Sami
Abbas Zaki

A second letter from Kahan on Friends of Fiji letterhead, under the signature of Mohammed 191366, dated June 15, 1988 was addressed to the Ambassador, Libyan Embassy, TUNIS. Marked at

the bottom of the letter was "Received in Tunis By: 'Jubeed' June 16/
88 12.45p.m."

Dear Mr Ambassador,

*I, Mohammed Kahan from Fiji and executive member of Friends of Fiji, a special
envoy of the Democratically elected Prime Minister Dr T. Bavadra and my
passport number 253848 issued in Suva, Fiji do urgently seek visit to the capital
of Libya, Tripoli with a Fiji delegation to discuss urgent matters pertaining to our
struggle, oppression and means of seeking assistance, guidance and support.*
*Initially we thought that we could do it alone and not seek assistance from other
government but we were wrong. Now that foreign government like Israel is openly
helping the illegal government of Rabuka, we are forced to seek outside help and
guidance.*
*We would like to travel to Tripoli from Tunis and not from London but for the
matter of communication, we could use the London office of the Tripoli Government.
Your speediest attention would be greatly appreciated.*

Sincerely yours,
Mohammed 191366

There was a knock on the door. My time was just about up. "Well
Mohammed, I will not be back for a while. If you need to
communicate with me write it down and Carolyn Wood can fax it
to me." I stood up and put the tape recorder and papers back in my
brief case.

We shook hands. For a moment our hands clung together as if we
might not see each other again. I had made Mohammed no
promises. I would tell the story as best I could. I would hold him in
the best light on the face of the evidence. I would not make him a
saint. He agreed he would have no say in what I wrote. The
information I had I was at liberty to use as best I saw fit.

Back at Bond Street Carolyn and I went into Alun Jones' office on
the main floor of his chambers.

"I am adamant that all three of us go to Fiji when the time comes.
You know the place and the people, Christopher. It will be all or
none," said Jones in a fiery outburst. This case made Jones seethe.

A traitor trying to extradite an Indian who tried to take back with a gun what Rabuka had gained with a gun.

"I'll see you early for coffee, Christopher. I will take the depositions home tonight to read. If you and I could meet in the morning so that you might brief me on some of the background, I would be in your debt."

I looked forward to seeing Jones over a fresh brewed cup of coffee in the morning. Kahan was in court tomorrow.

A Diary Of Intrigue

I put my feet up on the bed back at the hotel and began to look through the rest of Kahan's diary. It was blank for seven days between April 15 and 22. Saturday, April 23, Kahan was back in Delhi. The next day he went to Katmandu. For the rest of April and up till May 24 his diary indicated a quiet existence renting video's, sending fax messages around the world and making telephone calls.

May 24 was headed "Sydney, Phone Ratu Mo 71533 off." His diary continued to record monies spent on expenses. It appeared Mohammed Kahan was being required to account for what he spent. No free ride here, at least not yet. On June 22, the day I was arrested the page recorded something about used tires for Ben's Used Tyre Com Jersey City/N.Y. and a couple of U.S. phone numbers.

The diary recorded an entry for Mr Bajpai. "385-166/11: a.m. 27 June, 1988."

Ishwari Bajpai was an Alliance member who had funded a significant portion of the party's last two Alliance elections and had held ministerial positions in the Alliance government. At the time of the gun discovery Bajpai was a member in the Mara cabinet.

He has a supermarket in Nabua, not far from Rabuka's church and just down the road from the Queen Elizabeth Army barracks. Two days before the first coup Bajpai closed his shops and sent staff home. After the staff had left Army trucks pulled up and removed all his food stock. The supplies were returned in the same army trucks three days later. During the riots none of Bajpai's shops were damaged.

Kahan had talked to or been involved with all manner of Alliance party supporters and Mara confidantes. He had also done an amazing amount of travel. Thursday June 30 recorded Dr Vasdu Abdul No. 52 Connaught Circus, New Delhi 11 000 India.

June 30 was the date of the letter addressed to Chairman Arafat of the PLO and signed with the forged signature of Dr T. Bavadra.

The last entry in the diary was the day Mohammed Kahan was arrested. Friday, 22 July, it showed some more travel details: "Air India/ RF H3L3L Quantas: QF O94/ FJ918 / 29 July Ref JH VEVL / M. M.S.A. KHAN"

The exhibit list was another maze of intrigue. This man was an accomplished traveller at the very least. And for emergency he carried a back up Fiji Passport No. 2455 in his own name.

His hotel bills included the Seaview Hotel in Singapore on the first two days of June. The Hotel Ashoka Deluxe, New Delhi from 23/6/88 to 25/6/88: Kahan had been in New Delhi when I was arrested in Fiji. But that weekend he moved to the Kailash Hotel, also in New Delhi. By Monday night he was booked into the Hotel President, in Madras, where telex and telephone bills left a trail. An Australian ticket from Sydney to Brisbane on June 1 suggested he had an accomplice or an alias. It was in the name of a McMOHAN. Later that day a Quantas Airlines ticket from Brisbane to Singapore in the name of Kissum suggested Kahan either collected used airline tickets or had a chameleon bent.

Exhibit BW/28 was airline reservations, a pen, bills from the Bureau de Chane corres. relating to his visit to Tunis in June 1988, via Tunis Air, in name of CHEDY and KAHAN. Photo's of KAHAN in Tunis . . .

Part of Tunis Air ticket No. 199 4202 669 891 4 KAHAN — Sydney —Nadi — Sydney. June 6 to 15, Sydney, Nadi, Sydney.

In addition to Kahan's odyssey of the last few months the diary had thrown up some remarkable personal coincidences.

His Vancouver address was in the suburb of Burnaby, only a few blocks from where my grandparents lived. I flew into Fiji with Philippa and the two children for a holiday March 28. It was the same weekend Kahan had arrived there from Bombay, via Sydney. And the day we returned to Auckland, April 11, was the day the guns had arrived at the port of Lautoka.

From the Fiji prosecutor's depositions I already knew that Kahan had spent time in an Edmonton, Alberta jail in 1975. Thinking back I too had been in Edmonton then, but I had been involved in some intense local politics rather than doing time in that city's jail.

Bow Street Business

Glass doored book shelves line the front wall behind the bench in the Number One courtroom at Bow Street. The sitting magistrate walked into the court through a door directly behind his Edwardian backed chair.

There was nothing extraordinary about him. Earlier inquiry from Alun Jones indicated that His Honour was a reasonable chap and not prone to extremes. I had been warned about one judge who was supposed to be strongly right wing and totally unpredicatable, we didn't want to go in front of him. A most important rule of thumb in criminal law is to always know which judge you will appear before. It helps to get the measure of your man so you know where to pitch your submissions.

"Order in the Court" called out the Jamaican born, British registrar. "All rise."

Everybody stood. The prosecution and defence counsel sat to the right as I looked forward. I thought of the time in Fiji when I was watching the robbery trial with the three Fijians and the Indian taxi driver. It would be interesting to see if this court lived up to my expectations of British Justice.

The Queen's counsel, Mr Clive Nicholls, acting for the Fiji government, sat next to Alun Jones in the elevated box to the right of the court, up by the magistrates bench. The case number was read out by the crier: "Mohammed Kahan".

The door to the right giving direct access to the cells opened and suspected gun runner Mohammed Kahan walked into the court and stood behind the big thick wooden railings of the dock. Standing in the raised dock he looked taller than his real height of about five foot eight. He was dressed in a smart blue suit, clean white shirt and dark tie. He looked just like any other successful Indian businessman you might run into on day to day chores in New Zealand, Fiji or London.

The prosecutor, Clive Nicholls, rose first and introduced himself to the court on behalf of the 'Republic of Fiji'. His chambers were in the same building as Alun Jones for the defence, just across the road from this very British courtroom.

Alun Jones rose and declared his appearance for Kahan. Nicholls began his opening address by explaining that Kahan was arrested on July 22nd 1988 on a provisional warrant. Authority to proceed was given on September 26th. The offences: conspiracy to possess arms, possession, conspiracy to obtain property by deception, conspiracy to possess ammunition and possession.

Evidence had been taken in Fiji and submitted to the Foreign Office yesterday. Mr Jones had received copies late yesterday. There was also evidence taken in Australia which the applicant hoped to have before the court in 7 to 10 days. In addition live evidence would be called in court.

"Matters before the court today do not include an application for bail": Jones and Nicholls had already reached agreement.

"Mr Jones says it is impossible to say when he will be ready. The Department of Public Prosecutions (Fiji) expects to be ready soon. It is difficult to say how long the hearing will be, certainly at least two weeks." Nicholls went on to say it was quite plain that important matters of law and fact would be determined, Section 4 of the Fugitive Offenders Act concerning offences of a political character would be among them.

"May I say the Government of Fiji has already confirmed to the instructing solicitors that they will put no difficulties in front of the defence in preparing the defence including that Section four. If Mr Jones requires the assistance of the DPP in relation to dealing with Fiji we will do everything we can to help."

Alun Jones interrupted "You said you want live evidence. It would clearly help to know the nature of this evidence." Jones quickly seized on the chance to cement the legal concept that no obstacles should be put in our way. On the 9th of September counsel for Kahan had called for assurances that the defence would receive the same facilities with regard to taking evidence as the applicant for extradition, Fiji's number one prosecutor, had done. Now we asked for cross examination of witnesses. One witness would say the defendant was planning an insurrection, a statement with political implications.

"Can Mr Nicholls therefore assure us that we will have facilities for cross examination of witnesses who may have been ill treated."

Nicholls climbed back into the ring by announcing that the instructing solicitors already had a letter saying that no obstacles would be put in their way. The witnesses would go to the political issue, but such requests should be in writing so they could be considered in Fiji by the DPP. "The prosecution knows fully the duty placed on it even though it is instructed by a foreign government of disclosure."

Jones: "My question hasn't been answered. We propose to go to Fiji and we want written authorities to cross examine." Because bail had not been applied for, such was the gravity of the offence, and because there were no sureties Mr Jones argued that the court should determine whether the extradition claim was of a political character within a few days.

"Schtracks" was quoted as authority for a magistrate of the High Court to consider whether the offence was political."

In the Schtracks case of 1962 the court had decided that Israel did have jurisdiction over Jerusalem where the offence had been committed, although it did not have sovereignty there.

British extradition law dates back to an Act of Parliament in 1866. During debate on the bill British philosopher and Member of Parliament John Stuart Mill suggested the guidelines should be whether the offence was committed in the course of or furthering of civil war, insurrection or political commotion.

Subsequent court cases ruled that Mill's definition was too wide and that to escape extradition the offender would have to also have been politically motivated.

The Kahan case was unusual. It concerned allegations of the shipment of arms. Kahan was suspected and left the country. Twenty one had been arrested, of which 19 got bail only the week before the authority to proceed with the extradition case was issued.

On the face of it there was evidence to suggest that Kahan had armed the supporters of an insurrection against the regime. When

Detective Sergeant Waterman arrested Kahan he is alleged to have said that he helped people and 'there wasn't only me.' One of the principal suspects of the twenty one arrested, Mohammed Rafiq, was charged with conspiracy to instigate invasion.

However, Fiji didn't seek Kahan's return for the possession of guns but for allegations of treason. In June the Internal Security Decree was declared in Fiji. Its draconian measures, although passed in June, were backdated to March 1 and gave power to detain indefinitely.

At first reading it seemed the power to detain was for two years when it was renewable if release was considered prejudicial to the safety of the state.

The backdating neatly covered the shipment of arms that had reached Fiji in April. Life imprisonment was the new penalty for possession of illegal arms and military no go areas could be designated where it seemed people could be shot. The decree was clearly designed to encompass Kahan and his ploting.

Jones then presented a thumbnail history of Fiji since independence in 1970. Until 1987 there was a parliamentary government. But Rabuka disbanded it with the help of armed soldiers. A republic was declared and Ganilau, who had given an oath to the Queen, was made president All along Rabuka had carried the honour of a military list OBE.

It was quite extraordinary that a traitor pardoned by Ganilau, a man who himself had repudiated his oath to the Queen, should be seeking extradition, said Jones, it was an affront to justice. Poor Kahan, arrested in July and had been in custody since. Christopher Harder, the barrister who had defended native chiefs from Rotuma charged with sedition because of their oath of allegiance to the Queen had been to the Home Office this week. While he was in Fiji for the Rotuma case the Internal Security Decree was passed. Mr Harder had written to the government, he was then detained and while in detention personally witnessed bullying and mental torture at Queen Elizabeth Barracks, Jones said.

When under house arrest after his release from the cells Harder had been told there was an amnesty for the co-conspirators, but that the DPP wouldn't be able to extradite the 'gun guy' if they (the guns accused) were released. Jones restated the point that they were bailed only days before the authority to proceed was issued. The case was an important matter of public anxiety, the Queen had been repudiated but they still wanted to extradite Kahan. It was not a matter of dishonesty as the applicant claimed, but an offence of a political character. The defence would have to consider the material available and if necessary go to Fiji to obtain futher evidence.

Next Jones brought up the disappearance of Kahan's briefcase after his arrest. Kahan was so concerned he wrote his own letter to the court asking them not to disclose that there was evidence in the briefcase, including letters of contact to political bodies from the Friends of Fiji asking for help from Yassar Arafat and the Tamil Tigers.

This indicated the political nature of the case said Jones. But the evidence had been sent to Fiji, without any authority from the defence or court. Absolutely no authority to proceed had been issued. It therefore seemed the information had been sent unlawfully and could have been used to detain Kahan if he was acquitted on the direct charges.

Nicholls: "I am against the fixing of a swift date. We should hear all evidence to be adduced by the court, evidence to issue, and other matters of a prima facie case. It is difficult to divorce these from the political issues. We should do it at committal." But the Fugitive Offenders Act said the defendant should not be returned if it appeared to the committal court or High Court that the case was political, Nicholls conceded.

The matters raised by Mr Jones were also considered by the Secretary of State, when he decided the proper course was to issue an authority to proceed and the matter should be determined at the committal hearing at one and the same time.

"Mr Jones has spoken of going to Fiji. I want live evidence. It is proper that all the evidence should be before you. Schtracks limited the authority of whether fresh evidence can be put before the House of Lords on the political issue."

"The briefcase — if Mr Jones wants to raise the unlawfulness of this, this court is not the proper forum to decide. Only in so far as

244

the admissability of the evidence is concerned. It is a sensitive and difficult case."

Now it was Jones' turn and he choose a classic point by point prosecution.

"One: In the matter of the briefcase Kahan has been in custody since 22nd July. He is concerned about friends in Fiji. When he wrote he assumed the contents had not been shown to the Fijians. He has been told in the last 10 days that they were shown to a police officer. We would ask Mr Nicholls to tell the court on the next occasion on whose authority.

Two: Fiji was actually expelled from the Commonwealth on 22nd October.

Three: Mr Nicholls has been in Fiji. Why is it necessary for the Q.C. to go there on what he says is an ordinary case. We do not expect to be ready to go ahead for about six months, we must collect evidence and speak to people. We would like the court to benefit from seeing the whole case. We have not been told what live evidence is to be brought. This is the court of committal. The name should be considered at any stage. The only difference between the Extradition Act and the Fugitive Offenders Act is that the 1970 Act says that we must satisfy the police or the magistrates, the Fugitive Offenders Act says that it must be at the court of committal. It is clearly a political case. Kahan is at odds with the state."

Finally the Magistrate, Mr Robins, entered the fray:

He did not propose to go into the briefcase at all at this stage. Nor was the early magistrate court hearing a place to discuss the political nature. With regard to Mr Nicholl's point, the live evidence from Fiji and Australia had to be before the court before it can say if it was a political offence. These matters had to be decided when all the evidence was before the court.

Jones: " We will be going to the High Court to make an application for Habeas Corpus and the above Fugitive Offenders Act doesn't apply. We may not be coming back before your court."

Robins: "The case is remanded to 7th October with the defendant to be produced on 28th October 1988.

Was this what New Zealand High Court Judge and ex-Fiji Appeals Court Judge, Sir Graham Speight, had meant when he referred to my determined advocacy once I'd taken up a cause. This case could go for years.

On June 14 Sir Graham had written a brief, but persuasive testimony for me when I was seeking admission to the bar in Fiji. Addressed to the President of the Fiji Law Society it simply said:

Re — Christopher Harder

As you are probably aware, the above named Auckland practitioner is applying for temporary admission so that he may appear in some criminal matter relating to affairs in Rotuma. I do not know and do not wish to know anything about the merits of the case.

I am however, writing to you to say that Mr Harder is a well known and respected practitioner in Auckland, and anything which you can do to assist him would be appreciated. I have always found him reliable, though he has a fairly forceful manner which does not always endear him to others. He practices his profession in the best traditions and is a determined advocate on behalf of those whose cause he espouses — which is of course the proper role of a conscientious lawyer, especially in times of oppression.

I send you my warm personal regards.

Yours sincerely,
Graham Speight.

Remuera: October 17

I was back at my office desk, heavy with a dose of the flu which had found me easy pickings after dashing halfway around the world and back in the space of a few days to lend support on Kahan's behalf.

Radio Pacific's talkback show was booming into the office at a time when I would normally be listening to music as I worked. But with the interest I had developed in Fiji this particular talkback show was a must — the guest was deposed Prime Minister Dr Timoci Bavadra.

I could hardly believe what I was hearing. Ratu Meli Vesikula, the former Taukei stalwart who only a couple of weeks ago had joined forces with Dr Bavadra's political organisation, had sworn an affadavit linking Ratu Sir Kamisese Mara to the first coup.

Vesikula had delivered the affadavit to the British High Commission in Suva. This was a talkback show with some real messages for the world.

Soon after this revelation Dr Bavadra hammered home his message when a caller bluntly asked him if corruption was the main them behind the coups: "I have a feeling that was one of the reasons the coup was staged — corruption," said Bavadra.

Perhaps I was also getting somewhere in my campaign to challenge the continuing validity of Rabuka's military honour. I had just received a letter from Mr M.G.B. Plumb of the South Pacific Department in the Foreign and Commonwealth Office in London. He had been asked to reply to my letter to Mrs Thatcher on September 14 and to the private secretary of the Prime Minister on September 21. He assured me that "very careful consideration" would be given to the views I had expressed.

Within days I had learned that in June 1987, two months after the first coup, a group of Fijians flew to Kuala Lumpur, via Singapore. Rabuka had gone on a big recruiting drive increasing the military from 3000 to 6500. They needed more guns to equip the new soldiers. Present in the group were Ratu Sir Kamisese Mara, representing the cabinet and second in command Colonel Pio Wong, who was acting on a brief from Rabuka to spend $2 million on United States made M16 rifles and other military handiware from the Israelis. The purchase price of $3.6 million in the U.S. arms deal was discounted to $2 million because of "friendship".

Making up the numbers were several other army officers, body guards, a mystery man and Isikeli Mataitoga, who later became the Director of Public Prosecutions.

The money for the arms was to come from the Reserve Bank of Fiji. But the bank did not really think it had enough funds to cover the transaction, being at that time basically broke.

Reserve Bank Governor, Savenaea Siwatibau, since retired to obscurity in Australia, refused to part with the money until Rabuka 'ordered' the bank to hand it over.

The next development was a full knock down fist fight at their hotel between Mara's people and Wong and his military. Trouble apparently erupted when the arms deal was completed and a point of delivery had to be nominated. Mara wanted the weapons to go to his home province of Lau; Wong insisted they go to Suva.

The hotel management, who do not wish to be identified, called the police who arrested the parties to the brawl and took them downtown to the police cells. Ratu Mara was able to make some diplomatic telephone calls and was released within a couple of hours. The rest had eight hours of room-and-board courtesy of the local law. Mara may have been the first one back out on the street but the guns went to Suva.

When I interviewed Kahan in Britain he said Pio Wong and another man named Johnnie Veisamasama were involved in Kahan's scheme. Vaisamasama died earlier this year from an "accidental" gunshot wound from a .22 calibre pen-gun made in Lebanon, just hours before an appointment with the British High Commission in Suva to tell his side of the story involving the guns and the coup. If Wong was really Rabuka's man then the question that must be asked is: did Rabuka use Colonel Wong to con opportunist gun running Mohammed Kahan into the biggest political crime the South Pacific had ever seen.

Did Wong encourage Kahan to get guns for Mara and the Indians. Then use the discovery of the arms in Lautoka to justify the Internal Security Decree. Rabuka's big lie was that two-thirds of the container of arms was still missing. The military knew within days of the Australian discovery that only six crates had been shipped to Fiji because they beat it out of the prisoners.

Some years before the Fijian army had obtained some Soviet weapons from the Middle East as spoils of war. Was it possible that Rabuka had produced some of these weapons when the press had been shown caches of supposedly confiscated equipment after the security decree was announced.

The soldier who knows for sure is the soldier who helped Kahan at the Lautoka wharf and who actually checked out the container when Kahan opened it. This man has not been charged or bailed, nor has he appeared in court. Did he survive the interrogation that

Fiji security forces are so expert at. If so he will be subpoened as one of the critical witnesses in Mohammed Kahan's defence.

To complete the defence of Mohammed Kahan we required the following witnesses to be made available for cross-examination: Mahendra Patel, Hari Punja, Ishwari Bajpai, Pio Wong, Colonel Budromo, Sitiveni Rabuka, Adnan Kashoggi and the chief, Ratu Sir Kamisese Mara and the pathologist and his report on the death of Johnnie Vaisamasama.

I called out to my secretary Ameta. "Phone Foreign Affairs in London about our Fiji visas, then get Susan Judd at Air New Zealand. I want to book three seats to Fiji for Roscoe, Jones and myself for December 15."